Risking Liberation

Middle Class Powerlessness and Social Heroism

Paul G. King
Kent Maynard
David O.Woodyard

Foreword by Donald W. Shriver, Jr.

D0166685

Acknowledgment is made for permission to reprint:

To Fortune 500 for excerpt from "The Fortune 500 Special Report" (27 April, 1987). © 1987 Time, Inc. All rights reserved. Reprinted by permission.

To M.E. Sharpe, Inc. for excerpt from Lars Osberg, *Economic Equality in the United States*, "Table 2, Wealth Distribution by Percent." Reprinted by permission of M.E. Sharpe, Inc. Armonk, New York 10504.

To Oxford University Press and Cambridge University Press for excerpt from the New English Bible. © The Delegates of the Oxford University Press and the Syndics of the Cambridge University Press, 1961, 1970. Reprinted by permission.

To the *New York Times* for excerpt from Marian Burros, "Diet Game, Where Chances of Winning are Slim" (16 July, 1986). Copyright © 1986 by the New York Times Company. Reprinted by permission.

To *The Rotarian* for excerpt material (June 1987). Copyright 1987 The Rotarian. Reprinted by permission.

To Time for excerpt from Evan Thomas, "Growing Pains at 40" (19 May, 1986). Copyright 1986 Time, Inc. All rights reserved. Reprinted by permission from Time.

To *The Wall Street Journal* for excerpt from Amanda Bennett and D. R. Sease, "Getting Lean" (22 May, 1986). Reprinted by permission of The Wall Street Journal, © Dow Jones & Company, Inc. 1986. All rights reserved.

Library of Congress Cataloging in Publication Data

King, Paul G., 1940–
    Risking liberation.

    Bibliography: p.
    Includes index.
    1. Liberation theology.   2. Middle classes—
United States.   3. Middle classes—United States—
Religious life.   4. Heroes—Religious aspects.
I. Maynard, Kent, 1947—   . II. Woodyard,
David O.   III. Title.
BT83. 57. K493   1988   261.8'0973   88–45431
ISBN 0–8042–0842–5

Preface

We have written this book with an extended audience in view. It has been our aspiration to reach in print the people upon whom our research has focused. We hope that the same middle class readers who so appreciatively pondered *Habits of the Heart*, by Robert Bellah and his colleagues, will be engaged by our work. For that reason we have muted the disciplinary code words which for professionals convey meaning while making arguments opaque for others. Yet care with form and style has not led us to be naive about our accountability within the academy. We would be especially delighted if "town *and* gown" would find each other through these pages.

Over the last four years we have tested fragments of our arguments with professional and lay groups. We are indebted to many for encouragement and critiques. At a crucial point, Donald W. Shriver, Jr., enabled us to see that the fragments could form a book. His vision and support were important, and our gratitude is substantial. At a stage near completion Janet Greene, a professional journalist and layperson in the First Baptist Church of Granville, made valuable suggestions. There also have been many thoughtful responses from professional peers when we have presented parts of our analysis and argument at professional meetings and conferences.

With inestimable patience and good spirits Linda Payne typed, retyped, and endlessly revised our script at the computer. Elaine Hensley and Alan White helped immensely on several early drafts. We thank them all deeply.

Mutuality and reciprocal relationships have been at the center of our writing project. But they have also characterized the interaction between three persons of differing persuasions and disciplines. In both the creative exchanges and tedious processes of authorship we have experienced the very collectivity and solidarity that we envision for American society.

Dedicated to
James H. Cone

in memory of
Donald E. King
Katherine C. King

and for
Susan Diduk
Arthur and Pauline Maynard
with love

Foreword

Whatever their income, polls say, the great majority of Americans define themselves as middle class. In the past fifteen years the "middle" in America has been deeply troubled, especially by their precarious economic position. Further, if they are churchgoers, middle class Americans have probably heard much about the "oppression" of the poor by world economic systems. Middle class citizens of the world's largest capitalist country, they surmise that they are "pharaohs in everyone else's liberation story." Some reject this notion by resort to some version of old-fashioned Americanism. Others—for whom this book is written—wonder what liberation might mean for them. Is there a liberation theology for middle class Americans?

This book is an early "yes" to this question. Other books, and many a discussion group in churches, will have to take up the themes of the book if they are to acquire power for change in American society. *Risking Liberation* expands the agenda of two earlier books which set the stage of my own profound interest in this volume. The one book, *Spindles and Spires,* by two sociological colleagues and me, explored the mystery of how the churches of Gastonia, North Carolina, could have such tangible influence on race relations in that city and such negligible influence on economic relations. The other, *Habits of the Heart,* by Robert Bellah and his colleagues, documented the theme of individualism which we and numerous other students of American society find woven so deeply in our national cultural fabric. Missing from the Bellah book was studied attention to one of the great exceptions to individualistic religion in American history: the experience and achievement of the Black churches of America. Such attention is not missing in these pages.

King, Maynard, and Woodyard have written a book that connects our individualistic culture and religion to the social class situation, the economic anxieties, the political perplexity, and the possibility for action that face middle class Americans. If we could re-understand what it means to call ourselves "middle class," if we could look closely at the ties that bind us to the "working classes," if we could glimpse anew the social vision of the Bible, and if we could find new ties with each other for a collective pursuit of that vision, we might, these authors say, "renew our potential for heroism." We might do so by taking clues from the experience of the Black churches of America and the theologies that have emerged from them. No "paralysis by analysis" here, but an interweaving of social science and theology aimed at freeing us to be American, middle class, and religious with a new personal integrity made possible by new social relationships and new political vocations. This is a tall order. No wonder the book required three intelligences for the writing of it! And no wonder that many ordinary American readers will find in these pages reason to abandon the adjective "ordinary" for themselves and to explore instead the role these authors hold out for us all: heroism.

> Donald W. Shriver, Jr., President
> Union Theological Seminary
> New York City

Contents

Prologue
Three Journeys

For bourgeois classes as such have seldom before [the Protestant Reformation] and never since displayed heroism. It was "the last of our heroisms," as Carlyle, not without reason, has said.[1]

—Max Weber

As middle class academics and Americans, we have felt the need to come to terms with the experience of living in our own time. Much of that experience seems splintered and contradictory. Middle Americans generally seem unbelievably affluent by their parents' and grandparents' standards. Measured by the number of electrical appliances in the house and clothes in the closet, our prosperity rightfully dumbfounds us. Yet, it is easy to see how much closer to the margins we in the middle live than our parents did. We might have more, but we're paying for more of it on credit, and losing it much more quickly through default. Despite the camouflage of conspicuous consumption based on borrowing, many in the middle are experiencing real economic hardship and over the last decade have felt a shrinkage of real buying power.

What is true of economic experience is also true of the sense of control over existence. One of the distinguishing marks of the middle class in the past was said to be their degree of autonomy.

Unlike typical working class occupations, middle class professions were not just jobs; they were creative, involved real skill, and allowed for flexibility in how time was spent. Much of this seems to be ebbing, along with any feeling of power and control. We in the middle still want to think of ourselves as set off from the working class, as idea people who do not have to work with our hands. Yet in the stories we tell about our work we complain about our boredom and frustration. Metaphors about the "rat race" or "treadmill" abound. In an aptly mechanistic image taken from computerese, we worry about our inability to make any input. If not angered and combative, we are often resigned, cynical, or aloof, and we use absurdist humor to describe our lives as a circus or zoo.

In addition to our economic instability and decreasing power, we experience a feeling of estrangement. As a transitional middle class, we have typically been unsure of ourselves as a coherent group. With our upwardly mobile aspirations it is no wonder we also have a sense of rootlessness. But our search for identity seems increasingly frantic, desultory, and given over to fads. "Life in the fast lane" for many seems to start earlier and accelerate. The increasing rates of teenage suicide and drug abuse in American society are but two measures of this wider sense of isolation and uncertainty.

This book represents the efforts of three academics to analyze and try to clarify our position as Americans in the middle. It also represents a personal collaboration and journey among the three of us who are from quite different disciplines. One compelling reason for our joint venture has been the sheer complexity of middle class issues. No one discipline could do this topic justice, and certainly we do not claim to be exhaustive in any sense. Yet if we of the middle sector are experiencing such diverse patterns as increasing economic precariousness, a lack of control and autonomy, and a feeling of estrangement, we need to consider multiple views about our dilemma.

Another reason for a cooperative undertaking is that each of the authors aspires to understand middle class life and to work with others for possible solutions. It is because of such a commitment that Weber's reference to middle class "heroism" is so appealing. If we of the middle are to solve our problems—of economics, power, and identity—and solve them collectively, we will have to become heroic once again. This, of course, does not mean the usual romantic and individualized notions of bravery or altruism, a curious melange of Clint Eastwood and Mother Teresa. It means, instead, the willingness as part of a social class to reclaim control of our collective destiny and to work for change. Only as we realize that things do not have to be the way they are, that economic instability, powerlessness, or angst are not ordained in heaven, nature, or our genes, can we begin to consider a different future.

Recapturing social heroism won't be easy. Unlike the old middle class of the Reformation era who helped to create a radically new order, we have been born into ours. They espoused a new economic system and new religious ideology; we are the inheritors of what is now largely received wisdom. It is no accident, therefore, that much of the folklore that we entertain about ourselves as a class derives from the Reformation and the later era of the Industrial Revolution. From that period we continue the flattering images of ourselves as masters of our own destiny. The old heroism of the European burghers, thus, has become a shibboleth reinforcing today's conformity and obscuring the real circumstances of our lives. Living on the borrowed bravery of our forebears can mask the importance of being heroes in our own right.

To alleviate the dilemmas of the middle class will require, ironically, that we give up seeing ourselves as a separate class. Because of the economic changes in America, particularly over the last century or so, we in the middle are far closer to the working class and the poor than we often think. To be sure, there are real differences. But there is good evidence to show that the middle layer, the workers, and the poor represent different constituencies in a larger laboring class. If our similarities outweigh our differences, and we are growing more similar with time, then only by recognizing common interests do we stand a chance of making changes. This isn't one more call for the middle class to be generous to those less fortunate. It is a recognition that as a laboring class we all share a common plight. Only by working together as a political coalition can each constituency hope to change its life collectively.

Essential to the thesis of this book, then, is the claim that the traditional American label of *middle class* is inaccurate and misleading. It leads to a narrow focus on certain occupations which, on their own, do not constitute a class. A pernicious outcome of this is that middle Americans often do not see the extent to which they share interests with the poor, or those in the working class. The opportunity is lost to act together as a coalition working on common problems. Viewed as a coalition, those in the middle, the workers, and the poor are all "fractions," "sectors," or "layers" of a single, wider laboring class.

Throughout the book, then, such terms will be used systematically in two different ways. The term *middle class* will always refer to how those of us in the middle income range have tended to think about ourselves and others. A reference to the *middle fraction, layer,* or *sector,* in contrast, denotes the kind of action and thinking that should follow from a recognition of and membership in a wider laboring class.

One of the reasons it is so difficult to think about *social* heroism is our overriding preoccupation with the ideas and values of individualism. Any appeal to social or communal issues tends to be read as a sacrifice of the individual on the altar of some faceless mass society. Despite its many different forms, socialism for Americans is equated with the gray anonymity and lockstep mediocrity of state Big Brotherism. To move beyond this we need to challenge the applicability of individualism to our present existence and look for alternative stories or ideologies.

This book is by no means the first attempt to work through such complex issues, even from an interdisciplinary perspective. The most recent attempt was made by Robert Bellah, Richard Madsen, William Sullivan, Ann Sundler, and Steven Tipton in their collaborative book, *Habits of the Heart.* Bellah and his colleagues have presented a wide-ranging survey of middle class values and attitudes about our private and public lives. Perhaps one reason so many American readers responded to *Habits of the Heart* is it held up to us our allegiance to individualism while revealing how it prevents our deeper need for community. The courage to be separate can deter the courage to participate in the creation of the common good. The ambiguity and anxiety in American experience are brought into focus by Bellah's suggestion that "individualism may have grown cancerous. . . ."[2] The energies devoted to becoming distinguishable individuals have been directed toward excessive self-interest, which finally alienates and isolates persons from one another. For many, if not most, any impulses toward social solidarity are stillborn. The determination to be self-reliant and assume responsibility for self-enactment leaves many with diminished capacity for community. None of us would want to say we do not need others for a coherent and purposeful life. But, when bonding and caring are something to be achieved rather than assumed, the flaws in individualism begin to emerge. There is an increasing suspicion that the quest for a common good and the creation of social orders which would sustain it are a futile exercise. We may no longer believe we can do anything to create a world where "justice roll[s] down like waters, and righteousness like an ever-flowing stream" (Amos 5:24).

Bellah and his colleagues have presented a clearer vision of the isolation that excessive individualism has created. At the same time they have disclosed our painful struggles as Americans (through therapy, management, and manipulation) to reach out and establish connections that are genuine and are linked to some common good. *Habits of the Heart* assumes that our present isolation is the result of having lost faith in the best of our national and religious heritage. Only by restoring such traditions and mores, sacrificed to modernity, can we achieve real social renewal. The appeal is not to the good old days but the good old traditions. Bellah is in a real sense an evangelist calling for conversion to the best that has gone before, and believing deeply that personal transformation is the ground of our quest for "a new heaven and a new earth." A reconstruction of consciousness, being "born again," can lead to the formation of social contacts that are authentic and to the development of a social order that is just.

We agree with Bellah and his colleagues that "finding oneself means, among other things, finding the story or narrative in terms of which one's life makes sense."[3] But the scope and assumptions of the story make a difference. Some stories give rise to personal ambitions and achievement, while others promote social solidarity and compassion. We are not persuaded, however, that the American national, or even religious, heritage is inevitably redemptive. Stories that do not link with middle class social reality cannot transform it or even provide the means for resisting its encroachment.

Consider the following story from *Time* magazine,[4] which raised the issue of citizenship in relation to those now known as the "Baby Boomers." The bind in which many find themselves is reflected in "[t]he personal odyssey of Joyce Maynard, 32. . . .

". . . A precocious *New York Times Magazine* article she wrote in 1972 titled 'An 18-Year-Old Looks Back on Life' made her a minor figure of her generation and led to a frenetic reporting job on the *Times* after a year at Yale. Only a year later, however, she fled the bright lights and big city and moved to New Hampshire. . . . 'I dropped out,' she says. 'I wanted to do nothing but raise three children, make a good life for them and preserve their . . . sanity as we moved into the 21st century.' " That is a familiar story, an individual trying to escape from systems and institutions of power. Then, sometime later, she said, ". . . 'the [Federal] Government announced that it has chosen my town as a proposed nuclear waste dump site.' " What her story reveals is that trying to reclaim a past without discerning the social realities leaves us at the mercy of systems and institutions from which one presumes to have withdrawn. "Now, says Maynard, 'I do nothing but talk nuclear waste all day long. I have come to realize there is no way to tend just one's own backyard. There is no escape, even in New Hampshire.' "

The flaw in *Habits of the Heart* is that it moves from an analysis with which we agree toward a future that we desire without the means of transition or implementation. Bellah provides no means of enabling Joyce Maynard to resist her fate. Thus, while we think Bellah and his colleagues have eloquently summarized the feelings of many in the middle, they have not coupled that with an exploration of our underlying economic and class realities. In our own thinking about the situation of the middle class, we have been drawn instead to models that try to examine what the middle class as a *sector* thinks about things, and the degree to which that meshes with actual social and economic circumstances. We have also sought to explore models that offer new images, ideological stories, on which the hope for future laboring class coalitions could be built. Here we have been influenced by the work of liberation theologians from Latin America and by those such as Rosemary Ruether, and especially James Cone, who are writing from a North American perspective. We are not, however, simply grafting liberation theology onto the middle sector experience. That would be antithetical to the methodological spirit of liberation theology; American middle class reality departs significantly in many aspects from that of the Latin American peasantry. Yet in its concern for economic issues and political powerlessness, and certainly its call for a solidarity of class, liberation theology has much to offer.

Just as a liberation theology of the middle sector will differ from that of Latin America, or of Black Americans and women, so, too, we realize that it is not the only model available for change. One of the defining features of existence in the middle is its fractured and heterogeneous quality. Not all are religious, and those who are, come from many points of view. Nevertheless, as polls constantly show, Americans do believe in a Judeo-Christian heritage. This creates the potential for profoundly moving images of change. It is no accident that the synagogues and churches have been significantly involved in such largely middle sector campaigns as the anti-war, anti-nuclear, environmental, and consumer movements, or have influenced participation in the civil rights and feminist movements. Religion is by no means *the* bedrock for a new social heroism of the middle sector, but it does give one solid basis from which to begin.

As we were writing this book together we were often asked

to explain what unites a theologian, an anthropologist, and an economist. We are in part bound by the conviction that any significant transformation of the social order in America must begin with an analysis of the real position of the middle class. The middle class needs a persuasive sense of who it is, what drives the conditions of its existence, and a recognition of those realities which control its possibilities. It is only in relation to that shared sense that the middle class can envision and plan an alternate future.

Some knowledge of the authors' personal and academic histories might enhance understanding of our joint analysis of the middle sector. Our experiences have changed and shaped our stances on social issues and career choices; our collaboration has led to even further changes. The analysis does not mirror our personal and intellectual journeys, but without them we never would have begun.

A Theologian's Journey

I became a theologian because I needed to. Religious symbols and stories were important in my family. In time they became more important for me personally. As a college student I was driven both to understand the faith and understand myself at a level an avocation would not satisfy. "Getting the faith straight" for me meant achieving clarity about its true meaning and linking my existential needs to it. For a decade, that was all I needed.

In the late 1960s events forced a wedge between my theological security and the most important impulses awakened in my life. My theology was lodged in the private sphere, while my heart, spirit, and body were engaged by the public sphere. It was not personal authentication but social transformation that set my agenda. The attempt to bring my life and my theology back together found expression in writing *Beyond Cynicism: The Practice of Hope*.

James Cone was there in print when I needed him. He was my first and most durable mentor in liberation theology. The most compelling arena of my life was transforming the American social reality. Cone enabled me to see how the very stories and symbols

I had embraced in my personal life also informed my social self, which was defined by political and economic structures. The Exodus and the Christ event inform and expose the established orders of the world, leading to their transformation.

But Cone is Black and I am white! I might be responsible for racism, but oppression obviously did not define my existence. I needed to do for my own social reality what Cone had done and continues to do for his. At the point of that recognition an economist, Paul King, came into my intellectual horizon. We began reading and then teaching together on the interface of Third World development and liberation theology. As the need to bring it home became more prominent, we found very little literature to guide us in thinking through the relationship between our fields and how that connected with our shared experience as white, middle class, male Americans.

We struggled to think, teach, and write together in ways that eventually took the form of *Journey Toward Freedom: Economic Structures and Theological Perspectives*. In that book we developed the theme that theology was "agenda setting" for economics. It was, in our view, the theological task to expose injustice and suggest the contours of a future in which justice was implemented. It was the economist's task to analyze what was wrong in the present arrangement and suggest how to fix it.

It was not too long before the paradigm King and I developed was unsettled by the stimulation of an anthropologist. Kent Maynard was reared in a strong Methodist home largely informed by the "Social Gospel." Concern for the social remains prominent in him, though a secular orientation prevails. Bringing an anthropologist into the mix eventually caused King and me to see the imperialism embedded in our claim that theology was agenda setting. That posture was not even good liberation theology! I should have known that theology is the second step in that tradition.

I have moved from "getting the faith straight" to theology as "agenda setting" to understanding theology as "emerging within our social reality." That journey brings us back to James Cone and the recognition that my mentor is not where he was when he began to shape my theology. He is moving beyond racism as the sole category for understanding the condition of Black Americans. ". . . [B]ecause race appeared to be the most dominant manifestation of injustice in the United States," he had ignored class and its economic origins as a dimension of the American experience.[5] Cone now feels that "we cannot continue to speak against racism without any reference to a radical change in the economic order."[6] The agenda of the Black church and Black theology is to understand the immersion of us all in the political economy, and the control it exercises over our lives. This begins in our addiction to private property and the structures of capitalism. Class analysis has become for many of us a necessary and important prelude to doing theology.

An Anthropologist's Journey

I was led into anthropology as a discipline for at least two reasons, each related to my parents. With both my mother and father as teachers, I had an early and abiding feeling of the great diversity that there is in the world. They gave me the intuitive understanding that other societies and cultures were not simply quaint, but to be taken seriously as real alternatives. Both my parents are Christian, and from our home and the church I also received a lasting concern with social issues of peace and justice, if not a personal religious commitment. I have been interested for a long time in ways to define what I would now call a "good quality of life." Much of this was really brought into focus for me during my undergraduate years through involvement with the anti-war movement, and then with my alternate service as a conscientious objector.

Out of this came a great deal of my early interest, especially in anthropology, in the study of religion, and more generally with belief and identity. From a childhood interest in Latin America I went on to do a doctoral dissertation on what it means to be an evangelical Protestant in Ecuador. Coming to Denison University fresh from graduate school had a deep impact on how I looked at such matters. To begin with, I came to a Department of Sociology/Anthropology, and that integration of disciplines alone broadened my perspective. From anthropology I had always received the dictum that we live and study with other societies in order to learn more about our own—that was one of its earliest attractions for me, and still is. Through working with my departmental colleagues I have developed a framework by which to explore much more fully both indigenous *and* Western societies. My colleagues have also helped me to articulate my own position on what it is to do social science. Our lively debates and lengthy conversations have given me a much fuller grasp of what it means to say that a scientist is also both a person and a citizen. To hold certain values and to do hardheaded social analysis are not incompatible. It is only by clarifying my values, in this case being up front about my humanism and commitment to social change, that any sort of objectivity is possible.

Being able to work at a liberal arts institution such as Denison has also influenced me, because of the readily available opportunities to work with colleagues in other disciplines. From the time when David Woodyard first approached me about teaching a "religion and society" course together seven years ago, I have been pushed to work through the potential for both common ground and differences between the social sciences and theology. When Woodyard and King asked me to think about the joint venture that has resulted in this book, it gave me the added opportunity to learn in a much more detailed way the economic underpinnings of my own society. Economics and sociology/anthropology, of course, are much closer in their world views than either is to that of theology. Woodyard's commitment to a liberation theology, however, and my own interest in its role in Latin America, have brought home to me the real potential of the church and synagogue as agents of change.

I am a humanist, rather than a religious humanist. Liberation theology along with other religious symbol systems have primary interest for me as ideologies by which we in the middle might join with others to renew our potential for heroism. There are other such stories and beliefs, which we point to occasionally throughout the text, that are non-religious. There is an appropriate symmetry, however, in that we begin our work on the role of religion in social change today by drawing on Weber's work on the heroism of the middle class in defense of Calvinism in the sixteenth century.

An Economist's Journey

I am not sure why I became an economist. I do not believe I ever felt driven to do so. For an undergraduate and graduate student in the early to mid-1960s, it was a comfortable choice. Economists were held in high regard because the society connected so much of the unparalleled economic success of the sixties to the policy prescriptions of prominent economists. Sharing in that regard seemed both a natural and wise thing to do.

My economic education was in the neoclassical tradition with its claim that the unfettered market ought to make all economic decisions. No one raised the issue of the way institutional arrangements interfere with the free flow of the market. I did, however, learn about development economics. My observation of a continuing and growing gap between the rich and poor nations was my first inkling that neoclassical economics did not have the answers to all the questions.

The civil rights and anti-war movements in the late 1960s made me aware that some serious gaps also existed within the United States. But my economics training did not equip me very well for exploring those gaps. Fortunately, my interest in the history of economic thought had introduced me to what some considered to be "kooks and crazies" in our economic past. Did they have anything enduring to contribute to an understanding of the difference between economic reality and neoclassical theory? Thorstein Veblen, at least, seemed to point the way with his careful exploration of the difference between the conditions established by our existing economic institutions and those assumed by neoclassical theory. But, he left me with nowhere to go. I could use his approach to expose the failure of the theory, but it provided me with no framework for constructing an alternative vision of reality.

The resulting frustration led me to bury myself in applications of neoclassical theory. I increasingly ignored both development economics and the problems of poverty, maldistribution, and discrimination in my own society. If I could not figure out what to do about them, then I wanted to ignore them altogether. My intellectual concentration was reserved for questions of energy use and environmental quality, both of which were areas where neoclassical approaches could be used to explain conditions and to propose viable policy alternatives.

An unexpected exposure to liberation theology while on a research leave at Oak Ridge National Laboratory jerked my chain and pulled my attention back to the problems of the Third World and the poor in general. Theologians in Latin America and the United States were breaking new ground both by calling for the downfall of institutional arrangements that held the poor in oppression and by suggesting that the reconstruction of the economic and social system must be based in justice. They had made the break with tradition and with existing conditions that I had been afraid to make. They were proving that stepping outside one's inherited intellectual paradigm might be very hard, but it was essential if meaningful change was ever going to occur.

As a result, I have been struggling with a break from the neoclassical model for the past ten years. That the struggle still goes on indicates that breaking with the old paradigm is by no means easy. Continued collaboration with a theologian and an anthropologist convinces me, however, that the effort is necessary. My intellectual world view has been opened up, and it can never again be closed back down. Interaction with my colleagues has convinced me, for example, that any economic analysis that ignores the role of class cannot really explain the way in which economic decision making occurs. Any reconstruction of an economic system that allows for the unchecked accumulation of power will inevitably give rise to new sets of class conflicts and, more importantly, to the re-emergence of economic, social, and political injustice.

I was raised in a religious tradition that I would describe as working class Irish Catholicism. While my personal background includes sixteen years of Catholic education, and I remain a practicing Catholic, my involvement in our project and my commitment to change in our society flows only peripherally from that background. There have certainly been individuals in the church—parish priests, missionaries, liberation theologians—who have influenced me, and the general "opening up" of Vatican II helped to make more bearable a conservative institutional church dedicated to the status quo. I am convinced, however, that my family contributed far more to the development of a set of values that does not allow me to accept things as they are. My father, who was not Catholic, had a particularly profound influence on me. He was a practicing humanist without any formal or religious trappings, and he taught me a profound respect for justice and for the welfare of other human beings. I am also convinced that it is my background as an economist that allows me to reflect analytically on the conditions I find in my world and to see in them an essential injustice which has finally, if belatedly, prompted me to action. While I do not see the church as an institution that has driven me toward a fundamentally different value system, I do see it as an institution that contains some of the seeds of the counter-institutions needed to enact a society that reflects that value system.

1
Identifying the Middle in American Society

The Protestant Reformation, the rise of capitalism, and the Industrial Revolution are all connected by the thread of substantial middle class involvement. The old bourgeois middle class triumphed because they were able to tear themselves free from feudal ties. Max Weber claimed that the Reformation and the attendant rise of capitalism were the last examples of middle class heroism. He is not alluding by this to the highly individualized gallantry of a John Wayne. Heroism for Weber is a social act. It occurs when a group of people no longer simply stand up for the system, but stand out against it. They critique the present and act to reclaim control over the future. The bourgeoisie of the Reformation era changed the circumstances of their existence and freed themselves from the dominance of aristocratic, social, political, and economic structures.

Our thesis is that the new middle class, caught in the wake of all the changes brought by the rise of industrial capitalism, finds itself in a position analogous to the old bourgeoisie on the eve of the Reformation. That old bourgeoisie went on to define the present power structure. We in the middle class of today, ironically, are largely a by-product of that structure with its industrialism, urbanism, and tremendously increased bureaucracy. The very fact that we call ourselves "the middle class" and use images drawn from the old bourgeoisie is part of the problem. For we are neither a class nor a continuation of the old middle class. Our only real point of similarity, indeed, is the need for social heroism.

In this chapter we briefly sketch out the argument that is to appear in detail throughout the book. We will contend that (1) there is a growing structural similarity between the new middle class and what is often called the working class and the poor. Indeed, all three groups essentially form "fractions" within a larger laboring class. Members of this class earn wages or salaries, rather than deriving income from ownership of productive resources. (2) The similarity in position and interests of these three groups is evident especially in their increasing economic insecurity, lack of political power, and loss of control over significant areas of work life. (3) The "professional-managerial" group or "middle layer" of the laboring class has a firm belief in the ideological stories of individualism, a belief that is less typical of either the traditional working class or the poor. People in the middle layer have a fascination with the myth of the self-made individual, access to a modicum of wealth, the traditional prestige derived from their knowledge as "white-collar experts," and real dependence upon the property-owning classes; these have prevented the middle from seeing similarities with other segments of the laboring class. (4) Current social circumstances no longer fit either past realities or present ideologies. Working for change can no longer be in that long tradition of middle class volunteerism and altruism for those less fortunate. It is in the best interests of the middle sector itself to work jointly with other laboring class fractions to achieve political and economic justice. Recall here the terminological distinction introduced in the prologue. The term *middle class* designates those traditional views that associate class with an income range; *middle fraction, sector,* or *layer,* in contrast, refer to the argument that the middle in fact constitutes one part of a wider laboring class. (5) To create an effective political coalition of the laboring class will require new ideological stories concerning the *reciprocal* interdependence of each of its fractions. We develop a liberation theology of the "middle layer," which provides one ideology for thinking about a common plight. It will be one source, among others, for collective heroism in creating a more just and inclusive society.

The Middle Class in Historical Perspective

The middle class heroism to which Max Weber refers is the rise of the bourgeoisie in the nation-state. This was due to a fundamental shift in the relationship between economy and society produced by the change from feudalism to capitalism. In non-capitalist societies, including feudal Europe, economic production is principally instrumental; work in such societies is valued for how it sustains the social fabric and values of community. It supports other aspects of social life while being constrained by them. In capitalism, the equation is reversed. Social relations are now put in service of economic production for the achievement of profit through the rational maximization of self-interest. People are less valued for who they are than for what they can do for you. In non-capitalist societies individuals are defined by their relationships within the community. Capitalism, on the other hand, creates a dichotomy between the individual and society. It assumes that society exists to promote individual social mobility.

We argue that there is a necessity for a new middle class heroism. The new conditions under which the middle sectors live are not consistent with cultural conceptions of them. There is a discrepancy between the actual nature of a bureaucratic capitalist system, and the middle sector's commitment to individualism and sense of social mobility. These new conditions form a barrier to aspirations, which requires heroic action in the creation of new social forms. Can we in the middle develop an ideology that can undergird and promote such social heroism?

Religion provides a rich tradition from which to draw stories about the need to restructure society. The Judeo-Christian heritage draws upon the biblical message as one foundation from which to examine contemporary structures and institutions. The category of hero, however, seems conspicuously absent from the Bible. Its patriarchal focus is not on good men, and sometimes women, doing good things, but on God's purpose being worked through them. Yet that does not preclude using the category of heroism if we mean by it reclaiming the sense of empowerment to create new social worlds. In this definition heroism means putting our apparent individual and social interests at risk before the promises of a better order for all. Authentic existence is not individual but social.

Biblical illustrations abound of a willingness to sacrifice present circumstances for a future whose contours provide benefits to the human community. Consider an analogy drawn from a Hebrew narrative. The story of Abraham has some similarities to our own. When Abraham lived in Ur of the Chaldees, he had extensive material benefits. Flocks, servants, and other forms of wealth provided comfort and security. These were given depth by a network of family ties and friendships. The prevailing logic might suggest that Abraham had nothing to gain and everything to lose by seeking out a new land. Indeed, he and his family gave up a settled and comfortable existence for the nomadic life of the desert. He was called by a promise with no guarantees:

> By faith Abraham obeyed the call to go out to a land destined for himself and his heirs, and left home without knowing where he was to go. By faith he settled as an alien in the land promised him, living in tents, as did Isaac and Jacob, who were heirs to the same promise. For he was looking forward to the city with firm foundations, whose architect and builder is God. (Heb. 11:8–10, NEB)

What is interesting to note is that this biblical passage about Abraham comes from the New Testament. The early Christian church recalled the story not simply to give content to faith but to underscore a sense of hope for the future of the community. When the early church looked to Abraham as a model of faith, it was not an elevation of a remarkable individual. The Judeo-Christian community did not make a sharp separation between the individual and the corporate community. It is not the individual who brings the faith to the community, but the communal faith is represented in the faith of an individual. The author of Hebrews is embracing the people of Israel by invoking the memory of Abraham. The memory of the Abrahamic "city" makes the community of faith "strangers and exiles" upon the earth. It reminds them that they are at odds with all that is, because God is summoning "things that are not yet in existence as if they already were." (Rom. 4:17, NEB)

To a remarkable degree Abraham is who we are. Abraham's journey is our journey, and his risk is our risk. In the words of Robert McAfee Brown, "[o]ur displacement may not be geographical, as was Abraham's, but it will surely be ideological, theological, political, economic, and social."[1] The journey of the middle sector is Abrahamic in that we are called to place immediate benefits on the line with the hope of a new order in which our deeper interests will be manifest. While the story of Abraham is elliptical it is evident that he and his followers sacrificed structures that appeared to be in the interests of some for the promise of a new social order shaped by the interests of all. They moved from immersion in structures that defined them, and over which they had lost control, toward the creation of structures humanly fulfilling. The story of Abraham can provide one foundation for an ideology that reveals *our* immersion in a present-centered and individualistic society. Like Abraham we must break free from that immersion before we can begin to create new structures and a more open future. We are not asked as individuals to be heroes, but as part of a wider class we *can* be heroic.

Consider how this applies to the middle sector. Its traditional liberal sense of injustice has focused on the obvious inequities suffered by the poor, racial or ethnic minorities, and women in the United States. Some people in the middle sector think of themselves as collaborating in that injustice because of their links to the upper class. The middle class is said to be a buffer that softens the contradiction between the upper and working classes. Or they are the paid minions carrying out the orders of the property-holding class. Yet if the power and wealth achieved by the old bourgeoisie now deny economic security to even the middle layers of American society, then those in the middle class must rethink their own interest in movements of fundamental change. Indeed, we would suggest that the present economic order deprives middle Americans not only of economic security, but of that personal identity and sense of sociocultural well-being that characterize non-industrial societies. The middle sector can no longer afford to think of itself as a junior partner of the upper class, a bystander to the class difficulties of others, or even as a humanitarian helper of the poor. We in the middle have a stake in the struggles of the poor, whether we realize it or not.

What are the conditions for such a "new middle class" heroism, one that recognizes we alone are *not* a class but part of a wider laboring community? In what circumstances and by what means would the middle sectors construct and act on a new conception of a better, more just society?

Robert Bellah offers "civil religion" as a necessary ideology for the transformation of American society. The symbolism of America as "the new Israel," of "sacred covenant," suggests to Bellah a source for a new socialist vision of communal values. These would provide the grounds for contradicting the individualism and class inequalities that dominate our capitalist society.

This view is challenging, but inadequate. It recalls an ideal but vapid image of the communal past rather than an analysis of present inequality by class, race, and gender. Its search for a renewed covenant based on a common civil religion is commendable. But it shows little understanding of the way in which cultural ideas are used ideologically in connection with particular social interests. To have meaning for people, symbols must have a specific content, which can be related to particular human experiences and interests. With a highly diverse, institutionally differentiated society, the few symbols all might agree upon are too general to bind us together as a people. Civil religion does not call forth any compelling images or stories with which to identify, because it does not proceed from an investigation of the ambivalent position of the American middle sectors, and the diverse and conflicting nature of their interests. It fails, thus, to account for how such a vision would be attained given the existing structures of power.

We reject civil religion as a basis for a new heroism of the middle sectors and turn elsewhere for strategies of change. The most successful movements of social renewal and revolution in the twentieth century have been implemented by peasant groups. Such movements have involved ideologies of change often based on Marxist views of the social order and those of liberation theology. It appears, indeed, to be no accident that liberation theology has occurred extensively in those Latin American countries with large subordinate peasant classes and a rural proletariat.

In Latin America there are serious problems of economic deprivation. These leave the vast bulk of the population in crippling poverty due to the land tenure system, the power of traditional elites, the almost complete lack of social and economic mobility, the dependence upon single crop economies, and a variety of other issues. On the other hand, an extremely small segment of the population owns and controls virtually all of the means of production. In El Salvador, for example, fourteen families wield both economic and military power.[2]

The problems in Latin America are so stark, the marginated classes form such a huge majority, and the villains are so plainly evident that it is not surprising a powerful movement for liberation has emerged in many places. There is a clear recognition among Latin American revolutionaries that putting good men and women in authority would not change people's lives very much. It is the arrangement of the land tenure system, the means of conferring social status, and the maldistribution of economic and political power that are the root causes of the extreme inequality and its associated economic deprivation.

We believe that there are lessons for the United States in these revolutionary movements in Latin America. There are many sources of disaffection in our system as well. Blacks, women, and other poor in the United States are at the margins in terms of economic rewards. Much of the middle sector lacks any real control and power. There are profound differences between the United States and Latin America; yet there are also important common socioeconomic causes that push people into these marginal situations. An awareness of that can help focus and unite the needs for change.

Addressing the necessity for a *laboring* class heroism and a model for liberation in North America will begin with an analysis of the middle sectors and their position within the wider American class structure. Foremost among the issues to be considered will be the redefinition of justice and liberation within a nation that superficially appears to include both. Present middle class notions of justice presume a capitalist system in which the market is considered to be the only legitimate arbiter of equity and freedom. There may be individuals who fail in the market, but the market itself is never blamed for their impoverishment. Yet the inequality of income distribution that is an essential feature of modern bureaucratic capitalist economies means that economic well-being is systematically denied those at the bottom. The stagflation of the seventies and the continuation of extensive unemployment into the eighties have extended the experience of precarious economic conditions to much of the middle layers as well. Our economic aspirations as part of the laboring class have been seriously impeded and our ability to control our circumstances dramatically reduced. Faced with this situation, we need a new ideology that gives new specific content to the symbols of justice and liberation. Such an ideology calls us to reclaim economy as part of society and culture, to right the equation reversed by the old burghers. It calls us no longer to live in order to work, but to work in order to live.

Religious symbols offer one important means of defining a new movement for change. The Christian tradition obviously is not the only potential ideology for such a movement. Other symbols of change can and must be drawn from the rich traditions of humanism, Marxism, feminism, civil rights, and the ecological and consumer movements, to name but a few. We begin with Christian sources in part because of their familiarity to us. Yet they also have an importance in American history as a force both standing up for, and standing out against, the past. We wish to outline their participation once again in a new social heroism.

Defining the Middle Layers of American Society

In order to think more clearly about our experience as the

middle class it is important to define the term. Part of the problem is that while Americans intuitively point to a "middle" segment, they find it difficult to define. Talking about the upper, middle, and lower classes is a part of the vocabulary of most of us; really isolating a definable middle class is much harder. The problem stems, in part, from its heterogeneous character. Take occupation as one example, often used by Americans to locate themselves and others by class. Steelworkers, physicians, secretaries, the owner of a paint shop, or a sales manager at IBM, all commonly identified as middle class, are an unlikely mixture to include in one group. Putting together all of those with certain types of occupations in a single statistical category can be misleading. While it might disclose some similarities of lifestyle, it doesn't show if "occupation" is the basis for social interrelationships and common interests.

Most definitions recognize that to be a social class requires at least two necessary but not sufficient criteria: classes are hierarchical as structures, and they involve interrelations. Classes by definition are unequal in power. Some definitions also point to differences in wealth or prestige, and they usually imply inequality in access to and control over resources and experiences. Classes also refer to relationships among individuals, or subgroups such as families, rather than statistical categories. Those in the same class are dependent on each other and have similar world views. Occupation alone, then, is not a very accurate measure of class location. The secretary, paint store owner, and steelworker may all be called middle class, but that masks some significant differences, and even real antagonisms.

This raises a crucial issue in assessing the importance of class. In thinking about how society is organized, should most emphasis be placed on what its members say about themselves or what outside observers may see? Most discussions on the importance of class stem from either Max Weber or Karl Marx, who epitomize this split in concern by making common cultural styles or economic relationships the bases for social organization. Marx defined class in terms of the relation of different groups to the means of production. As an outside observer he could see how control over land and capital gives greater power to owners than to those who must sell their labor as workers or employees. The nature of our economic activity, whether we are aware of it or not, creates real differences in every other aspect of our social and cultural lives. This view can also recognize the importance of a class becoming aware of itself and its difference from other groups. To have one's consciousness raised and act explicitly in terms of class interests is necessary for social change to occur. Any real change in class alignment, as happened to the old middle classes with the rise of capitalism, requires a recognition of who you are as a class, identification of class interests, and concerted efforts to advance those interests as a group.

While Marxists can appreciate the importance of self-understanding as a class, it was Max Weber who emphasized that the way people think about themselves can be important for organizing social groups.[3] Differences in "cultural style," measures of prestige, or social activities bind people together or create deep divisions and mistrust. Living in the "right" neighborhood, for example, might be an important basis for social ties. Weber sees these status markers, however, as being different than class per se. Indeed, they can be even more central at times to the ongoing organization of society and obscure actual class alignments. Weber agrees with Marx that whether or not one owns property is the basic criterion for establishing classes. Most of the time, however, we are largely unaware of this as a basis for group identity. Far more important will be other status markers related to cultural lifestyle, ethnicity, or perhaps religiosity. Our common-sense labels in American society for the upper, middle, and lower class, with such fine-tuned variations as upper middle, lower middle, nouveau riche, or "old money," exemplify this point.[4] We think that we are referring to social classes, when in fact they are often status groups. The social activities and cultural values that define these status groups are not determined by class; in fact, they may even influence class relationships.[5]

There is much truth in the Weberians' position that no simple tie exists between one's class as objectively defined and the cultural lifestyle to which one subscribes. All workers, for example, are not necessarily identical in their activities and cultural views. Yet the ownership or non-ownership of property does tend "in the long run" to be a criterion of status "with extraordinary regularity."[6] There are exceptions, but economic position fundamentally influences both prestige and life chances. That is not an accident; it points to the essential importance of property relationships and the means of production for defining who we are in a capitalist society.

The point remains, however, that in any contemporary capitalist society there are a number of ways in which group status or identity can be established. And these may obscure or even contradict basic economic relationships. That we tend to think so much about blue-collar, white-collar, "yuppie," and other kinds of occupationally based status groups is evidence for this. The proliferation of lifestyle groups as well as subdivisions within classes has occurred for many reasons. Yet such groups are also clearly related to the increasingly complex division of labor and intricate bureaucracies that typify our lives today.

In the end, this means that analyzing middle America cannot rest exclusively on either objective economic class relationships or what Americans subjectively think about their own social groupings. Both factors are involved and mutually interacting. Note, for example, how the Weberian and Marxist views complement each other in explaining the development of industrial capitalist societies. Both positions see such societies as being essentially composed of two great classes. For Marxists, of course, these are the proletariat and bourgeoisie. Marx argued that the drive for profit-taking in capitalism would create an ever greater concentration of wealth. This would lead increasingly to stark conflict between owners and workers. As a consequence there would be a decrease in the importance of the "middle" groups of the mid-nineteenth century such as small-scale business owners and farmers. Marx has been largely correct in this latter prediction. He failed, however, to predict that the expansion and centralization of industry, which led so many of the members of these peripheral classes to become wage laborers, would also greatly expand the bureaucratic structures. These bureaucracies became the bastion of the managers, other white-collar employees, and professionals, who make up much of what is generally labeled today as the middle class.

Weber's conclusions about the expansion of bureaucracy and the way in which such complex occupational divisions promote different lifestyles help explain why Marx's prediction of class conflict never materialized. With the growth in the economy since the late nineteenth century, middle class Americans have seen tremendous increases in both their numbers and economic prospects. As a consequence, they often forget or deny just how much they now share with other segments of the laboring class. Each fraction engages in different types of work, under different conditions. The middle sector refers constantly, for example, to the supposed distinction between "hand" work and "head" work. We use this as a status marker of our higher prestige and even at times our supposedly greater intelligence. Higher education becomes a badge symbolizing intellectual, moral, and cultural superiority. The very use of the term *culture* to denote a cultured individual is correlated with the rise of the bourgeoisie and the subsequent proliferation of "middle class experts."[7]

These status distinctions were produced by the economic system. Yet they conceal the growing similarity between the middle and other segments of the laboring class, which has been caused by more recent forces at work in the economy. As a result, it is more and more difficult to keep up the old pretenses. If that is true, it is necessary to clarify just what is meant by these middle layers of American society. If we are not a class, and our cultural values as a status group do not accurately reflect our real position in society, how are we to define ourselves? The sociological literature alone on the characteristics or even existence of a middle class is complex and fractious to say the least. We will touch here only on the main features of the debate that bear most directly on our argument. There are, however, some guidelines and matters of consensus emerging from the fray, which parallel our own sense of the increasingly tenuous position of the American middle sector.

Much of the argument about the existence of a new middle class has focused on whether or not there are recognizably separate interests by which to define it. If control over property is central to social class, as we assume, then does the middle class have a distinctive relation to the means of production? Are these class interests different from both those of the capital-owning class, and the working class and poor?

There are three basic positions that attempt to interpret the place of the new middle sectors. (1) The middle sectors are a distinct new class, separate from both the working class and the elite. There are definable middle class interests that are in opposition to the interests of both the workers and owners. (2) The middle sectors are not a distinct class, but instead are located with one foot in the working class and the other foot in the owning classes. Interests are sometimes aligned with the working class, sometimes with the owners. (3) The middle sectors are a part of a single larger class. In fact, the middle layers, working proletariat, and the poor are three class fractions belonging to a general laboring class. All its members earn their income through wages or salaries; though there are internal differences, they have much more in common with each other than they do with the elites.

The Middle Sector as a Distinct Class

Barbara and John Ehrenreich have attempted to define the middle sector as a distinct class. This position argues for the existence of a "professional-managerial class" (PMC) made up of technicians, managers, and "culture producers." The latter are all those who create, or socialize us to believe in, the dominant ideologies of our society, e.g., advertising and media executives or teachers.[8] Members of the PMC are said to have distinctive economic interests that are antagonistic to those of both workers and owners. That is, they are "salaried mental workers who do not own the means of production and whose major function in the social division of labor may be described broadly as the reproduction of capitalist culture and capitalist class relations."[9] For the Ehrenreichs the PMC is quintessentially the bureaucrats, technocrats, and purveyors of information and popular culture who are not essential to production per se, like the working class. They are the ones who ensure that the system of production runs smoothly, either through managerial control or by making people believe in it.

The PMC is characterized by more than just its common economic position; it has a similar cultural style as well. "At any moment in its historical development after its earliest, formative period, a class is characterized by a coherent social and cultural existence; members of a class share a common life style."[10] This argument as a whole may seem similar to the earlier discussion of the Weberian position on class. The Ehrenreichs, however, have essentially collapsed the distinction between class and status group. The PMC is considered to be a separate class because it has both a coherent economic position and a self-identified status.

There are real difficulties with this argument. First, does the PMC actually share a "coherent social and cultural existence" apart from the working class? Certainly people in many laboring occupations that the Ehrenreichs would exclude from the PMC would define themselves as middle class. On the other hand, there can also be deep cultural divisions between supposed members of the PMC. The Ehrenreichs themselves note the suspicion that can exist between individuals in the liberal arts, service professions, or especially education, and those involved with business and industry.[11] Academics, for example, may assert their moral purity as experts, while viewing "Madison Avenue types" or business managers as having "bought into the system." The elitism and disdain, of course, work as well from the other direction. Those in the business world might dismiss the academy as the ivory tower and academics as incompetents— "those who can't do, teach."

People in the same status group, therefore, do not necessarily represent a single class. "Yuppies" may be an easily recognizable group, but they are hardly a class. American society has a highly complex division of labor which creates many different economic statuses. This is coupled ironically with the machinery of commercial mass media, which makes for a very homogeneous popular culture. As a result there are bound to be many contradictions in our consciousness; many may *call* themselves middle class, but this might not fit easily with their objective economic positions.

The Middle Sector as "Trapped Between Classes"

If the PMC does not have a particularly distinctive cultural style as a class, what of the proposition that it occupies a similar economic position? In fact the PMC refers less to a common economic position than to those who perform similar economic functions. Unlike workers and owners who engage directly in production, the PMC is said to reproduce the capitalist system; it provides the cultural images and technical expertise that sustain the system and make it run.

Erik Wright points out two problems with this view. First, "*every* position determined by capitalist relations of production to some extent or another contributes to the reproduction of those relations."[12] That is, the working class and capital-owning class, as a consequence of their positions within the structure, also perpetuate the kind of society in which we all live. People in certain positions, such as teachers, managers, or advertising executives, may specialize in promoting ideas or structures that ensure that we all act to maintain the status quo. But this does not distinguish the PMC as a class from the working and owning classes. Second, it is not true that the PMC is concerned only with "reproduction" and maintenance of society. It is also engaged in productive activities. "Engineers, for example, do not merely function to reproduce capitalist class relations. They also design bridges and in other ways perform clearly productive functions."[13] If members of the PMC are engaged in both productive and reproductive functions, then there is no basis for distinguishing them from the owning and working classes.

Wright's solution is to reject the need to place every position in the division of labor unambiguously into a given class. Certain occupations have conflicting interests that pertain to several classes, not fitting easily into any. "[T]hey represent positions which are torn between the basic contradictory class relations of capitalist society."[14] Two positions, for instance, that share interests with both the working and owning classes are managers and semi-autonomous employees.[15] The quintessential example of the former would be the technocrats. These are the technicians and professionals who, like many workers, have only limited control over their own work and other employees. With owners, however, they do control aspects of the work process and share some authority in the company.[16] They, thus, represent a position combining characteristics of large-scale owners and workers.

Semi-autonomous employees, on the other hand, occupy a position straddling that of workers and small-scale owners. This includes occupations such as laboratory researchers, professors at elite universities, and other highly technical white-collar employees.[17] We might add other professions here such as physicians, who have increasingly lost control over their work situation with the proliferation of corporate medicine and Health Maintenance Organizations.[18] The ambivalent position of these semi-autonomous workers is largely the by-product of the prole-tarianization of independent professionals, skilled workers, and artisans, which occurred with the expansion and centralization of the economy in the nineteenth century. Once self-employed small producers, like merchants and artisans, they are now employees in larger concerns. They retain a significant amount of control over their immediate daily work routines, unlike the classic proletarian position of an assembly line worker. Yet, they are no longer independent producers. They may call themselves em-ployees, rather than workers, and receive a salary rather than a wage, but with other workers they *are* dependent on the owner for the basic conditions of their working lives.

The Middle Sector as a Fragment in the Laboring Class

There is a certain logical movement in the development of these views on the place of the middle sectors. Where the first claims that the PMC is an independent class with its own interests, the second suggests that the interests of these middle positions are drawn from both the owning and working classes. There is yet a third position, one that we will adopt. In this view the middle layers are a *part* of a wider laboring class, though with some significant *internal* contradictions.[19]

The argument for this position rests on the changing nature of control in the workplace throughout the history of the United

States. Since the Industrial Revolution in this country, not only the kind of jobs but the conditions under which they are carried out have dramatically changed and become more complex. Richard Edwards documents three types of control over the workplace: simple, technological, and bureaucratic control. Simple control evolved in the initial stages of the Industrial Revolution, a time when firms were generally small and the individual entrepreneur exercised personal and arbitrary power over workers. An Edison or McCormick could go into the plant and with a small group of foremen effectively dictate working conditions.[20] Workers had virtually no power in such a system, but neither was the control simply naked coercion. "[The owner's] success depended on his ability to get work out of his workers, whether by harsh discipline or by inspiration; undoubtedly, most attempted to use both."[21]

While simple control evolved first, it still provides a major source for the complexity and contradictory character of American society today. Simple control is particularly characteristic of the labor market in such areas as small manufacturing, service and retail sales jobs, and temporary and typing-pool office work.[22]

Technical control came about primarily as a response to the increasing size and complexity of the firm, coupled with the shift to assembly line production. It was no longer possible for a charismatic employer like Ford to exercise personal authority. With the assembly line, itself a by-product of the search to increase productivity and reduce costs, workers found themselves ruled by the requirements of the machines rather than the personal whim of the owner, straw boss, or foreman. Edwards notes the impact of this even in industries like meat packing: "By establishing the pace at which hogs were driven up the passages and onto the slaughter platform, managers could set the pace of work for the entire workforce."[23] Supervisors no longer had primary responsibility for directing the workers. The requirements of machinery and the line severed the old personal though unequal relationship between owner and worker.

There are three further consequences of technical control: the number of supervisory workers needed to control other workers is vastly reduced, the work force becomes more homogeneous, and the degree of control by owners is generally increased.[24] A contradictory result of the increased homogeneity of the labor force is that workers could more readily see their common interests as workers.[25] The great union movements from the late 1800s up until World War II are precisely correlated with the rise in assembly-line industries. It makes sense, thus, that technical control today is characteristic of jobs in assembly-line production work, such as the auto and steel industries, or machine-paced clerical work.[26]

The increasing power given to owners by technical control is particularly evident with the coming of the computer. Computers vastly increase the ability to monitor the quality of work and productivity of each worker. But they also "de-skill" workers, since jobs require less knowledge and training. This increases the tediousness of many occupations. Furthermore, if virtually anyone can do your job, then you lose the ability to negotiate with employers. With computers entire new areas of *information*-oriented jobs, whether performed by clerks or physicians, become increasingly subject to the technical control of automation. The loss of control that the traditional working class experienced with the Industrial Revolution, the middle class with our presumed monopoly as experts and "head workers" is experiencing with the information revolution.

The third type of control, bureaucratic, grew out of the formal structures found increasingly in large-scale national and even transnational firms. The shift away from assembly-line industries to service industries and the increasing centralization of firms, with more and more employees in areas other than direct production, led to a radical increase in bureaucracy. Such companies control the workplace by creating intricate divisions of labor which circumscribe each position with complex rules. Bureucratic control "is built into job categories, work rules, promotion procedures, discipline, wage scales, definitions of responsibilities, and the like. [It] establishes the impersonal force of 'company rules' or 'company policy'. . . ."[27]

In companies such as IBM and Polaroid, bureaucratic con-

trol resulted as well from explicit attempts to avoid the unioniza-
tion that could result from technical control.[28] Bureaucratic rules
split the work force into highly specialized categories, immediate
work conditions, and elaborate differences in pay. Polaroid, for
example, has fifteen hourly and ten salaried grades for jobs. This
divides the workers' short-term interests and limits their ability to
think about common issues around which to organize.[29] In
addition, loyalty to the system can receive real rewards. The
higher pay, increasing rights, and job security with longevity
encourage workers to compete with each other individually for
benefits, rather than organize collectively.[30]

By instituting the "rule of law" coupled with incentives,
firms and organizations can reinstitute the old loyalties of simple
control. The worker's allegiance, however, is no longer given to
the owner but directly to the company, university, or other
organization. We even wear the institutional logo on our clothes
as a sign of prestige. To think of organizing or, worse, striking is
a betrayal of the "family." A new paternalism is established in
which working for rights collectively is thought of as rude or
uncivil. Unlike the obvious conflict engendered by a straw boss or
assembly line, bureaucratic rule becomes invisible. The subtlety
of its control allows it to be taken for granted as natural,
necessary, or even just.[31]

Such control, nonetheless, produces consequences that paradoxically may lead to greater power among workers. Bureaucratic
control began with the white-collar employees of large-scale firms.
With the tremendous increase in industrial and governmental
office work, however, blue-collar positions are now bureaucrati-
cally regulated as well. As a result, the traditional barrier between
head and hand work is being broken down. The work of technical
and professional workers, or those in private or public bureaucracies, may differ little from the assembly line. All of these jobs
increasingly are characterized by highly specialized and routine
tasks.[32]

The rise of bureaucratic control, therefore, provides real
evidence for the position that the middle class is essentially
similar to all other workers. It is not an independent class, nor is

it caught between classes. Edwards, in fact, argues that the forms of control are correlated with, and in part produce, three different "fractions" in a larger working class: the *working poor,* who are found in jobs with simple control; the *traditional proletariat,* who are often ethnically based manual workers, clericals, and factory operatives; and finally, the *middle layers,* who tend to be white males and stand between all lower-level administrative and production workers on the one side, and capitalists and the various echelons of high management on the other.[33]

We would prefer to label these fractions the *laboring class,* since the term *working class* seems too close to only fraction two, the traditional proletariat. All laboring class fractions lack control over their labor. Each may have different immediate interests, but they also have common long-term, more basic interests which put them into conflict with those who buy their labor. On the surface, the type of jobs done by the middle layer and their suburban or "gentrified" lifestyles makes them seem different from the working poor or proletariat. Much of this, however, is due to higher wages rather than any basic difference in economic position. All fractions in the laboring class have to work for others and are dependent on them. This gives each fraction in the laboring class two basic interests in common: it raises the specter of *economic instability* and signals a *real lack of power.*

The Middle Layers and the Laboring Class

Historically, of course, the American middle class has experienced an economic boom as a result of the technical and bureaucratic expansion to which we have referred. It has been a source of pride in the United States that the middle class has been able to own its own homes. Education has been a ticket to the good life of material prosperity. Yet, the 1970s have recalled a sense of economic tenuousness. "Specific groups have been threatened by depression in the stock brokerage business, the cancellation of military contracts . . . and the decline in school enrollments, and all groups have been made more nervous by the deep recession starting in 1974."[34]

This threat to the economic well-being of a large portion of the middle layers, the proletariat, and working poor is not a temporary downturn. As we will argue, the move away from assembly-line industries to high tech automation promises higher levels of chronic unemployment in all areas of the laboring class. This cannot be separated from the increasing centralization of wealth and internationalization of the division of labor which have occurred with the rise of transnational corporations. Large corporations can close down domestic plants and reopen them in the Third World to take advantage of "free trade zones" and cheaper labor. This increases the economic instability of all workers in any given country and effectively undermines what little power local or even nationally based unions have. Such transnational economic forces underscore the similarity of the different fractions in the laboring class domestically and point to the common interests of workers in both the first and Third worlds. As a result, we are likely to see more and more efforts at cooperation between workers internationally, such as the recent Coca-Cola strike in Guatemala.

The increasing economic precariousness of many in the middle fraction is reflected in the loss of earning power since the 1960s, the greater necessity of two-income families, and the fact that a college education is not as accessible. In part, this is due to the previously mentioned "de-skilling" of many middle level jobs; the ascendance of automation either reduces the level of education necessary for the job, and therefore its pay rating, or does away with the job altogether. This leads to what has been called the proletarianization of middle level jobs—it not only reduces their financial remuneration and number, but also makes them more dull and repetitive. The traditional working class has often felt this estrangement from their work. There may be a real pride in actually producing something with your hands. But there can also be boredom and indifference induced by the assembly line and a feeling of inferiority because the person is "only" doing hand work. The American belief in individualism may lead to a particular viciousness here; those in the laboring class who "don't make it" may be stuck with the feeling that it is their own fault.[35] This seems summed up in a sign found occasionally in proletarian establishments: "If you're so smart, how come you're working in a place like this?"

The middle layers are coming to experience these same feelings of estrangement. We express this in terms of being caught in the red tape of bureaucracy. With the rise of automation and bureaucratic control, many of us find ourselves in jobs with little room for creativity or flexibility. We think of our life's work as "paper pushing." There does not seem to be much difference between the autoworker, insurance assessor, secretary, lab technician, sales representative, or an employee in any government agency. Even people in the professions, such as teachers, engineers, lawyers, and others, are losing autonomy as they become employees. Our daily lives are characterized often by saying, "I don't make the rules; I only work here." This signals an underlying sense and reality of *individual powerlessness* in all fractions of the laboring class.

There does seem to be evidence that we are defining ourselves much less in terms of jobs than by the type of leisure styles they will support. Work is essentially viewed as a means to other ends. Like the working class who "pay their dues," we say we "put in time" and "live for the weekend." "T.G.I.F."(thank God it's Friday) is learned by every school child, and "deferred gratification" is rapidly disappearing in favor of an individualized search for pleasure now. Accompanying this cynicism and sense of hopelessness about the possibility of change is an even more commonplace and debilitating isolation, loneliness, and depression. Two particularly agonizing examples of this are the marginal position of the elderly in our society and the dramatic increase in teenage suicide attempts, now the second leading cause of death among American teenagers. But the search for "Mr. [or Ms.] Goodbar" and the preoccupation with discovering "who we *really* are" appear to be constant expressions of individual restlessness and lack of power.

This belief in individualism is related to the rise of bureaucratic control and the proliferating division of labor in American society today. Under bureaucratic control the world is seen as one in which individuals are players in large overarching companies or organizations. The task is to be tough competitors who can individually make it up the ladder of success. At times, however, this can even work against bureaucratic control. We admire the corporate image, but we may not have much loyalty to individual companies. Corporations complain of young executives who look for splashy short-term successes to promote their own career trajectory rather than the longer-term interests of the company.

There is no doubt that the ideology of individualism has been particularly pervasive among the middle sector; indeed, it has been one of the main impediments to the middle class's thinking of itself as part of a wider laboring class. We think we have raised ourselves up through a good education, hard work, and careful saving; poverty and powerlessness are taken to be individual failures, not collective traps.

Yet, the roots of individualism go much deeper than bureaucratic control; they reside in the very character of industrial capitalism as an economic system. Individualism affects *all* of us. In large part this is due to the fact that capitalism removed much of economic production from the family.[36] The workplace took on the imagery of the battlefield or nature. Every day we would "go off to the wars" or "the jungle," while the home became our castle or refuge from the storm. Work was a place we had to go, where we were on "company time," to earn our living. Home was a place where we could do what we wanted, when we wanted. It is no wonder that when a woman has worked in the home, without pay, her work has become subordinate to the man who supports the family. Since she did not have to go out and do battle, her role was to give aid to her "knight in shining armor."

The split between public and private, working and leisure, attended the individual's loss of control over labor and personal circumstances. The world became a place where a person did not count for much, and mysterious "social forces" reigned. The individual and society were thought of as two distinct, even opposed, things. With the utilitarian logic of capitalism, *everything* has a price. The marketplace and public sphere generally were considered to be crass; personal life came to seem more lofty and genuine. Thus, while we know we have to make a living, we put down those who revel in it as nouveau riche. We distinguish between commercial artists and the fine arts; the one is vulgar, the other creative. Those in the public sphere, such as politicians, are judged on the basis of effective and charismatic personal style rather than commitment to the public good.[37]

This elevation of the personal leads each of us to search constantly for our "true" self, away from society.[38] We presume in others and ourselves a single, "real" person— "I want to get to know the real *you*"—which can be found only by getting beyond the superficial masks of public roles. Our world is one that led to the rise of existentialism, a concern about meaning-lessness, and a fear of angst and doubt. It is we who buy all the books on personal growth and have filled the dictionary with words that begin with *self*.

Yet, the middle sectors are the joiners in a nation of joiners; we make up the ranks of every kind of voluntary association imaginable. It is telling, however, that such groups *are* voluntary. They are premised on the autonomy of the individual, on the creation of social links to serve special interests. Single issue clubs as well as politics abound. Whether they be groups for animal rights, lower tax rates, or the owners of Airstream trailers, chances are they will exist.

Any of the latest best-seller lists with the seemingly endless stream of faddish books on "getting yourself together" make it obvious that we look for sources of meaning in what first appear to be the most bizarre corners. That diet plans or "personal management" techniques dominate the mass media should not be surprising given the emphasis on individualism in American society. At last count, for example, there were 29,068 "theories, treatments and outright schemes for losing weight."[39]

There are, however, at least three sources of identity that seem especially prevalent among middle Americans. The first is consumerism as a way of life. With the nineteenth-century origins of the department store in France, buyers were encouraged to "invest objects with personal meaning, above and beyond their utility. . . ."[40] Goods became a way to achieve personal fulfillment rather than satisfy some utilitarian need. Is it any wonder, then, that we spend hours browsing through catalogues and go to malls on Friday night for entertainment? Our children would rather die than be dressed in the wrong brand of denims. It was Marx who suggested that "you are what you do." We seem to have changed that into "you are what you consume."

A second source of identity and meaning is nationalism. Indeed, many in the middle layers and some from the ethnic-based proletariat have been among the most ardent supporters of nationalism, one of our few enduring ascribed identities. This may be, in part, because of the past history of substantial growth in the middle sector. As it expanded in the years between 1850 and 1960 with rapid industrialization and bureaucratization, it was easy to be thankful that we were either born an American or were able to come over on the boat. Patriotism may also be coupled with lack of consciousness as a class. It certainly may lead us to blur class consciousness by forgetting our similarity to people in comparable positions in other countries. Yet we can also act with an awareness that our interests are not always best served by those who shape national policy. A hint of that occurred during the Vietnam War, when there was far more doubt about our national purpose than during World War II. A significant number of the laboring class questioned whether or not the Vietnam War was a "rich person's war"; were their sons and daughters really dying for the national honor?

A final source of identity for the laboring class has been religion. Americans are increasingly becoming members of churches. Certainly mainstream churches are growing, but it is the evangelical groups that are expanding most rapidly. These are precisely the churches that seek to establish the least ambiguous, all-embracing social identity for their members. They do this, however, *within* the dominant ideology of individualism. Pat Robertson, Robert Schuller, or Jerry Falwell, for example, provide people with a personal sense of identity, but not one that allows for the interpretation of problems as having real structural causes. Solutions are seen either as a process of personal adjustment—the permanence of problems sent by the devil—or as a result of individual effort. In either case the problems and their resolutions are couched in individualistic terms; *you* may become better off, but the structures that produce inequality for entire classes of people remain firmly in place. This is true of even our most charitable moments. We will hold hands with others for "Hands Across America" or give millions of dollars to "Live-Aid" or "Farm-Aid" concerts, but these largely ignore the underlying structures that produce poverty in the first place.

We have argued, thus, that with the centralization of the economy, the rise of transnational corporations, and the coming of the information revolution, there is a growing similarity in the interests of all fractions of the laboring class. This is particularly evident in an increasing economic precariousness and sense of powerlessness. Each fraction may be controlled in different ways, but there is a common sense of apathy or cynicism about collectively changing the workplace or political agendas. The indifference stems from the bureaucratization and ideologies of individualism produced by capitalism itself. They prevent us from seeing that the old individualistic ways to move up the ladder no longer work for most of us. While many are stepping on each other to try, most are falling farther down the rungs.

There is another irony in this situation. Just as individualism emerged originally with capitalism, changes in economic structures today are creating the conditions for a new sense of reciprocity. The rise of capitalism produced and was in turn fostered by the reality and ideologies of individualism. But contemporary capitalism is beginning to cut the ground out from beneath that individualism. The economic insecurity and sense of powerlessness, created by capital accumulation, have pushed each of the fractions of the laboring class closer together. Each group will continue to have its own immediate interests, but the underlying economic structures assure a growing set of more basic long-term interests held in common. These unite us as a wider class in opposition to the elites who own so much; "the chief adversary of each class fraction is not another fraction within the [laboring class] but rather the business community."[41]

The new commonality in laboring class positions provides a

basis on which to build socially oriented ideologies. As alternatives to individualism, those ideologies more accurately reflect what is going on today. By no means are we suggesting a simplistic and misguided return to Marx's original two-class model, staring at each other across the brink of class warfare. There are, and will remain, significant differences in the day-to-day appearance of the middle layers, traditional poletariat, and working poor.

But we no longer want to be deceived by appearances. Deep and abiding changes have occurred in our economic position, changes that make our beliefs about individualistic heroism resemble tilting at windmills. We need to think about changing those beliefs because they are so destructive to both ourselves and others. The old individual villains are not the source of the problem; sin can indeed be institutional.

2

Plight and Promise in the Middle Sector

Modern industrial nations such as the United States are dominated by their economic institutions. In this sense, at least, it is correct to say that economic forces drive the society and shape its institutions. The contemporary fascination with the "bottom line" is testimony to this economic domination. The central importance of the economic, over time, has contributed to hopelessness for the poor and effective powerlessness for the middle sector.

There is a certain irony in the development of industrial societies. Many observers would argue that such development has occurred most forcefully and fully in places like the United States where capitalistic modes of production have been dominant. These societies have been able to generate long-run surplus, which has allowed extensive improvement in standards of living relative to non-industrial societies. The irony is that industrial societies with such a great capacity for eliminating poverty still have both relative and absolute deprivation, together with a distribution of income that is becoming less rather than more egalitarian.

The incidence of poverty in the United States, for example, has been increasing over the past decade. In 1970, 25.4 million people, or 12.6% of the population, had incomes that fell below the poverty level. By 1983, the numbers had risen to 35.3 million people, which was 15.2% of the population. During the same period, the distribution of income shifted so that the middle part of the income distribution got relatively smaller while the extremes increased. The median real household income fell over the same period by 6.8%, from $22,410 in 1970 to $20,885 in 1983.

Table 1

Percent Distribution of Income by Households, 1970 and 1983
Income Measured in Constant (1983) Dollars

| | | Percent Distribution | | |
| | Number of | 0– | $15,000– | $35,000 |
Year	Households	$14,000	34,999	and over
1970	64.8 million	32.6%	47.7%	19.7%
1983	85.4 million	35.9%	39.8%	24.3%

Source: U.S. Department of Commerce, Bureau of the Census, *1984 Statistical Abstract of the United States*, p. 442, Table 734.

Many of the non-industrial countries in the world are so poor that even with equal distribution of income and wealth, everyone would live in poverty. For example, the thirty-five poorest countries in the world in 1983 had an average annual income of $260 per person.[1] It is obvious under such circumstances that the powerful might seize luxury for themselves in part to escape the impact of poverty. Conditions are quite different, however, in the nineteen industrial market economies. These countries had a 1983 average annual gross national product of $11,060 per person. Why should countries this rich have people still living in poverty? In the United States, for example, the bottom 20% of the population receives only 5.3% of the income.[2] That translates into an annual average income of $3,740 per person. This is well below the poverty line officially defined by the Bureau of the Census. In contrast, the top 10% of the population received 23.3% of the income or an average of $32,875 per person. (For more information about the United States' income distribution, see the appendix to chapter 3.)

Not only is there a large gap between the rich and the poor in the United States, but as was suggested above, the gap has actually been widening since the middle 1970s. There are more people living in poverty in the United States now than ever before. Why have the rich seized so much that the poor cannot have enough? How do the rich manage to keep their very large share? Can it be otherwise?

Structural Entrapment in the Economic System

Most middle Americans are bound to a structural logic that the old middle class created but we cannot control. This leaves us powerless, *as individuals*, to make meaningful changes in the way society creates output and distributes rewards. The Protestant Reformation and the rise of a private ownership market economy established the conditions for a new individualism. Our own history and socialization process in the United States have raised the ideology of individualism to new heights.

As long as both the logic of individualism and that of a private ownership market economy are accepted, one is stuck with the consequences that flow from such a system. Unequal and often inequitable distributions of income, wealth, and power come about because private ownership and control carry with them the possibilities for accumulation. Significant differences in accumulation mean significant differences in the distribution of wealth. Control over the decision-making processes of the economic system rests with those who own and control the means of production. Thus, those with large amounts of accumulated wealth also have large amounts of economic power. And large differences in income can flow from those differences in wealth and power. If the logic of individual private ownership is inviolate, then most of us must face a social existence in which we are economically insecure and powerless to change things. In fact, all we are able to do is use minimal income redistribution programs to apply Band-Aids to some of the deepest wounds caused by income disparity.

When one talks in these terms, it sounds as though the only negative impact of the existing system is that some people are poor. But the structures under which Americans live are not only limiting the freedom and choices of the poor, they are entrapping the middle sectors as well. As a result of the scale of corporate enterprises in our economic system and their concentration of wealth, they have become semi-autonomous and partially in control of the nation-states in which they nominally reside.

To illustrate, in 1983 total wealth in all forms in the United States amounted to $3.9 trillion. Of that total, 62% was held by businesses, 21.2% by government, and only 16.8% by households.[3] (The appendix to chapter 3 provides additional data about the wealth distribution.) To be sure, one can make the claim that most of these businesses are technically owned by their stockholders. That is, formal ownership of the assets of the corporation is represented by the holding of stock certificates. Since many stock certificates are owned by individuals, this reintroduces ownership by households, at least by proxy. Of course, in today's complex financial markets, the bulk of corporate stock is owned by foundations, financial institutions, and other corporations. That moves individual ownership at least one step further away. Even then, it is important to note that of those assets owned by businesses, over 75% are owned by those very large businesses with more than $250 million in asset holdings.[4] Such giant corporations are really under the control of their management and feel almost no influence from the individual small stockholder. It is increasingly naive to think that somehow the middle class exercises any degree of autonomy or control in these circumstances.

To further illustrate this point, consider the fact that each of the 200 largest industrial corporations in the United States had 1984 sales that were larger than the entire gross domestic product of each of the fifteen poorest countries in the world.[5] There were only sixteen countries in the world whose GDP[6] was larger than the annual sales of Exxon, which in 1984 was the largest industrial corporation, with sales of $90.8 billion.[7] To put that differently, in terms of its generation of economic activity, Exxon would have been the seventeenth largest country in the world in 1984. Such concentrations of wealth and power are not simply docile in the face of reform. It is equally unrealistic to imagine a voluntary sharing of power by the existing elite. Where, then, is the supposed power of the "silent majority" who constitute the middle sectors of the United States socioeconomic system?

During the Industrial Revolution, the bourgeoisie seized effective control of the society from the aristocracy. But in the ensuing two centuries, the bourgeoisie themselves have become a new elite. In fact, the old bourgeoisie have already been transformed into an international class whose interests transcend national boundaries. Virtually all the Fortune 500 companies in the United States have very significant international operations and subsidiaries. In addition, there are other international giant corporations, based elsewhere but which impinge on the United States through their operations and subsidiaries. The world has become an international marketplace; capital but not labor is highly mobile both inside and beyond national boundaries. That means that a corporation can move its plant and production to a foreign country in search of cheap labor or preferential tax treatment, leaving American workers jobless. Workers do not have that same ability to change locale and improve their economic well-being. Thus, it is the highly concentrated ownership of capital that confers mobility, status, and power on its holders.

Because of this concentration of wealth and power there are ever greater restrictions on economic and social mobility for the laboring classes in the United States. The contemporary middle sector, for example, travels more and changes jobs more than any generation in history. Yet the ability to change social class or relative position in the income distribution is less than it was in the eighteenth and nineteenth centuries. As an example of this, the middle 50% of the wealth distribution (leaving out the top 20% and the bottom 30%) owned around 26% of all wealth assets at the time of the American Revolution. In 1973, that same group owned just a little over 15% of all wealth assets. The bottom 30% owned virtually no wealth assets in either time period, which means that the losses for the middle group went exclusively to those in the top 25% of the wealth distribution. The upper class gained considerably in wealth terms at the expense of the middle sectors.[8] And, of course, virtually all the wealth assets owned by the middle 50% are now in the form of residential property and farmland. In the nineteenth century, the ownership of farmland may have conferred some power on the middle sector, since agriculture was the principal form of economic activity. But as the society became increasingly industrialized, the locus of decision-making power and control shifted to those who owned industrial assets. Such assets are almost non-existent among the wealth owned by the middle 50% in contemporary America. Even this view significantly understates the concentration of wealth, since it ignores the still wider wealth gaps that exist between the first and Third worlds.

Industrialization led not only to increasing accumulation of wealth, but also to a change in the nature of work by dramatically redefining the number and kinds of jobs that were available. The Industrial Revolution of the nineteenth and early twentieth centuries accomplished the automation of unskilled labor, the creation of technical control that was discussed in chapter 1. Because industrial economies grew so fast, however, it was possible to create enough new jobs to absorb both labor force growth and the workers released by the automation of their old jobs.

Of course, some of the control of unemployment in the late nineteenth century resulted from pushing women and children out of the labor force rather than from new job creation. The social legislation of the last half of the nineteenth century outlawed child labor and drastically reduced the possibilities for female labor force participation. That permitted economic growth to absorb the expansion of the labor force without creating large-scale unemployment. Such social legislation moved women to an even more subordinate position in the economic hierarchy as it took them out of the labor force. The higher levels of skill required for automated jobs allowed the rates of pay for factory work to rise high enough that men could afford to take on those jobs and still support their families. The social legislation ensured that women would not be competing for these now more rewarding occupations.

Nevertheless, overall economic growth in the manufacturing sector during the last half of the nineteenth and the first half of the twentieth centuries was extensive in part because of automation's impact on productivity. For example, the auto industry became a highly automated sector of the economy between 1910 and 1920. That caused large increases in the productivity of labor employed in the auto industry. Those productivity increases, in turn, allowed the industry to begin to pay much higher wages. Workers earning high incomes were not only producing cars, but they also became an important part of the market for cars. Automation allowed a given number of cars to be produced with less labor and thus caused a reduction in the demand for labor. But the higher demand for cars flowing from higher wages completely overwhelmed this depressing effect of automation. The net result was a rapidly expanding industry that created many new jobs.

This phenomenon continued well into the twentieth century. For example, potential employment (essentially equal to the total labor force) grew at an annual rate of 1.55% from 1948 to 1969.[9] During the same period, national income grew at an annual rate of 3.85%.[10] The rapid growth of national income relative to the labor force occurred because labor productivity was rising. Productivity rises, in part, as a result of the use of better capital equipment and technology. The use of new equipment and new technology indeed was allowing fewer people to produce the same output. But that same phenomenon gave such a boost to both production *and* demand that employers were hiring more, not fewer, workers. As a consequence, the rate of unemployment stayed low, 3.8% in 1948, and 3.5% in 1969.

This contrasts with the thirteen-year period from 1970 to 1983, when the potential labor force grew at an average annual rate of 2.24%, but output grew by only about 2.7% annually.[11] This growth in output was not fast enough to absorb all the new entrants into the labor force, and as a consequence unemployment rose from 4.9% in 1970 to 9.5% in 1983. This problem was caused, at least in part, by slow productivity growth. It may be investment in new capital that creates the conditions for growth sufficient to allow for new jobs. From 1948 to 1969, however, the annual rate of growth in net capital stock was 4.1%,[12] while the comparable rate of growth during the 1970–1983 period fell to

3.4%.[13] Despite the economic recovery that began in late 1982, the unemployment rate in 1987 is still well above 6%.

Economic growth in the United States over the past 150 years was, until the 1970s, accomplished with relatively low unemployment and with rising absolute standards of living. The rise in standard of living was even more pronounced in the twenty-five years following World War II as the United States became the predominant economic, political, and military force in the world.

However, while economic growth did play a positive role in job creation and in raising standards of living through much of this period, its benefits were by no means evenly distributed among the population. Many Americans discovered in the 1960s that despite the incredible rise in average incomes, not all were sharing in the bonanza of economic growth even in the United States. The rapid growth in postwar population, the dearth of unskilled jobs, and the increasing entrance into the labor force by marginal groups pointed out sharply that the cornucopia was not to be shared with Blacks, Hispanics, women, or the elderly. Even with more jobs available in general, these marginal groups found that their access to jobs was blocked.

In 1967 the median income of Black households was about 58% of that of white households. In response to this and other conditions of minority and female economic disadvantage, liberal politicians created a plethora of tax and transfer programs. But despite temporary improvements, the conditions of most in these groups are no better in the 1980s than they were in the early 1960s. In fact, by 1983, Black median household income had shrunk to only 56% of that of white households. What makes that situation even worse is that in 1983, both Black and white median incomes were lower in real terms than they were in 1967. Both groups had suffered a decline in their real purchasing power. In the face of such stagnant growth in real income, society is unlikely to create and maintain tax and transfer programs that do much to redress the imbalance in incomes between whites and Blacks, men and women, or the young and the old. Now, the neo-conservatives who have come to power in the 1980s want to claim that the income redistribution programs themselves have destroyed incentives and created lasting poverty for many. It is in the context of the reductions mandated by these conservatives that social programs have been cut and minorities have lost much of the ground they gained during the late sixties and early seventies.

Neither the liberals nor the conservatives have explained what is really going on. By no means do we want to imply that the anti-poverty and anti-discrimination programs of the 1960s and 1970s were failures, useless, or without good moral intent. They simply did not go to the heart of the problem. In a system with private ownership of the means of production in a market economy, there is bound to be increasing concentration of power and wealth. In our society, roughly 80% of the income arising from production is paid out in wages and salaries, while the other 20% is property income in the form of rent, interest, and profit. This property income is paid to those who own the means of production. For example, in the United States today, fully 60% of that ownership is concentrated among 1% of the population. In fact, 90% of the population owns no such assets at all.[14] Therefore one-fifth of all income goes to a very small segment of the population.

It is this small part of the population that effectively controls our surplus production. They are the only ones with large enough incomes to allow for any meaningful accumulation. Not only do they control the existing means of production, but their control over surplus and their ability to accumulate make them the only creators of new means of production. Over time, therefore, they increase both their control of wealth assets and their economic power.

It was this group of wealth owners and accumulators whose acquisitive goals led to the automation of production which replaced unskilled labor. Since technological advance allows at least a temporary advantage to the innovator, new technology was pursued in an effort to make more profit. The successful businesses found themselves getting larger and placing more capital investment at risk each time they attempted an innovative change. That led them to try to achieve greater control over both the production activity and the market in order to reduce the risk. The combined pursuit of growth and control led to the current situation: an economic system dominated by monopoly and oligopoly business firms.

As has been suggested, earlier attempts to automate, while they eliminated some jobs, created far more because of the rapid growth in output that accompanied them. Besides, the middle sectors were not concerned about such automation. After all, a lot of the new jobs being created were in management and supervisory positions, and that enlarged the size of the middle fraction. Rather than facing competition for their jobs, middle level managers found themselves in a wonderful world in which the numbers of new jobs exceeded, at least for a time, the development of the management personnel needed to fill the jobs. So, we all nodded sagely and talked about the blessings that our private ownership market economy was bestowing on us as a result of our unprecedented burst of technological innovation. After all, it was the working fraction and the poor who were at risk under these conditions, not the middle sectors.

When one compares recent experience with the past, it is easy to see that things have changed dramatically. For example, during the period from 1900 to 1950, the availability of jobs in the manufacturing sector of the economy increased at an annual rate of 2.1%, while the service sector grew slightly faster at 2.5%. From 1950 to 1970, the manufacturing sector continued to grow, but much more slowly, with new jobs being created at an annual rate of only 1.2%. Meanwhile, the service sector accelerated its pace and created new jobs as a rate of 2.9% per year.[15] With the stagflation of the 1970s, growth in manufacturing jobs disappeared, leaving the service sector to bear the burden of absorbing new labor force members. That sector continued to expand job opportunities at a rate of 2.9% per year from 1970 to 1985, but it was not enough to absorb all the labor force growth, and as a result, unemployment increased from 3.5% in 1969 to over 7% in early 1986.[16] (The appendix to chapter 3 provides detail about both unemployment and job growth.)

Using white-collar jobs and blue-collar jobs as a rough

indicator of the division of the laboring class between the middle sectors and the working and poor fractions, it appears that the middle sectors are doing well. White-collar jobs have continued to grow both in absolute terms and in relation to blue-collar jobs throughout this century. The 1980 census, for example, showed for the first time that there were more white-collar than blue-collar jobs in the society.

It is not clear, however, that this translates into a labor force that is economically better off. The most recent growth in white-collar jobs is occurring in the midst of an economy that has real growth only is the service sector. In fact, four of the five largest manufacturing industries had net job losses during the recovery from the recession of the early eighties. Virtually all the new job creation associated with the recovery came in the service industries.[17] Accompanying this trend in new job creation has been a reduction in worker incomes. Jobs in the goods-producing sectors of the economy have average wages of around $10 per hour, while the service sectors have much lower wages, averaging closer to $7 per hour.[18] Even if the service sectors tend to create more white-collar jobs, allowing the ratio of white- to blue-collar workers to rise, the lower average incomes mean that the new white-collar workers are earning smaller incomes and have even less ability to control their economic circumstances. We in the middle sector might still have the prestige of wearing a white collar, but it does not seem either to increase economic security or to reduce powerlessness.

As suggested above, the new jobs that have been created during the past fifteen years have been almost exclusively in the service industries, not the goods-producing industries. For example, from 1970 to 1985, there were approximately 27 million new jobs created. None of those jobs were in manufacturing, and only 1.8 million were in the other goods-producing industries, construction and mining. By contrast, the service sector added about 25 million jobs over the same period. Unfortunately, the labor force grew by more than 30 million people, so that even with record numbers of people employed, the numbers and the rate of unemployment increased significantly.

There is no reason to believe that these recent trends in industry and job growth will be substantially altered in the near future. That has continuing implications for the laboring class, particularly for the middle fraction. Computer technology is the wave of the present and future for information management. It is a capital-intensive technology, however, and that means we need fewer information managers than in the past. Replacing human information managers places much of the middle sector at risk in terms of job security, income, and standard of living. Because information-managing activities are being automated at a rate that far surpasses anything that occurred during the nineteenth and early twentieth centuries, there is no way we can re-employ all those who lose their jobs in a serious recession and create enough new jobs to absorb all the new entrants into the labor force.

To illustrate, the recovery period (November, 1982–May, 1984) from our most recent recession had the highest rate of economic growth for its first eighteen months of any postwar economic expansion. It also created 56% more jobs during the first eighteen months than the next most powerful expansion.[19] Despite this fact, the unemployment rate in 1984 stood well above 7.5%. Only the service industries were expanding, and their expansion, while extensive, was not at a fast enough rate to take care of labor force growth when the goods-producing industries were stagnant. And, as we have said, the goods-producing industries have been virtually stagnant since 1970.

This problem is exacerbated by the changes in real income discussed above. It is difficult for the goods-producing industries to experience much growth when the effective demand for their products is being consistently reduced by falling real incomes caused by the job and demand shift from the manufacturing to the service sector. The auto industry provides a particularly useful example. The recession of the early 1980s led to the largest industrial losses in history in the American auto industry. Each of the "big three" had at least one year in which their operating losses exceeded $1 billion. In the recovery, 1982–85, each of the "big three" experienced all-time record profits. General Motors' profit in 1985 exceeded $5 billion. That does not translate, however, into records for numbers of units sold and employment. In fact, the best year for domestic production of autos was 1973, with 9.7 million units. The 1985 production amounted to only 8.2 million units. Some of this drop can be accounted for by imports, but even with that, total sales in the United States in 1985 were some 400,000 units below their 1973 peak.[20]

In terms of employment, the peak year was also 1973, with 369,000 people employed in the auto industry. By 1982, in the deepest part of the auto recession, employment had fallen to 239,000. The recovery (1982–84) increased sales from 5.7 to 8.1 million units, but jobs have climbed back only to 307,000. That means approximately 60,000 auto industry jobs were lost over a period of ten years with no real hope of long-term job recovery. This is true despite the fact that the value of sales in constant dollars increased by $9 billion from 1973 to 1984. The numbers of new cars demanded has simply decreased because of the changed economic circumstances of the buying public. The recovery of profits has come about not because the market is so strong, but rather by means of wage and salary cuts, other cost-cutting measures, improved technology, and the oligopoly power of the industry, which has allowed it to raise the real price of a car even in the face of weaker demand.[21]

Unemployment and the threat of unemployment are likely to be a permanent and indeed worsening condition for many in both the working and middle sectors of the laboring class. Since industries have the resources and power to move their operations elsewhere, regionally or internationally, workers lose their ability to bargain in a world of corporations that operate across national boundaries (transnational or multinational corporations). There have been many recent threats of shutdown if workers do not agree to wage concessions. Of course, wage concessions generally mean lower incomes for all employees, with only top management being protected by bonus and profit-sharing agreements. This is already clear for the unionized skilled and clerical workers who make up a large portion of the working fraction of the laboring class. But it can also be seen in the increased commercialization of the professions and in the computerization of functions formerly performed by middle level managers.

Thus there is a parallel between the position of the middle sectors now and that of the working class in the nineteenth century. The inability to influence the decision-making process coupled with the threat of income and even job loss were important issues for the working class then and are important for the middle sectors today. Does that imply a similarity in the class *interests* of the two groups? There is a danger that today's middle sector is beginning to face the same chronic insecurity of finances, of jobs, and of lifestyle that has afflicted the working class and the poor since the nineteenth century, when the concern of the working class was not just that machines might take away their jobs. The more overriding fear was that machines would reduce the skill required to do the job and allow the employer to hire a less skilled and thus cheaper work force. In fact, it was not until very recent times that new technology became so complex that it simply allowed no room for the unskilled or semiskilled. But it is this latter phenomenon that is at the heart of both the continuing threat to the working class and the new and emerging threat to the middle sector information managers. If information technology can allow jobs to be done more efficiently and cheaply, then the elite who control the means of production will choose that technology, substituting smaller numbers of people skilled in the use of new technology for the larger numbers using the present technology. Such choices threaten both the security and the existence of many in the middle fraction. What is important to recognize in this situation is that the threat to our security does not come from the technology. We should not become modern day Luddites, breaking up the computers to keep them from taking our jobs. The technology is only a symbol of the powerlessness that arises from an inability to control the means of production.

Impediments to a New Social Heroism

One might expect in such a situation that there would be an increase in class consciousness, along with a greater awareness of the similarity of middle sector interests to those of the other class fractions; an ideology based on the concern for distributive justice should gain a far wider audience among the middle fraction. It is laudable, but *not* in our own best interests, to be altruistic, to give to the poor without apparent benefit to ourselves. This is the great difficulty of present liberal programs of reform. It *is* in our own best interest to be reciprocal, to unite with the poor in the demand to own rights in the public property of all, to reclaim control over our economic livelihoods.

Responding to this kind of non-individualistic ideology and achieving a real change in society do call us to heroism. It is not, however, the heroism of the individual, but of social class. The last heroism of the middle class, at the time of the Reformation and the Industrial Revolution, resulted in the dominance of the individual over society by achieving mobility, and of the economy over sociocultural values by elevating accumulation and profit. Reversing this process is certainly not likely if we rely on the nostalgia of modern conservatives. Their vision of the golden past is one of a triumphant individualism and unbridled laissez-faire · economics, a vision that is surely out of synch with the large-scale corporate bureaucracy of the modern world.

Instead, we ask for an emphasis on the social nature of the individual and a concern for the just production of the means of living. Relying on the golden past creates a society that is not open to change; it suggests a history that is doomed to repeat itself. If structural entrapment is to end, then the middle sectors need to become aware of their commonality with the rest of the laboring class. They need to become involved in a radical reordering of society, a movement that is liberating for justice, not for individual greed. That means building *toward* a new future, not *out of* a bankrupt past. Removing structures that create oppression and powerlessness cannot be accomplished unless heroism arises out of reciprocity, not altruism. Altruism maintains the barriers of class and privilege; reciprocity breaks them down.

The conservative individualistic approach to justice, which relies so much on a blend of self-reliance and altruism, has been called the "fair play" argument. It leads to a view of inequality as the inevitable consequence of fair competition in a game to which the players bring different skills. The poor in this model possess fewer skills; in one sense they deserve their poverty, while in another they must be helped altruistically by those of us who are more fortunate. That contrasts with a "fair shares" position, which views inequality as the source of an unfair disadvantage for some in the game. If you are born into the upper class your financial success in life is not simply due to superior ability. To alleviate the impact of this source of inequality will take more than individual initiative or altruistic alms. It will require a restructuring of classes based on an understanding of the reciprocal interests of all in the laboring class.[22]

What interests are reciprocal? How would the middle actually benefit from cooperating with the working and poor fractions? Whether one thinks it is morally right or wrong, it is clear that the most distinguishing feature of capitalist societies is the elevation of the economic elements of existence to the place of prominence in the cultural hierarchy. To draw the middle sector into social renewal, then, we must appeal to their economic interests.

It is in this dimension of their existence that middle sector people are, paradoxically, most vulnerable to powerlessness, yet most resistant to change. The resistance arises from the fact that the middle fraction in the United States today lives a far more comfortable economic existence than all but the very wealthiest in any other epoch of human history. Striving for radical change puts that comfort at risk in ways that are unmeasurable and unpredictable. But it is the very terms under which people in the middle layer have accepted that comfort, of dependence on others for employment, that create vulnerability. Despite fancy job titles, and often large salaries, they are in reality not much different from wage laborers in the inability to control their own economic destiny. For example, General Motors and Ford have announced that they will reduce their white-collar work force by 20% over the next five years. During its retrenchment, Chrysler permanently laid off 20,000 workers. DuPont has eliminated over 11,000 jobs, and Chevron recently announced that it was cutting its white-collar work force by 9,000.[23] The steel industry has engaged in extensive layoffs and salary cuts for management personnel in the past five years. Several computer companies have moved their entire production operation to work environments in South and East Asia, which have lower labor costs. The existing structures and their own lack of control leave middle sector white-collar workers no source of redress when the elite make these kinds of decisions.

The income rewards for middle sector white-collar workers and lower level managers in the modern corporate world are still extensive. But job security is becoming increasingly tenuous, and even material rewards are being eaten away by the drive for cost reductions and increased profit. That is the trade-off to which the middle fraction has consented. As long as we in the middle cling docilely to material benefits, we can do nothing to change our own vulnerability and dependence. Nor can we effectively alleviate the injustice, economic and otherwise, that the economic system metes out to the poor, to Blacks and other minorities, or to women.

Again, there should be a sense of reciprocity arising here when the middle sector realizes that although our material conditions are better we, too, are powerless, victims of polluted air, of callous indifference in the location and use of chemical waste dumps, of nuclear saber-rattling and its associated defense expenditures, of defective consumer products, of bureaucratic corporations and governments, and of a host of other systemic problems. The most we can hope for as individuals is to be able occasionally to "beat the system." We cannot prevent the system from constantly infringing upon our well-being and rights, nor can occasional victories prevent the same injustice from being imposed on someone else.

The old bourgeoisie broke with the feudal order by instituting the highly competitive system of capitalism. They pushed its impress into every area of life by adhering to Protestantism and other ideologies promoting a new individualism. The present-day middle fraction is steeped in this tradition. The institutional structures of our society, however, make individualism more apparent than real. There *are* areas of our lives in which we are free to make meaningful decisions and choices, yet we do not have the power to establish or control the framework in which those choices are made. Far too often no one asks the questions: freedom for whom? freedom for what? who and what set the limits to freedom? It is clear in American society that most of us are free to say what we want or to worship as we please. But many people are not free to earn enough income to fulfill basic human needs. We tell stories about the triumph and freedom of the individual, but even for the middle fraction the reality often is tight control by corporate and government bureaucracies.

We have tried to document the growing similarity of all fractions of the laboring class. The time may again be approaching for all these sectors of society to consider real alternatives to present socioeconomic arrangements and the corollary ideologies of individualism. It is once more a time for social heroism. It would be arrogant to imply that we in the middle sector should play a leading role in such a movement. But we do have a role to play by virtue of our numbers and involvement in key areas of society and the economy. This same involvement, of course, also restates the problem of our structural ambivalence. While we do have much to lose in changing the status quo, we may too easily forget that we also have much to gain by cooperating with the working proletariat and the poor.

To claim that the middle class is in reality a part of a wider laboring class along with the working class and the poor is not to equate the three sub-groups. There are real differences among a chemical engineer, steelworker, part-time clerical worker, and a "street person." Quite clearly the middle fraction has both a modicum of economic leverage and areas of derived power that the working fraction and the poor cannot approach. There is, thus, a vexing ambivalence about the middle position in society. We are both oppressed and oppressor, controlled and controller. It would be at once presumptuous and condescending to suggest that we share fully the experience of the working and underclass of American society. Whether we realize it or not, however, our structural position is becoming similar to theirs.

It is in the area of lack of control over the structural framework of their lives that people in the middle layer, people in the working fraction, and poor people find a similarity in the objective conditions they face. But again it is too simple to argue from this premise that commonality and solidarity exist among these groups. It is true that jobs at the bottom end of the middle spectrum have not provided any more income than unionized blue-collar jobs in the "smokestack" industries. Yet it is not simply the objective economic conditions that separate the middle sector from the working fraction. Rather, it is the economic setting and stability, and the seeming potential for upward economic mobility in the middle sector, which really set it apart from the working fraction and the poor.[24] The blue-collar worker faces a constant threat of layoffs, industrial relocation, and business failure, any of which can severely threaten the economic well-being of workers and their families. The middle fraction, while not immune to such problems, has traditionally been more secure in its economic condition.

Any new symbol system promoting change in the position of the laboring class must recognize both its internal fractional differences and the difficulties that will constantly attend such a broad-based coalition. In several senses, the laboring class, and certainly the middle fraction within it, does not have the same power as our middle class forebears of the sixteenth century. The old bourgeoisie emerged during the Reformation in part because the new uses of religious symbols supported individualism. That allowed ownership of the means of production, pursuit of economic profit, and the accumulation of wealth to become acceptable, status-conferring activities in the society.

Under the old order, the economy existed to serve the society, with the interests of that society defined and determined by the aristocracy and their supporting bureaucracy. Yet, while feudalism was a stratified order, the economy was still essentially subordinate to the social weal. The middle class, certainly, and even the peasantry and other classes to some degree, could count on the nobility to fulfill some social obligations. Under the old system, as well, the bourgeois merchant middle class owned some assets, giving them a modicum of power. The resources that conferred most power—land, for example—nevertheless eluded their control. The middle class remained subordinate to the aristocracy and its bureaucracy. Under current conditions, however, the modern middle sectors own or control even fewer sources of power and are at the mercy of the now entrenched bourgeois *upper* class and *its* bureaucracy. The middle fraction does not have a position of power at all independent of the dominant system; our status is as employees rather than producers, and our ideology of individualism allows the market to dictate the nature of our social life.[25] Recall, for example, that 60% of the productive assets are owned by only 1% of the population; 90% of the population own no such assets at all.[26] Control over these assets is actually even more concentrated; the corporate form of organization puts that control predominantly in the hands of a small cadre of top-level corporate management. Thus, an extremely small segment of the population has effective control over all aspects of our lives. They dominate decision making about the nature of economic goals and the strategies for meeting them.

The American middle sector faces what we term a *tri*-lemma. General economic conditions leave us increasingly like the other segments of the laboring class, vulnerable to the bite of poverty; low-level participation in corporate decision making, however, leads to middle sector cooperation in the oppression of both the working fraction and the poor; finally, our structural powerlessness as employees and our individualism create a sense of isolation and meaninglessness, of being unable to change either our vulnerability to or our cooperation in that oppression.

The power of the middle fraction to engage in change is also limited in another way. Given the immense centralization of wealth in the West, one can argue that the real source of power today does not rest in the nation-state, but in transnational economic institutions, such as ITT, GM, or the World Bank. People see themselves more readily as part of a nation-state than as part of an economic class based on an international division of labor. They are thought of as members of a largely democratic system in which everyone has very real possibilities for significant upward social and economic mobility—there is a strong

American belief in the potential to be in charge. Unfortunately, when this belief is coupled with the corresponding value of individualism, we are led to view problems of poverty, joblessness, discrimination, and powerlessness as the responsibility of the individual. At best they are seen as political problems rather than as class related or transnational economic issues.

Finally, in considering what hope there is for involving the middle sector in fundamental social change, we must recognize that the middle fraction includes such diverse groups as professionals, managers, technicians, clerical workers, and bureaucrats. Many professionals with their traditional independence cling to a sense of being an educated elite rather than workers. Members of bureaucracies, such as lower and middle managers, still derive some power from those positions. But such power is always subject to the framework established by those who own and control the system. While many technicians and clerical workers are increasingly being sought out by unions, or are organizing themselves, they too often remain divided by issues of gender, job description, or status.

In light of such a litany of barriers to middle fraction effectiveness and a larger labor class movement, from where do we derive any power at all to participate in a reordering of our society? In part, it comes from our sheer numbers as the largest segment of American society. But it also comes from the key positions we occupy in the system. Although we do not control the system in the sense of deciding where to go, nonetheless, the laboring class does make the system go by managing the bureaucracy and producing the goods and services.

As it stands, of course, the middle fraction value system, in particular, is not set for a role of radical social criticism. It would *seem* that changing the society operates directly against the best interests of the middle class. Our position in society, the assets we own, and our material comfort all flow from our participation in the existing system. How can we contend that risking those benefits is a reasonable and indeed desirable thing to do?

We claimed earlier that the pre-industrial bourgeoisie faced both a potential gain and a risk of loss as they contemplated fundamental change in the society. The apparent loss they faced, however, was less real than it seems. The loss they might sustain was the degree of material comfort they had managed to amass in their world. Their relative lack of power made that material comfort vulnerable in any event. Their apparent sacrifice of self-interest actually resulted in the creation of the conditions of genuine security.

A similar argument can be made with regard to the apparent material well-being of today's American middle sectors. The deep recession of the early 1980s illustrated this as it touched the lives of many in the middle fraction. Managerial and technical employees as well as skilled laborers have found themselves suddenly without jobs. The poverty and sense of hopelessness that they have traditionally ascribed to the "lazy" poor have become a very real part of their own existence. Middle level managers who have themselves escaped the more dramatic recessionary impact can still sense the problem of increasing insecurity, since their jobs have forced them to cooperate in the creation of unemployment, income loss, and despair for others. And in a society in which economic values dominate, loss of economic security tends to strip people of personhood. If middle sector economic conditions have become so tenuous, is it not in our best interests to cooperate in a societal restructuring which not only increases security for all, but also redefines the value system in ways that avoid identifying humanness with economic success? Certainly, the middle fraction, working fraction, and the poor all have a stake in creating a social system that is both more secure and more humane.

The Church as One Agent of Social Heroism

It is not surprising that persons committed to significant change in our society include both those who count *on* and those who count *out* the church in relation to their expectations. There may be as many who see religious institutions as integral to their hopes for the human community as who see them perpetuating a future that will repeat the past. Communities of faith have a history of both accommodation and radical resistance to the prevailing order. One can find evidence of both criticism and concessions.

In recent decades the civil rights movement provided a conspicuous example. Some recall the charge that eleven o'clock on Sunday morning was the most segregated hour of the week. Others want to remember that in the same time frame the church also nurtured and supported integration as well. Central America is also a compelling example of double vision. The silence of the Central American church at best and co-option at worst can be documented effortlessly. Yet anyone familiar with very recent times has to name the church as an agent of the future for the masses.

Without denying the long history of duplicity, a connection can be made between the church and the middle sectors in the journey toward a new society. There are indeed religious roots of rebellion deeply planted in the community of faith; there is a prophetic tradition there that fosters an alternative community with a consciousness "not of this age." There is an important distinction between "royal consciousness" and "prophetic imagination" as they have funtioned in the Judeo-Christian communities.[27] The "royal consciousness" nurtures the security and well-being of the present order; it encourages communities to embrace the structures and realities at hand as permanent and beneficent. The human tendency is to settle down and settle in. The "royal consciousness" is perversely stated in the slogan "America, love it or leave it." Realities of exploitation and oppression for some can be made to co-exist with the privileges of others through a "religion of static triumphalism."[28] Within such a position there is no place for criticism; it becomes unchristian, unpatriotic, uncivil! God is the Lord of order and to be disorderly is blasphemous.[29] Of course, "the religion of the static gods is not and never could be disinterested, but inevitably it served the interests of the people in charge, presiding over the order and benefiting from the order."[30] Contentment for some and despair for others are the inevitable consequence.

The "prophetic imagination," in contrast, disrupts numbness by revealing the source of both privilege and oppression and holding out the prospect of new realities dimly perceived. "The task of prophetic ministry is to nurture, nourish, and evoke a consciousness and perception alternative to the consciousness and perception of the dominant culture around us."[31] Criticism of present realities occurs in anticipation of a historical alternative made possible by cooperation with the "freedom of God." The "prophetic imagination" unmasks the fraility of what lies at hand before the promise of what is to be. The promise of newness crushes the pretense to permanence, as in the assumption that a particular class structure is natural or ordained by gods. Jesus cleansing the temple, for example, announces the forthcoming destruction of the temple because of its support of dominant power structures and its failure to create the conditions of the new age.

It is tempting to cast the two "consciousnesses" in the categories of good versus evil. And there are some reasons for doing so if the situations are clearly defined by oppression and liberation. But order is not inherently demonic. An element of order is a necessary condition of social existence. We need social, structural forms for our common life. The church is a historic institution, and part of its mission has to be preservation of its own forms as well as those in the society. The community of faith has no affinity for chaos. Yet anarchy is not the only alternative to "idolatry." The problem for the church is that the "royal consciousness" tends to dominate and submerge the "prophetic imagination." Order can preclude critical reflection upon its perversions. The issue with which we need to contend is nurturing the "prophetic imagination" and restraining the "royal consciousness."

One approach is to ask why there is in America an important link between the middle sectors, the church, and a new society. A simple way of answering that is to say that the church is a mainstream institution with a heritage and capacity for acting as a counter institution. It can bring into public discourse the force of arguments that are at odds with the direction of society. Recent examples of that in American Catholicism have been the Bishops' letters on "The Challenge of Peace" and "Catholic Social Teachings and the U.S. Economy." The church is important not only because it is there, but because it is an institutional form of resistance to the institutional forms of dehumanization. Albert Einstein, reflecting on Nazi Germany, acknowledged it was his anticipation that the university would be the center of resistance to Hitler. What surprised him was not only its failure to do so but the emergence of the church as the principal institution to say "no."

But the deeper meaning of the church for the middle class and the new society is in its relation to a religious symbol system. The symbols of the Judeo-Christian faith still function in oursociety, and the church may be the only institution with a mission for monitoring their interpretation and application. The symbols are used to make sense of our common life in history. They are a means of affirming that the forms and substance of our existence are meaningful. The problem is that those symbols can be used for a variety of objectives. They can be manipulated ". . . to illuminate or to blind, to make one soar or to paralyze, to give courage or to make afraid, to liberate or to enslave."[32] Sacred symbols once detached from their origins can function to facilitate freedom or to justify slavery.

Not only is the church an institutional factor in society, but the symbols of its faith are at large, lending legitimacy indiscriminately. It might even be argued that the "royal consciousness" functions independently of the church. For example, near the beginning of his second term President Reagan argued his case for an arms build-up by appealing to a parable in Luke 14:31–32. His paraphrase and commentary were as follows:

> Jesus, in talking with his disciples, spoke about a king who might be contemplating going to war against another king with his 10,000 men. But he sits down and counsels how he's going to do against the other fellow's 20,000 and then says he may have to send a delegation to talk peace terms. Well, I don't think we ever want to be in a position of only being half as strong and having to send a delegation to negotiate, under those circumstances, peace terms with the Soviet Union.[33]

A reading of the complete parable reveals that it does not have to do with military strategy but with preparing oneself for discipleship. Reagan draws the parable off its context; this frees him to use it in ways that serve his purposes. Jesus is talking to a "great multitude" about the stringent claims of following him, an allegiance that subordinates one's loyalty to family, comfort, and privilege. The enemy is not a nation but one's own immersion in the gifts of the world. The issue is not military parity but spiritual capacity for sacrifice.

The church, then, not only has a position in a society significantly populated by the middle sectors, but has a responsibility for the sacred symbols that serve as agents of legitimation. The church can sever the alliance of these symbols with the old order and help free them to create a new society. That is a significant factor in restoring "prophetic imagination." Of course we need to acknowledge that the church, as most Americans have known it, is an institution whose promise is ambiguous. Mainline churches will have to undergo a radical conversion to the reality of their task in our society. Mainstream institutions do not easily turn on themselves and address their environments in that way without significant resistance.

If we turn to the church in Central America we may find some perspective. On the surface there does not seem to be anything paradigmatic, or transferable, to our situation. There the church *is* the church of the poor. True, it is controlled by others, but the people in the church *are* the oppressed. While they may have to learn their condition through a process that has been called "conscientization," the contrasts are sufficiently stark in the society to become accessible under critical reflection. The absence of ambiguity is conspicuous. The middle sector in America is in a more opaque position. Its condition superficially appears rather favorable; the reality of middle sector powerlessness is not as stark, is difficult to identify, and, therefore, is not as energizing for action. It also has more to lose economically than the poor in Central America. The question for the first world is, "What is the functional equivalent of becoming the church of the poor in the Third World?"

Gustavo Gutierrez, while writing about the poor and from within their oppression, engages in a subtle shift in terms. "Toward a Church of the People" is a subtitle in a chapter of one of his recent books.[34] While "people" and "poor" are inter-

changeable in the Third World, they are not synonymous terms in
North America. The church in the United States may include
those who are poor, but the dominant reality of *most* people in
Latin America *is* one of powerlessness. For the North American
middle sector in the church, religious institutions are no longer
able to set the conditions under which decisions are made.
Society is out of their control. However, Gutierrez summons the
community of faith "to battle injustice, spoilation, and exploitation, to commit oneself to the creation of a more humane society
of sisters and brothers. . . ."[35] The task is solidarity with other
victims. It is also recognition of middle sector complicity in their
oppression, and indifference to our responsibility for their powerlessness. We feel helpless. Yet the church of the people will
need to come to clarity, conscientization, about its own reality
and what it has done to others. We have been seduced as a church
by the myth of neutrality, the conviction that we should not
interfere in secular matters. And ". . . neutrality is the most
reprehensible partiality there is. It means choosing for those in
power, choosing for injustice, without taking responsibility for it.
It is the worst sort of politics and the most detestable sort of
'Christianity.'[36] The model of neutrality imposed by society
legitimates the "royal consciousness." Rejecting neutrality and
surrendering the "royal consciousness," however, present only
one dimension of the task of the middle class church. It must
cease being a middle class church and work in the interests of all
who labor and grow weary.

We are still left with the issue of strengthening "prophetic
imagination" in the life of the church. Again, there may be a
significant clue in the formation of "basic Christian communities" in Latin America and particularly in Nicaragua. Basic
communities arose out of the concerns of Vatican II to return the
church to the poor, to recreate a vibrant, committed grassroots-
level movement. They are not to be churches in the ecclesiastical
sense but in the more biblical one of being those gathered in
response to the Christ event. The participants want to find their
agenda in the Scriptures rather than continue to internalize the
reality the dominant culture would impose. This is not an act of
the elite in the church but the people of faith. Those "above" the

people do not own the "Word"; it is available to all. "In the basic-Christian-community process, both members and leaders make connections between the Scriptures and their lives. Underlying it all seems to be a basic change in attitude from one of accepting the world as it is to one aiming at transforming it. . . ."[37]

Central to that process is the recognition that the God of Moses and Jesus is not one who made things as they are but rather enlists *us* in the project of making them what God intends them to be. One of the reasons liberation theology is so threatening to the Vatican is that basic communities are not only non-hierarchical, but their interpretation of the "Word" may interrogate the structures and policies of the church. If "the Word" gets around, there can be no controlling what it will call in question.

The notion of basic communities recalls the image of "the remnant" which permeates the Judeo-Christian tradition. The concept of being a majority is alien to Scripture. The people of God are always a creative minority, a band of social deviants, who counter the consciousness and the institutional formation of the society. Theirs is not the conventional wisdom of the day. We need a significant modification of that concept in the present. The remnant is not the whole church but a minority within it. They are ". . . the handful within the church committed to God's liberating purposes, . . . [who] search for ways to keep a critical allegiance to what the church ought to be in spite of what it is."[38] While the church as a whole may not discern the reality of the middle fraction and its linkage with workers and the oppressed, the "remnant within the remnant" will as it reads the Scriptures with powerlessness in view. Hence, it is not an honored and elite remnant, but a despised minority. That remnant will not only engage in chipping away at the enculturation of the church as a whole but turn its prophetic imagination loose on the arrangement of the society until it dreams new dreams and gives birth to new forms in which justice can be served.

In one of the basic communities in Nicaragua nurtured by Ernesto Cardenal, the discussion centered on the categories of life and death. As we will argue in chapter 7, those categories reach beyond biology to define states of existence. One of the participants identified the meaning of those categories within his own experience. "The truth is that in today's world there are two kinds of people: some are on the side of life and others on the side of death."[39] The "remnant within the remnant" focuses upon a witness to life and a dismantling of the structures of death. Their task is "to plumb, comprehend, come to appreciate, and then insist upon . . . the right to a human life."[40]

Obviously not all will be responsive to the mission of critical reflection upon the reality of the middle class as being in fact a "middle fraction." Nor will all accept responsibility for radical change. But a remnant can reclaim the sacred symbols that call for revolutionary action. They can challenge the "royal consciousness" restraining the church and nurture the "prophetic imagination" which summons into being social arrangements that promote justice and a better quality of life for all. Those who can see clearly must act decisively to create an alternative consciousness and community. The "prophetic imagination" dismantles our "Jerusalem temples" because it has heard the claim of Christ in the poor and cannot compromise with the rich and the powerful. What links the church, the middle fraction, and social change is a symbol system that sets the middle class under judgment for its "immersion" in history. These symbols declare new goals of social change and appoint the church and other institutions to the task of mediating a new order for a new humankind.

3
Economic Institutions and Middle Sector Powerlessness

American society elevates economic goals and values to a pre-eminent place. That commitment to the economic has created dominant institutions and structures which support the accumulation of material well-being in the hands of some. That is, structures of production, ownership, and control determine the distribution of wealth, power, and income. What are those structures, and how are they formed and changed? Thus far we have argued that the poor are in a constant state of deprivation, that the working fraction lives with long-term insecurity, and that the middle sector is beginning to feel insecure as well. What are the economic institutions that feed this deprivation and insecurity? Are there ways to challenge the power inherent in existing arrangements?

The deep commitment of American society to individualism and to capitalism has encouraged and even demanded the emergence of a private property ethic. The rights to own and use private property are not only an important plank in the platform of individualism, they are also extended to property owned by business corporations. Private ownership of the means of production is both celebrated and sacrosanct, whether it is held by an individual person or a corporate conglomerate. Society mounts a staunch defense of private ownership and the rights of the corporate form of business organization. These two expressions of our individualistic ideology actively help to create the conditions of poverty and injustice for many.

Vast accumulations of economic power and wealth in the hands of corporate elite mean that effective control over resources and hence over economic decision making rests in those same hands. Claims about individual control or consumer sovereignty then become absurd. One of the reasons why poverty is so unevenly spread among the population rests with our inability as a society to move productive resources to those places where they could be effectively used to create jobs and eliminate poverty. That happens because society does not control the resources; private corporations do. Despite all of this, we continue to treat private ownership of the means of production as inviolate and tolerate increasing concentration of economic power in the hands of large corporations with only an occasional whimper. What is it about the nature of these institutions that leaves us so unwilling to challenge them?

Personal and Corporate Private Property

In the late eighteenth century, the United States included many small, freeholding farmers. Given such a beginning, it is not surprising that private ownership of land and homes holds a prominent place in the litany of values that form the backbone of our culture. In fact, that kind of private property does not seem to pose any threat in terms of the concentration of wealth and power that this book views as a predominant evil in our society.

Unfortunately, we have not been able as a society to distinguish between private property rights in the context of a freeholding agrarian society and the concentration of wealth in an industrial society. There is, after all, a vast difference between a farmer whose net assets may total $500,000 and an Exxon corporation whose 1984 net assets were estimated at $63 billion.[1] Concentrated private ownership of the means of production in an industrial society confers more power more inequitably than does dispersed ownership of farm land in an agricultural society. And, certainly, the ownership of homes and consumer durable goods does not pose a threat to the disadvantaged in our system. There may be something to the claim that widely dispersed landholding is a good defense against despotism if land and human labor are the bases for economic productivity and a source for political power. In an industrial society, however, where capital is the basis for productivity, the concentration of property in the form of the means of production may be an invitation to despotism. Latin America provides ample evidence of the connection between highly concentrated wealth and the emergence of political repression.

Institutions must be examined within a context to determine if they play a life-affirming role or one that causes and sustains injustice and poverty. For example, there was a class structure at the time of the American Revolution with a small coterie of very wealthy landowning elite who exercised a good deal of control in the colonies. Unlike today, however, many in the middle were able to gain a measure of security by owning their own small farms. Indeed, in the nineteenth century it was possible for anyone to acquire a plot of land and perhaps really take command of his or her own destiny as a result of the Homestead Act. But that liberating role was dominant only as long as the United States remained an agrarian society with power and status flowing from landholding.

When manufacturing and finance moved to center stage with much larger amounts of capital at risk, private ownership's role in control became dominant over its role in liberation. Ownership was no longer being dispersed in order to liberate, but concentrated in order to control and thus limit risk. The top 20% of wealth holders, who owned about 74% of all wealth at the time of the founding of the American republic, owned better than 84% of the wealth in 1973.[2] (Changes in the wealth distribution over time can be seen in the appendix to this chapter.) And that ignores the ways in which real control over the use of those assets has been even more concentrated in the hands of large corporations. The society has done virtually nothing to change the legal conditions surrounding private property ownership or rights. In the eyes of the law there is little if any difference between the property rights of a homeowner and Dow Chemical's property rights as a corporation.

There is a vast difference, however, in the respective abilities to use those property rights in ways that affect the general well-being of the society.[3]

Society elevates property rights to a prominent position, yet limits the middle class in owning any property that is economically important and almost totally prevents the poor from having any such rights at all. The distribution of "who owns what" shows an interesting pattern. In 1972, the top 1% of wealth holders in the United States owned about 60% of the corporate stock, 60% of the bonds, 53% of other debt instruments, and almost 90% of all trust funds. In contrast, they held only 15% of all real estate (how many houses can you use?), 15% of all cash (credit cards are easier), and 7% of all life insurance (their assets *are* their insurance).[4] Note that their ownership is concentrated in those areas in which they are likely to be able to exercise real leverage and control over the decision-making processes.

In fact, the way in which the elite exercises its control over the economic system through its ownership of the means of production makes certain that the poor remain poor and the middle class powerless. If a small group of elite owns all the important resources, how can the limited ownership of much less important assets confer any real power on the rest of us? It is here that the issue of evil embodied in institutional forms can be seen most clearly. It is not that the elite necessarily want the poor to be poor or the middle class to be powerless. Rather, the internal logic of the system dictates that they act and construct ancillary institutions in ways that protect the dominant institution, private property. The fact that property rights are concentrated in their hands ensures that others will share very little in the material benefits flowing from that property. Thus it is an institutional structure that has these unfortunate and, we believe, immoral side effects, not people choosing to create an immoral world.

Latin America shows clearly the connections among property, poverty, and powerlessness. Liberation theologians in Latin America are openly challenging the institutional arrangements that create those connections. We will leave a careful exploration of their theology until chapter 6, but some of their premises can be examined here in an attempt to understand the potentially negative role of private property.

One of the most obvious characteristics of liberation theology in Latin America is its location among the poor. Poverty is the pre-eminent condition within which we are to grasp the meaning of the faith, because poverty is the pre-eminent condition of the people. In Brazil, for example, the poorest 20% of the population in 1972 received only 2% of the income. In fact, the bottom 60% received only 16%, while the top 10% got more than 50% of the income.[5] Despite very rapid economic growth since then, the conditions of the very poor have worsened. Their average annual income per person has stayed virtually unchanged since 1964 while the average income per person for the whole society has nearly quadrupled. In other words, all the benefits of Brazil's phenomenal economic growth have been funneled into the hands of the small group at the top of the income distribution. Although Brazil is the most stark example, similar arguments can be made for other Latin American countries, especially Mexico, Panama, Venezuela, Peru, and Nicaragua before the 1979 revolution.

Liberation theology makes the claim that the weak, the powerless, those who live lives defined and controlled by others, have a privileged position theologically. The very people who are denied a full human life have a unique point of entering into a Gospel of freedom. God is with and among them in a special way because of their condition. "God loves the poor with special love because they are poor and not necessarily because they are good."[6] The poor do not necessarily embody righteousness, but a righteous God embraces their condition. The victims of injustice have a privileged position in relation to understanding the action of God in the world and the history of that action reflected in Scripture.

What follows from this is that solidarity with the poor becomes a necessary condition for entry into the meaning of the Christian faith. That includes the solidarity of the poor with each other. Not only within communities and nations but between them, a consciousness of linkage is necessary. Those in the movements of the poor need to understand themselves as participating in one movement in defiance of the sources of injustice. It has become a truism that "none are free until all are free." But solidarity also means that all the people of the church everywhere are called to Christ in the poor and are measured by their response. The defense of human rights is a project for all, whether or not they are part of "the wretched of the earth."[7] The daily struggle of some for survival is the struggle of all who understand their destiny through the biblical faith. "To be followers of Jesus requires that they [Christians] walk with and be committed to the poor. . . ."[8] God is embedded in the movement of the poor, and solidarity with the poor forms our relationship to that God.

In the context of Latin America, the things that keep the poor in their poverty include the concentration of the best agricultural land in the hands of a very small elite; land tenure systems that ensure that peasants will have, at best, only a marginal degree of ownership rights of a marginal amount of marginal land; and political structures that support and maintain the status quo. Thus, the institutions that allow private property rights to be amassed and exercised by the elite are dominant sources of oppression for the poor. The elite can use the means of production (largely agricultural) as a way of raising their own wealth and status, and that, historically, has meant paying wages and growing crops, such as sugar, that contribute very little to the welfare of the society at large. Josue de Castro's description of the sugar economy of Brazil in *Death in the Northeast*[9] is a chilling account of the human cost of raising the economic interests of a few above the human need of the masses. The ability of a few large landowners to monopolize land for sugar prevents the use of that land for subsistence, creating widespread malnutrition and poverty.

These economic interests of local elites in the Third World are fueled by the demands of the richer industrial nations of the world. It is little wonder that many in Latin America, seeking an end to the domination of privilege, have called for revolutionary changes that would bring a more socialistic set of economic and political structures to replace the highly concentrated and privatized systems which now exist. When wealth and income are so heavily concentrated, sharing offers a real possibility for improving the conditions of the masses. The standard of living of the masses in Cuba before and after the 1959 revolution points to the possibility that a different vision of who owns what can have a startling impact on the well-being of the mass of the population even when the overall economy is not performing particularly well.

In 1975, sixteen years after the revolution, gross domestic product per person in Cuba was the same as it was in 1952.[10] Measured in terms of the traditional economic output measure, Cuba was clearly not doing well. On the other hand, the percentage of the secondary school age population actually enrolled rose from 14% to 74% during the 1960–83 period. For the college age population, the enrollment percentages rose from three to twenty.[11] In 1960, there were slightly less than 1,100 people per doctor. By 1983, that figure had improved to 600 people per doctor, about the same as in Australia, Canada, and the United States.[12] In the years since the revolution, average life expectancy has risen from sixty-three to seventy-five years.[13] Even these limited data indicate that quality of life has been improving significantly for the masses in the Cuban population. The change to socialism led to a more egalitarian pattern of resource distribution that was able to counteract some of the effects of poor economic performance.

That argument is clear for Latin America but raises a different set of issues in the first world. Does solidarity with the poor mean we have to become poor? The middle sector has some material privilege; in relation to the Third World that privilege is substantial for many. How are we to assess our access to wealth, in many instances our possession of it? It certainly can be argued that Jesus called his disciples to relinquish their worldly goods as a condition of following him. "If we are to follow him, we are to freely separate ourselves from whatever separates us from the needy of the world so that we might enter into solidarity with them."[14] It hardly needs to be argued that in a world divided along the lines of rich and poor, it is precisely our wealth that fosters separation. Our riches are often gained through their poverty. Wealth in the form of ownership of capital is an agent of oppression.

The temptation is strong to press this argument only in individual terms. If you own a home while others are homeless, if you have an abundance of food while others are starving, if you have two coats while others have none, the solution is for the individual to divest. Traditionally, the Gospel gets constructed along lines that call for personal charity in relation to public deprivation. Generosity on the part of individuals is important, but it ought not to be conceived as an answer to the problem. Voluntarism in all its forms is meritorious, but it leaves in place all the orders that create and perpetuate poverty. Indeed, it is a by-product of such orders. Societies without our emphasis on private property, without surplus, and with a far more basic emphasis on reciprocity do not have a notion of charity or of altruism. Generosity in these societies is not an extraordinary act to be applauded; it is an expected responsibility of all members of society.

Some join the argument at the level of a diatribe against wealth. If the poor are loved by God because they are poor, then those who have some measure of wealth should be subject to wrath. One might expect an argument along those lines from José Miranda, who takes seriously the contention that the early church embraced and advocated communism. His agenda is set by Acts 2:44–45 (NEB), which reads: "All whose faith had drawn them together held everything in common: they would sell their property and possessions and make a general distribution as the need of each required." But Miranda is quick to affirm that "Jesus ha[d] no horror of wealth, neither in itself nor in its use and enjoyment."[15] He goes on to claim that when Christ says "[h]appy are the poor" and "[w]oe to you the rich" the intent is not to honor and condemn. It is not self-evident that the one is righteous while the other is unrighteous by virtue of their economic state. What is being condemned by Christ, according to Miranda, is wealth that causes poverty and creates differentiation between the rich and the poor.[16] The problem is not only the means by which wealth is accumulated but the degree to which it "suck[s] away at the quality of life of the poor."[17]

The notion of wealth that differentiates is an important one, but for us in the American middle layer it does not necessarily reveal the central issue. We cannot adequately focus upon our relation to possessions and the consequences of that relationship without exploring the matter of private property. If there is one thing about which the middle fraction tends to be clear it is that private property is central to the "American way." To suggest that it ought to be held up for critical reflection is perceived as an assault on "the sacred canopy," or the sacred cosmos. Most would sooner question Mother's Day.

Setting aside the norms of our society and tracing the treatment of property within the biblical tradition will erode any confidence in the sacredness of private ownership. Some might hope to find a divine mandate in the past that can be imparted to the twentieth century. However, that hope is not likely to be fulfilled in any unambiguous way. At the very least, private property is demystified and left without any self-evident stature.

Martin Hengel provides a guide by which to mark the history of the struggle by people of faith. Early church leaders were reasonably confident that private property had an integral relationship to the fall as an agent of alienation from one another. John Chrysostom wrote that ". . . when one attempts to possess himself of anything, to make it his own, then contention is introduced . . . we are eager to divide and separate ourselves by appropriating things."[18] Property and riches divide and cause a deterioration of what should be common to all. The church fathers certainly had in mind the Old Testament and the Jewish tradition. Within the Israelite community it was clear who really owned the land. "The earth is the Lord's . . ." (Ps. 24:1), and we are tenants on the Lord's property. As such it is a human obligation to imitate the generosity of God. Whatever right to property might seem to exist was "subordinated to the obligation to care for the weaker members of society."[19] The universe is on loan, and its inhabitants are responsible for one another. When one moves on to the teaching of Jesus one senses that earthly possessions may be subject to renunciation in the light of the imminent coming of the Kingdom. Of course, Jesus, his disciples, and the early church were in some measure dependent upon wealth. They were in fact supported by it, often by women of means. But any dependency upon possessions was an "egoistic self-assertion," Hengel wrote, and an impediment to the cause.[20] Once one reaches the Pauline community the eschatological framework is receding and the emphasis moves toward sharing. Paul was more concerned with that relation to worldly goods that occurs because the Kingdom is in our midst, while "we . . . are citizens of heaven" (Phil. 3:20, NEB).

What becomes clear in this summary is that private property by no means has an assured status. There is no divine right to property. The need of the neighbor makes all claims to ownership relative. The degree to which one can transfer biblical views on private property to society today cannot simply be asserted. Such transfer is a complex issue. The early Christian communities were relatively small, often urban enclaves, more separatist than revolutionary in intent. In an exceptionally hostile environment they were forced to focus on the conditions of their common life rather than the surrounding order. Our industrial society creates very different sets of problems than those faced by the early Christians.

There is a temptation to give too much ground to these dissimilarities. Differences of scale do not render the Christian tradition irrelevant to our society and the development of a social ethic. The problem with Hengel's study is that he focuses his argument on what the individual can do with the tradition. Acknowledging and transforming the supposedly "selfish heart" of humankind may be a significant step.[21] One cannot dispute that possessions can lead one astray and obscure the need for each of us to embrace some degree of austerity. Yet, it is not adequate to construct the issue of property as "the crisis of man, his selfish desire to assert himself, his struggle for power and his mercilessness."[22] The "selfish desire" takes institutional and systemic form, and the faith needs to address it on that level as well.

The Judeo-Christian community has an obligation not only to put brakes on any attachment to property but to call in question the legitimacy of private ownership of the means of production as integral to the American creed. It is precisely the assurance of what is mine and the force of accumulation in the economic sphere that impoverish others. Private ownership not only sustains but increases the separation between rich and poor and promises a theft from the poor that is no less real because it is facilitated by Adam Smith's alleged "invisible hand."

Poverty in the first world is not as visible and dominant a condition as it is in Latin America. The truly poor in our society comprise some 15% of the population as opposed to 60% to 80% of the population in Latin America. Because the group is so much smaller, it becomes an enclave, hidden away in ghettos and not in day-to-day contact with the rest of us. In Latin America the rich are the enclave, and they are surrounded by poverty.

Middle sector Americans cannot do liberation theology in the condition of poverty, but it can be done in the light of that which makes poverty inevitable. We cannot claim to be the poor but can claim our complicity in the homelessness, the hunger, and the nakedness of others. And an increasing economic uncertainty can be acknowledged in our existence. We may not necessarily have to become poor as a class, but we are obligated to identify and destroy whatever makes others poor in our midst and around the globe. It is not simply by personal divestment that things are going to be changed; although, for others to become less poor, we will have to give up our disproportionate use of the world's resources. We must bring the power of our numbers to bear on those institutional arrangements that not only create our own powerlessness as individuals, but also maintain the poverty and powerlessness of many in our own society and elsewhere. It is tempting to think of those arrangements as being limited to such things as racism, sexism, and other forms of discrimination. But the institutions of discrimination can arise and take hold only because the economic and political institutions confer power unequally. Exploring the role of those institutions leads to a reappraisal not only of private ownership of the means of production but also of the economic order that requires such ownership.

The Pervasiveness of Corporate Domination

It is important to reiterate that private property per se is not necessarily the institutional evil that plagues society. The fact that many of the people in the American middle layer own their own homes does not, for example, imply any particular pattern of oppression of the poor, nor does it by itself make the poor less powerful than the middle sector. It is rather the concentration of the private ownership of the means of production that confers immense power on a few and powerlessness on most. This concentration tends to take the institutional form of corporate business and thus subordinates the common interest of the society to the special interest of business corporations.

Chapter 1 explained how the middle fraction has both a complicity in and a susceptibility to injustice. This arises because the concentration of wealth limits the ability to change things, removes control over our own destiny, and creates powerlessness in the face of the system. The middle sectors are screened off from the sources of that powerlessness by their belief in the story of individualism, in the sanctity of private property, and, of course, by material well-being. An examination of the distribution of wealth in America, however, can begin to raise our own consciousness about our condition and that of the poor. The middle 25% of the wealth distribution, roughly the lower middle class, owns only 6% of the wealth assets. Fully half of all the wealth assets are owned by the top 6% of the population. The distribution is seen to be even more unequal if one concentrates on that part of the wealth assets that confers economic power, the ownership of the means of production. Then, as we suggested earlier, 60% of these assets are owned by only 1% of the population, and 90% of the population owns no such assets at all. Is it any wonder, then, that individuals are powerless to change or shape the system? With ownership of the means of production so concentrated, the vast majority have no tools with which to do the shaping.

Yet, even this description of the ownership of wealth assets does not give a complete picture of the concentration of economic power. It is true that the means of production are owned by the wealthy, but not directly. The means are owned, instead, by corporations; the corporations are in turn owned by the wealthy in the form of stock certificates. In 1974, for example, the top 100 manufacturing corporations in the United States owned 56% of all the manufacturing assets.[23] Assume there is an average of ten top-level managers in each of these corporations. Then 1,000 people controlled better than 50% of the productive assets in America. That is five ten-thousandths of 1% of the population! Those corporate managers make decisions every day that affect all of us. They can close a plant and move operations to Taiwan, as in the recent decisions of microchip manufacturers in Silicon Valley, instantly eliminating thousands of jobs. Their decisions can lead to a Sunbelt that blooms while the Northeast dies. They can make a mistake in gauging the public taste and help plunge the nation into recession as the auto industry did in the late seventies. Furthermore, the largest corporations are growing and becoming even more powerful. In 1965, 50% of corporate assets were owned by giant corporations, each of which owned $250 million or more in assets. By 1980, that group's share of corporate assets had climbed to 70%.[24] (The appendix to this chapter contains more information about the concentration of wealth.)

The incidence of corporate power spreads in two directions. The size and dominant position of corporations as employers give them great control over the labor market, both for blue-collar and white-collar workers. Their dominance as sellers of the products they produce gives them an even larger measure of control over the markets for products. The concentration of such immense wealth and market power in the hands of a very few people con- tradicts the assumptions of an atomistic competitive market that is supposed to be the benchmark for an economic system that serves the welfare of its members. It is small-scale competitors who must attend to the price and profit signals sent by the market. It is those signals that tell the producers what the consumers want.

Corporate giants do not merely listen and respond to the signals; they have the power to use their advertising budgets and their new product development staffs to create their own signals.

Their size and their assets allow them to borrow money and buy inputs more cheaply. Their lack of competition permits them to keep the benefits of that borrowing and purchasing rather than passing them on to the consumer in the form of lower prices. As a result, consumers get products they do not really want and pay prices that are higher than they need to be. Consumers are without an effective means to counter this power of the large corporation.

In the resource markets, particularly the labor market, the neoclassical argument is that competition among employers for employees and competition among the labor force for jobs will work together to "clear" the labor market. That is, unemployment will be eliminated by the force of market interactions among buyers and sellers of labor. Try to tell that to autoworkers or steelworkers who have been unemployed since 1980 and see no real prospect of regaining their jobs. The dominance of the auto industry in Detroit or the steel industry in Pittsburgh has been so complete that when those industries begin to lay off workers there is no "other part" of the labor market to pick up the slack. The problem is not merely recessions, which cause temporary unemployment. Chapter 2 showed that the American auto industry has rebounded from the bleak times of the early eighties to make record profits in the last few years, but that has not meant a return to work for many of those laid off in the recession. The steel industry has failed to recover and has been closing plants and moving operations in an effort to forestall further losses. Most Americans would be shocked to learn that there is not even one operating steel mill left in Pittsburgh. If the power of the big steel companies had not been so concentrated and dominating, then adjustment to steel's demise would not be so difficult.

One can see another example of corporate power in the ability of giant corporations to change dramatically their business interests through merger. For example, the Fortune 500 classifies U.S. Steel as an oil company, not a metal manufacturer. They are still the largest steel company, but their mergers with Marathon and Texas Oil have given them so many assets and so many dollars worth of sales in the oil business that petro-chemicals are now classified as their major activity. As a symbol of this diversification they have taken the "Steel" out of their name and become USX. In all, twenty firms that were part of the Fortune 500 in 1983 were not there in 1984 because they were acquired by other firms in the 500.[25]

Mergers among such large firms, of course, lead to even more concentration of economic power. But they are also a symptom of the failure of the market to direct resources where they are needed. Because of changed tax laws allowing more rapid depreciation of capital assets, companies like U.S. Steel have found themselves with large cash flows in the 1980s. The theory behind the tax breaks was that generation of these cash flows would lead to dramatic increases in new capital formation and that would spur more rapid economic growth. Often the reality has been that mergers and acquisitions have yielded a higher return to the corporations than investing in expansion or modernization of existing facilities. The result has been more concentration of economic power, but little or no improvement in society's well-being through increased productivity. That is one of the reasons why the recovery of the eighties has proceeded in such a stuttering pattern. Sustained economic growth requires extensive investment in new plant and equipment. The wave of large-scale mergers has soaked up the money capital that should have been used for that investment.

We earlier alluded to the fact that unemployment seems to have fallen about as far as it will. In mid-1987 it stuck at approximately 6.5%. Without the creation of new jobs that flow from capital investment, new entrants into the labor force cannot be absorbed at a fast enough rate to drive the unemployment rate lower. Indeed, one must worry about the paradoxical situation of rising unemployment and rising corporate profits. Mergers under favorable circumstances tend to pour at least short-term profits into corporate coffers, but they do not create jobs. In fact, they actually destroy jobs, at least at the middle, information-managing level.

The condition of powerlessness becomes even worse when this increasing concentration is coupled with the phenomena of multi-nationalization and the information technology revolution.

Each of these is increasing the pace at which the middle layer is losing control over its destiny. People in the middle layer are already relatively powerless and are becoming even more powerless. The most recent depression of the American economy has demonstrated that the middle fraction is also becoming increasingly vulnerable to unemployment and poverty. It no longer appears to be a long step from being powerless in the middle sector to being victimized within the rest of the laboring class.

William Dugger presents an interesting argument about the evolution and growth of corporate power. He claims that recent growth is invidious and not easily recognizable because it is not as naked as the monopoly-building activities of the late nineteenth century. Instead, as we have already suggested, recent corporate expansion has been in the form of conglomerate mergers, which have four distinguishing features: (1) operation in several different markets, (2) purely financial goals, (3) decentralization, and (4) the development of a conglomerate "culture."[26]

The market and financial features allow the corporate conglomerates effectively to by-pass the formal capital markets when they raise the financial resources for investment projects. This allows them to avoid incurring even that limited control over decision making. The overriding goal of the modern conglomerate is to make money, not products. Dugger quotes David Roderick of U.S. Steel: "The duty of management is to make money. Our primary objective is not to make steel."[27] Yet, the whole basis for the neoclassical claim about the superiority of the private ownership market economy is that it will efficiently deliver the goods that people want. If our economy is increasingly dominated by such conglomerates, and if they do not see their responsibility as production of goods, then why do we keep pretending that the system is serving the social welfare?

Not only service to the social welfare but also any real sense of individualism is lost as the conglomerate culture becomes more dominant. The successful managers—those who rise to some positions of real power—are the ones who serve most effectively the dominant conglomerate goal, making money. But by their very natures, conglomerates are organized in a bureaucratic, not an individualistic, way. Those who fit in best are those who work most effectively in a bureaucratic form of organization. "Free-thinkers need not apply." As a consequence, the next generation of power holders, the next top-level corporate decision makers, will be replicas of this generation, not innovative individuals.

Increasingly, the dominant organizations in American culture are conglomerate corporations that elevate profit over productivity, care passionately about making money, but are conspicuously uninterested in producing goods and services. These organizations are run and populated by bureaucracies that discourage the input and creativity of the individual. They do not listen to the demands of the consumer, because meeting demands is useful only if it makes more money than they can earn from another financial merger. Finally, such organizations are international in scope and will willingly impose poverty on large groups of people by closing or moving operations if that will allow them to move on to other operations that increase their cash flow. Accumulation of wealth and of power are far more important than serving any human needs in this institutional setting.

The Location of Justice in the Economic Sphere

Concentrations of power create injustice in the economic sphere. The concentration enables the powerful constantly to grasp more control and wealth, an action that leaves the weak increasingly subject to exploitation. While American society has recognized the existence of economic injustice, it has always acted as though injustice were strictly distributive in nature. Consequently, moves against injustice have taken the shape of tax and transfer programs, which redistribute income from one group to another in the society. Governmental policy has concentrated on making the distribution of income more equal rather than on making the economic system more fair.

The creation of a system marked by fairness takes placebefore rather than after production has occurred. The source of injustice is the concentration of ownership of productive assets and the consequent ability to use those assets to further the narrow aims of the elite rather than the well-being of the society. Those narrow aims are served within the production process and its generation of profit and control. Redirecting the economy,

then, calls for a reorganization of control over and direction of the
production process.

    Imagine a Southern town whose dominant industry is a textile
mill owned by a multinational conglomerate. The corporation may
create economic and other pressures that keep wage levels low and
trap the poor at the margins of society. The illegal efforts by J. P.
Stevens to prevent union organization and the refusal to bargain
in good faith with legitimate union representatives are examples
of such pressures. At the same time, the textile mill may
contribute to pollution and environmental decay in the town. The
middle fragment can address neither the injustice of the economic
margination of the poor nor the impact of environmental decay.
All the leverage is on the side of the textile mill. As the dominant
industry they have a direct or indirect impact on the economic
well-being of everyone in the town, even middle-level merchants
and professional people who seem not to be connected with the
textile industry. If the major employer decides to leave town,
everyone suffers.

    The combination of power and the pursuit of profit creates a
serious mismatch between the interests of the corporation and
those of the society. Solutions to the mismatch in the example call
for a pre-production redistribution of control over the use of
resources, not a post-production redistribution of income. If the
town were to gain control of the corporate decision-making
apparatus, it would be able to force decisions reflecting broader
societal interests rather than narrow profit interests. Any such
seizure of power is, of course, a radical change from the way
things are. Movements from "what is" to "what ought to be"
mean a serious disruption of the status quo and a challenge to the
entrenched elite.

    The civil rights movement of the 1960s showed how disturbing
such challenges can be. In the first half of this century, Blacks in
America had legal rights but were unable to exercise those rights
under the prevailing institutional conditions. "Equality before the
law" was a largely empty phrase for Blacks, particularly in the
South, because the political, economic, and social institutions of
the society were organized in ways that prevented equal access to

the tools of the law. Black Americans had to organize to end seg-regation in schools, restaurants, job opportunities, and public fa-cilities. One of the paths to changing things was the creation of Black political power through massive voter registration drives. As a consequence, and after a great deal of violence, Black politicians began to be elected for the first time since Reconstruction.

The change in the political institutions helped to end some of the worst expressions of racism in the South. It is important to note that participation of Blacks in the political system was not just an accommodation within the existing structures. It was a far-reaching and radical reordering of the structural arrangements that had pre-vailed since the Civil War. The empowerment of Black political leaders, both in elected and appointed positions, meant a corre-sponding decrease in the power of the traditional white elite. Having a Black mayor in Atlanta, Georgia, did not turn out to be just a mat-ter of changing the color of the political leader. It was rather the end of one way of ordering the world and the beginning of a different order. The seizing of political power by Blacks changed access to jobs and the ability to accumulate wealth. The new view was pro-foundly threatening to the old entrenched centers of power. It is little wonder that Black political emergence was accompanied by violent backlash.

Attacking racial injustice called for seizing and reorienting the traditional sources of political power. In a similar way, creating justice in the economic sphere cannot be confined to a post-production concentration upon income distribution. Modi-fying the income distribution represents only a change of heart, a new way of thinking about the outcomes that flow from the existing system. No change can be accomplished without that. But it is not enough; the more pressing need is for a change of location. This means that the issues of justice and injustice are addressed at a different level. The society has traditionally rearranged outcomes to achieve justice. The new approach looks to the structural causes of injustice and searches for structural remedies to create justice.

Another way to make that argument is to point out that the United States has made patchwork accommodations in an attempt to cover up the most obvious incidences of economic injustice. The welfare system provides a minimum subsistence level of income to those whom the economy precludes from earning a living wage. Unemployment benefits provide short-term relief to workers who lose their jobs because of an economic downturn or a destabilizing corporate decision. And the society provides education and minimum health care to the very poor. None of these accommodations, however, gets at the core of the structural arrangements that create poverty, joblessness, and economic injustice.

Most of the people on welfare face one of two problems. They are unable to work due to the presence of young dependent children. Or they bring only limited skills to the job market, and there are not enough jobs available at their skill level. American society views these problems as personal and individual. That is, the disadvantaged are the source of their own difficulties, and they could correct the deficiencies if they would only develop their skills and work harder. But the reality is that our educational system does very little to prepare those who are most at risk in these situations. Furthermore, society provides no effective and cheap means of child care to free those with dependent children for entry into the job market. And finally, corporations, intent upon private profit, see no advantage in training programs that raise skill levels and potential societal contributions. Low incomes and the necessity for welfare will persist as long as the society continues to try to solve structural problems with individual solutions.

Unemployment benefits are certainly a necessary and humane attempt to ease the pain of job transition and the geographical migration of economic activity. But they have no effect on the structural obstacles placed in the path of unemployed laborers. Most often unemployment comes about because jobs are being shifted from one sector of the economy to another, or from one geographic area to another. Sometimes the latter phenomenon means a permanent loss of jobs for the society as businesses close American production facilities and open them in foreign countries. Unemployment benefits by themselves make up part of the lost income of the jobless, but they do nothing to help the unemployed person prepare for or find new work. The United States lags far behind Europe, for example, in providing job retraining opportunities and subsidizing geographic relocation of workers. More importantly, our society does nothing to limit the ability of private corporations to make relocation decisions. With the control of investment decisions firmly in the hands of private businesses and financial institutions, there is no effective power to prevent relocation and loss of jobs. The society substitutes an unemployment check in place of efforts to create new job opportunities or prevent job loss. Once again, we as a society put the emphasis in the wrong place. We try to repair the damage after a private decision creates joblessness rather than preventing or changing the decision in the first place.

Modern conservatives claim that liberals have tried to solve problems by "throwing money at them." But as has been seen in the 1980s, withdrawing funding has profound consequences in terms of increased poverty and more extensive periods of unemployment. The problem is that American society has been putting its resources in the wrong places. Income redistribution to alleviate the immediate impacts of poverty is crucial, but it does not achieve the goal of ending poverty unless those structural obstacles that create poverty in the first place are also torn down.

Even our vaunted egalitarian public educational system with its provision of universal free schooling directs its attention to redressing results rather than altering structural causes. The system provides for a minimum level of education for everyone. But it allows those with the most resources to provide much more in the way of educational resources for their children. The result is predictable. The children of the white middle class and the elite almost always have a better quality education than children of the poor and minorities. Often, instead of creating the more egalitarian society claimed by our educational system, the result is increased division and disparity among the classes and the races.

What these structures in American society all have in common is their assumption that injustice can be cured by acts of charity and altruism. Creating economic justice within that system seems to mean making misery slightly less painful and visible. Such approaches do not eliminate injustice. They simply cover it up. What is needed is a different system, one that puts the question of justice at a different point. We have argued that the concentration of wealth and decision-making power in the hands of a very few is the source of economic injustice. The exclusion of Blacks and women from full participation, the widespread existence of poverty and malnutrition, and the powerlessness of the middle fragment to change things all stem from the particular ways in which the wealth and power holders choose to organize the system.

Their choices pose a pre-production problem that cannot be solved by any redistribution of the income arising from production. Redirecting the decision-making process involves both changing the hearts of people who make the decisions and changing the location, the stage in the process at which the decisions get made. That is a far more radical step than rearranging the resulting income. A major source of the difficulty rests with the structure of the modern corporation. The prevailing corporate ethic views the world as the place where the corporation makes a profit. A truly radical alternative would force the enterprise to view production as the place where the industry serves the welfare of the society.

Justice as a pre-production demand begins by challenging the two dominant institutional arrangements that have concentrated economic power: private property and corporate structures. The elevation of property rights to a pre-eminent position is a fact in American society. The assertion of human rights is difficult when it calls for any reallocation of property rights. Those at the bottom, the victims of economic injustice, have no property rights and thus cannot effectively push for human rights. The difficulty is exacerbated when the virtually unbridled right to use private property is extended to corporations. That compounds an already existing maldistribution of power and resources. If ownership of productive resources were limited to individual people, then the interaction among those people would place some brakes, both practical and moral, on the ways that resources were used. Unfortunately, those brakes are far less effective when very large concentrations of resources are owned by a corporation.

Restructuring institutions to create economic justice must, at the very least, break down the legal arrangements that identify corporations as being no different from individual persons. Those who suffer from dehumanization, insecurity, and powerlessness cannot even begin to address their grievances until the differential advantages of their adversaries, the economically powerful, are eliminated. The power to use and abuse corporate resources must be limited; the establishment of restricted property rights, subject to social control is one step in reducing corporate control over the economic lives of all of us.

Any meaningful attack upon the economic and sociocultural malaise, if it is to be successful, must alter the economic structures that are at the heart of society and therefore at the heart of the malaise. We have called this a pre-production approach to economic justice. That pushes us to look at the underlying structural causes of inequality. The dominant structures begin with economic institutions, particularly private ownership of the means of production and corporate forms of business decision making, which generate injustice and powerlessness. The society has attempted to correct the flaws by tinkering with the income distribution. This book calls for the development of a new set of production institutions that allow, indeed demand, that the production process itself be oriented toward and organized for justice.

Appendix

In chapters 2 and 3 we have argued that it is essential to understand the nature of the structural situation in which all of the fractions of the laboring class in the United States find themselves. We have used statistical evidence to support our argument but have avoided extensive tables detailing the data about the economic situation of the poor and those in the middle. This appendix provides some of that detail, including wealth and income distributions, patterns of ownership of productive assets, employment and unemployment, and the sectoral location of jobs.

Since one of the signs of the economic precariousness and powerlessness of the middle sectors is their deteriorating relative position in terms of command over resources by means of income and ownership of assets, this appendix will begin with current and historic data on the income and wealth distribution in the United States.

Table 2
Percentage Income Shares of American Families,
1950–1984, by Quintiles

YEAR	LOW 20%	4th 20%	3rd 20%	2nd 20%	TOP 20%	TOP 5%
1984	4.7%	11.0%	17.0%	24.4%	42.9%	16.0%
1980	5.1	11.6	17.5	24.3	41.6	15.3
1975	5.4	11.8	17.6	24.1	41.1	15.5
1970	5.4	12.2	17.6	23.8	40.9	15.6
1965	5.2	12.2	17.8	23.9	40.9	15.5
1960	4.8	12.2	17.8	24.0	41.3	15.9
1950	4.5	12.0	17.4	23.4	42.7	17.3

Source: U.S. Department of Commerce, Bureau of the Census, *Money Incomes of Households, Families, and Persons, 1984* (Washington, 1986), p. 37.

As Table 2 shows, the income distribution is becoming more skewed, with the share of the bottom quintile now the smallest it has been since the early 1950s, and with the shares of the top 20% and top 5% rising back to or above 1950s levels. The middle has also been squeezed, with the share of the middle 60% at 52.4%, smaller even than the 52.8% in 1950. These recent trends have reversed the pattern of greater income equality begun in the expansion of the 1960s.

Another important characteristic for measuring the degree of economic equality or inequality in a society is the distribution of the ownership of various kinds of wealth assets. Table 3 shows percentages of total wealth held by different groups of wealth holders at the time of the American Revolution and more recently. There is a long trend toward greater concentrations of wealth in a few hands.

Table 3
Wealth Distribution by Percent, 1774, 1962, 1973

% of wealth held by:	1774	1962	1973
Top 1%	13%	34%	32.6%
Top 5%	35	53	57.5
Top 10%	51	62	69.8
Next 10%	17	16	13.8
Next 50%	30	22	15.4
Low 30%	2	0	0

Source: Lars Osberg, *Economic Inequality in the United States* (New York, 1984), p. 44.

The difficulty with the concentration of ownership does not rest just with the fact that fewer people own a larger share of the assets. Rather, there is the additional problem that such owner-ship is becoming concentrated in the hands of particularly large businesses. See Table 4.

The concentrations of income and wealth have both resulted from and contributed to the slow growth in the United States economy since 1970. Concentrated wealth tends to look for conservative, wealth-consolidating, financial investment deci-sions. That has meant more mergers and fewer technological innovations. Conservative decisions slow down economic growth. And, of course, slow economic growth has meant fewer opportunities for creation of new, more dispersed, wealth and income. This has real impacts for job creation. For example, since 1970, the United States economy has been growing so slowly that the average rate of unemployment has been rising

Table 4
Percent Distribution of U.S. Wealth Ownership by Sector
Selected Years, 1929–84

Year	Total Wealth (billions of 1972 dollars)	Percent held by:			
		Households	Government	Business	100 largest industrial firms
1929	926	9.9%	15.2%	74.8%	na
1945	1170	6.6	43.1	50.3	na
1955	1545	12.1	26.7	61.3	na
1965	2203	12.2	26.2	61.5	28.6%
1970	2715	13.7	25.2	61.0	29.7
1975	3220	15.2	23.6	61.2	27.5
1980	3718	16.5	21.9	61.6	28.8
1984	4071	17.1	20.8	62.1	30.4

Source: U.S. Department of Commerce, Bureau of the Census, *Statistical Abstract of the United States, 1986*, pp. 462, 524.

even without the existence of an economic crisis like the Great Depression. Coupled with this has been an increasing number of discouraged workers who have left the labor force and are not officially counted as part of the unemployed. Finally, the part of the labor force that is employed only part-time as a result of economic conditions is also rising. Thus, the official unemployment statistics, bleak as they are, probably understate the job shortage. The employment data in Tables 5 and 6 illustrate these trends as well as contrasting them with employment trends in the earlier part of this century.

Table 6 clearly details the shift away from manufacturing and toward the service industries that has marked the post World War II American economy. In the forty years from 1910 to 1950, manufacturing and services grew at almost the same rate, with roughly one-third of the labor force employed in manufacturing and with between 50% and 60% in the service industries. From 1950 to 1985, employment in manufacturing declined dramatically to less than 20% of the labor force, while the service industries exploded and now employ almost three-fourths of all labor.

Table 5

Unemployment as a Percent of the Civilian Labor Force
Selected Segments of the Labor Force
United States, 1950–1983

Year	Total Civilian Labor Force	Unemployment				Discouraged[b] as % of LF	Part-time[a] as % of LF
		Total as % of LF	Male as % Male LF	Female as % Female LF	Black as % Black LF		
1950	62.2	5.3%	5.1%	5.7%	na	na	na
1955	65.0	4.4	4.2	4.9	na	na	na
1960	69.6	5.5	5.4	5.9	na	na	4.1%
1965	74.5	4.5	4.0	5.5	na	na	3.0
1970	82.8	4.9	4.4	5.9	na	na	2.9
1975	93.8	8.5	7.9	9.3	14.8%	1.2%	4.1
1976	96.2	7.7	7.1	8.6	14.0	1.0	3.7
1977	99.0	7.1	6.3	8.2	14.0	1.0	3.6
1978	102.3	6.1	5.3	7.2	12.8	0.8	3.4
1979	105.0	5.8	5.1	6.8	12.3	0.7	3.4
1980	106.9	7.1	6.9	7.4	14.3	0.9	4.0
1981	108.7	7.6	7.4	7.9	15.6	1.0	4.4
1982	110.2	9.7	9.9	9.4	18.9	1.4	5.6
1983	111.6	9.6	9.9	9.2	19.5	1.5	5.6
1984	113.5	7.5	6.6	6.8	15.9	na	5.1
1985	115.5	7.2	6.2	6.6	15.1	na	4.8

Notes: [a]Part-time includes only those part-time workers who would prefer to work full-time but cannot find full-time work.

[b]Discouraged workers are those who have left the labor force because they do not believe they can find any jobs.

Sources: 1950–1983, U.S. Department of Labor, Bureau of Labor Statistics, *Handbook of Labor Statistics, 1985* (Washington, 1985), pp. 8, 9, 38, 58, 64.
1984–85, Council of Economic Advisers, *Economic Indicators*, January, 1986, and U.S. Department of Labor, Bureau of Labor Statistics, *Monthly Labor Review*, March, 1986, p. 64.

Table 6
Millions of Persons Employed, by Sector
United States, Selected Years, 1910–85

Year	Total Employ- ment	Goods Produc- ing	Manufac- turing[a]	Service Produc- ing	Govern- ment[b]	Supervi- sory Posi- tions
1910	21.7	10.2	7.8	11.5	1.6	
1920	27.4	12.7	10.7	14.7	2.4	
1930	29.4	12.0	9.6	17.4	3.1	
1940	32.4	13.2	11.0	19.2	4.2	
1950	45.2	18.4	15.2	26.8	6.0	
1955	50.7	20.5	16.9	30.2	6.9	
1960	54.2	20.4	16.8	33.8	8.4	
1965	60.8	21.9	18.1	38.9	10.1	
1970	70.6	23.3	19.4	47.3	12.5	22.6
1971	70.7	22.5	18.6	48.2	12.9	22.9
1972	72.8	23.1	18.9	49.7	13.3	23.6
1973	75.6	24.1	19.8	51.5	13.7	21.5
1974	78.4	24.7	20.0	53.7	14.2	22.6
1975	77.0	22.5	18.3	54.4	14.7	26.0
1976	79.4	23.3	19.0	56.1	14.9	26.3
1977	82.1	24.2	19.6	57.9	15.2	27.2
1978	86.7	25.6	20.5	60.8	15.7	28.5
1979	89.9	26.6	21.1	62.9	15.9	29.5
1980	90.4	25.7	20.3	64.7	16.2	30.1
1981	91.1	25.5	20.2	65.6	16.0	30.3
1982	89.6	23.8	18.8	65.8	19.0	30.1
1983	90.1	23.4	18.5	66.7	19.7	30.1
1984	94.5	24.7	19.4	72.6	16.3	30.9
1985	97.7	25.1	19.4	72.6	16.3	31.7

Notes: [a]Manufacturing employment is a sub-category of Goods Producing employment.
[b]Government employment is a sub-category of Service Producing employment.
Source: U.S. Department of Commerce, Bureau of Economic Analysis, *Survey of
Current Business*, "Current Business Statistics," selected issues.

4
The Inevitability of Ideology

In any society there is a choice between holding to the status quo or recreating society anew. By no means is it equally possible to enact both choices. The dominant groups and forces in society are opposed to any new social vision arising outside their own ranks. We in the middle may decide for social renewal, yet have our actions defeated by the reigning powers that be. Or, a decision may simply be made for us by default; society often is maintained precisely because the issue of an alternative vision is never addressed. In either case, the future is something that has been seen before; it simply repeats the past. There are times, however, when significant segments of a society have attached themselves to a vision of what could be and acted successfully on it. Then hope has the power to relax the grasp of what has been, and a new future begins to emerge.

The Nature and Pervasiveness of Ideology

If we in the middle fraction are to deal with our condition of powerlessness and sense of isolation, we need to choose hope and develop ways to enact it. That is neither an easy nor a comfortable process. The call for change is usually viewed with trepidation, even by those who are most marginalized by present circumstances; there is a "fear of freedom."[1] For if one accepts the views of the elite as natural, as normal, even as sacred, then to reject them is to risk not just insecurity, but also insanity or immorality. Having a place, no matter how lowly, is comforting.

A commitment to the social order by the oppressed depends largely on their belief in it, their acceptance of a particular cultural view as absolute reality.[2] Social order is often maintained because we are deeply convinced of its legitimacy, its naturalness, rather than because of naked coercion. Yet, this persuasiveness of certain cultural symbols is tied to an underlying coercion that does exist in the relationships between social classes in society. Everyone may be capable of interpreting reality, but those in the upper classes are most able to enforce their version of reality. The dominant cultural ideas and values, those accepted most widely in society, are likely to reflect the interests of the most powerful groups. We are socialized into their cultural perspective, but we assume it as our own.

This understanding of how cultural ideas are based in society and help to defend the status quo has come traditionally to be called ideology. In this book we assume, however, a very different view of ideology. The traditional conception sees ideology only in a negative light, supporting the dominant power structure. Ideology is usually considered something to be avoided; in contrast, we contend that whether things remain the same, or significantly change, an ideology is involved. A given society may embrace one set of values, or opt for another, but all societies are accomplished by ideological "systems of means."[3]

Ideology can obviously support discrimination and inequality, but it also is necessary for being critical of such domination and fighting against it. Ideology can disguise or conceal the true nature of society, but it also is a necessary and revealing representation of the world in which we all live.[4] *Ideology, therefore, refers to the necessity of a perspective, a recognition that all knowledge is socially based.* We can neither perceive nor conceive of the world without a certain point of view. Our representations may not be accurate; we might accept as natural a reality that supports someone else's interests at our own expense. Yet ideology may also allow us to wake up and take notice, be critical, of what we used to take for granted. If we are to begin to act against domination and for justice, we need to be ideologically awakened to the possibility of a new and different society.

This echoes an argument used for Latin America, that a process of "conscientization" is the necessary first step for the overthrow of oppression. Conscientization is the ideological realization by the oppressed that they are oppressed. That is, the poor recognize that their own interests are not the same as those of the elite. They must discern the nature and sources of dominance and act collectively for a new order. Action is necessary to reclaim the human capacity to shape the world. However, all such action must begin with conscientization and a new ideology that takes the perspective and interests of the oppressed into account.[5]

Advocating an ideology of social renewal or revolution for the middle sectors calls for a more extensive definition of the term ideology. Both social science and theology have been afflicted with a definition of ideology that limits it to ideas that proceed from and support the interests of a particular dominant class or social sector. Since an ideology purports to be a universally accurate depiction of reality, but in fact represents only the concerns of one group, it carries the negative connotation of obscuring reality. It screens those not in the dominant classes from perceiving the true circumstances. Though other dimensions to the concept obviously exist, ideology is intimately associated here with the notion of false consciousness.

In this view ideology refers to the evaluative use of ideas in defense of a particular position, representing only the interests of one contending group against another. It does not disclose historically valid knowledge, but conceals the fact that human beings have constructed reality.[6] In this definition both ideology and human interests are obfuscating. The play of interests is contrasted explicitly with science; whereas ideology is linked to the pragmatic manipulation of ideas for ulterior motives, science is free of the perversity of personal interests.

There can also be a second and equally important aspect to the definition of ideology. Here ideology refers essentially to a non-evaluative cultural worldview, a symbolic system of ideas and values rooted in a particular society. Ideas are tied to particular historical circumstances. Because human beings always live under certain social conditions, they cannot understand these circumstances other than by taking a point of view. The necessity of perspective grounds ideas in social conditions; it makes the comprehension of reality ideological. Since social conditions are always capable of changing, the ideological conception of them can also be dynamic. It allows us to perceive the nature of historically mutable truths. This definition of ideology is non-evaluative because it acts to represent or reveal reality, rather than obfuscate it.[7]

This second conception of ideology rejects efforts to conceive of it as one sphere of cultural knowledge set off from other non-ideological spheres, such as science. Cultural meaning, in general, is said to be bound up with human intentionality.[8] Human beings construct meaning, whether in science, religion, or other areas, in light of the purposes at hand. Those purposes are based on what actors take to be their interests, an assessment of wants and how to realize them.[9] Yet both purposes and interests are conditioned by individual histories and the wider structures under which we all live. It is no wonder that the poor and the wealthy can come to quite different interpretations about what they value and how they should act. For culture to have meaning for us it must bear some relation to the familiar and to our own intent and interests. All knowledge, therefore, is socially based; any given type of knowledge is informed by life generally. Science, for example, may draw its metaphors or theoretical conceptions of problems and their solutions from the social circumstances of its practitioners.[10] If this is so, then neither ideology nor human interests are simply obfuscating. Without a perspective, knowledge and action—even living—would be impossible. The most basic task of ideology is to clarify, to provide stories that reveal a picture of the world. Some stories may be false; others, however, provide the basic images by which we live.

Ideologies, in this sense, refer to an essential aspect of all symbol systems. It would be most accurate to use the term as an adjective rather than as a noun. There are no ideologies, only the ideological use of symbolic orders.[11] Yet in emphasizing the revealing elements of ideology, we must not forget that the ideological can also conceal. For if interests inherently influence meaning, they may be purely sectional or class interests masquerading as being meaningful for society in general. Indeed, a principal ideological mode is the portrayal of specifically sectoral interests as valid for all social groups in society, the reproduction of the status quo as natural, and the denial of any existing contradictions in the system.[12] As part of social *interaction*, ideological forms relate to the strategic pursuit by individuals of their own wants in light of perceived interests. As ideologies become part of *institutional structures*, however, they preserve forms of domination inherent in the existing features of a society.[13] Ideologies, thus, can justify the interests of dominant groups, particularly as they become embedded in structures and institutions. Yet, at the level of discourse, ideology is also related to the discernment of such interests by the subordinate sectors of society. The institutions may be stacked against us, but in the course of living we can become critical of them. By realizing just what our position really is and the wants and interests that it entails, we can unmask the ideological disguises of the dominant. Ideology is bound up with both the dominant cultural forms and the counterculture of the opposition. Indeed, the very terms in which we are able to critique the existing structures, or envision new ones, are necessarily dictated in part by those same structures.[14] Ideology, therefore, both shackles and frees. It is as much a part of the defense of domination as the attainment of liberation. The issue is not the presence or absence of ideology, or even the possibility of moving beyond it. It is the nature and legitimacy of the particular human goals and interests that lead to any given ideological use of symbols. If ideology is inevitable, it matters all the more which ideology we choose.

Ideology and the Disciplines

In this book are suggestions that the ideological is an aspect of all symbol systems. There are no privileged, ideologically free zones of knowledge. Obviously, this includes our own disciplines in the social sciences and theology. While such a proposition stands in contrast to a good deal of tradition, whether of positivism or neo-orthodoxy, it also rests on a whole series of alternative epistemological moves being made in our fields. We need, therefore, to clarify our own assumptions in order to underscore how we could collaborate when our disciplines are often thought to be methodologically different, even antithetical. To do this we will sketch how our various disciplines have seen themselves in regard to ideology, and how we depart from these views.

Sociology/Anthropology, and Ideology

Both anthropology and sociology, from their inceptions, have been influenced deeply by positivism. Nineteenth-century thinkers viewed the disciplines as being essentially like the natural sciences. In 1895, Emile Durkheim established "rules of sociological method" which argue passionately in defense of the unity of all science, based on the positivist program for the discovery of natural laws of society. Natural and social science alike have been presumed to be engaged in a value-free, "objective" search for empirical regularities, which determine the natural and social world.[15]

Science is engaged in the pursuit of absolute truth through a scientific method assumed to be dictated only by universal standards of reason. Ideology in this view has come traditionally to refer to anything that is pseudo- or anti-science, or against the truth. Anthropologist Marvin Harris, for example, implies this in his particular version of cultural materialism. Harris speaks of "the struggle for a science of culture" and contrasts his own positivist view of science with "obscurantism," which ". . . arises only when knowledge obtained through nonscientific [i.e., non-positivist] means is deliberately used to cast doubt on the authenticity of scientific knowledge. . . ."[16]

The positivist effort to defend the objectivity of social scientific analysis portrays science as though it were based on principles of human action entirely unlike those in any other sphere. The scientist acts solely by appeal to reason, while human beings generally are passionate, committed to certain moral systems, and act with a wide array of social and specifically class-based interests. The positivist thus must embrace the implausible position of holding one set of assumptions about human nature and action for scientific practice, and an entirely different set for all other areas of human activity.

This further implies that ideology is conceived of as one among many spheres of knowledge, or falsehood. Ideology, like science, religion, or poetry, is thought to be identifiable as a certain type of symbol system. Breaking off ideology for consideration as a separate thing is not limited to materialists like Harris. Clifford Geertz, an anthropologist interested in more interpretive approaches, remarks, "Where, if anywhere, ideology leaves off and science begins has been the Sphinx's Riddle of much of modern sociological thought. . . ."[17]

The essential difference, however, between science and ideology in Geertz' view is one of "stylistic strategies" for coming to terms with the world, rather than any necessary difference in the truth of their conclusions. Where science is said to be "disinterested," ideology is committed to certain values. Science is "diagnostic," "critical," whereas ideology is "justificatory" and "apologetic."[18] Science generally uses a "literal" style of presentation, while ideology relies on a highly literary use of figurative language, such as metaphor, irony, hyperbole, or oxymorons.[19]

In spite of this listing of presumed differences, there is said to be an essential similarity between ideology and science. Both are symbolic constructions about the world, and both may express essential truths. Far from always distorting our perspective, the ideological use of rhetorical figures may provide the subtlety necessary for capturing the complexities of history. Ideology "might in fact draw its power from its capacity to grasp, formulate, and communicate social realities that elude the tempered language of science. . . ."[20]

This is an important point, and one quite compatible with our view of ideology as having the potential to reveal as well as conceal the realities of the world. Where we differ is in our insistence that all forms of knowledge have an ideological aspect.[21] The usual move is to separate ideology and science as systems, rather than considering the ideological dimension of

science. That repeats the positivist view that it is possible to be
disinterested in the pursuit of science. Certainly the distinction
between the literality of science and the figurative nature of
ideology will not hold up.[22] Metaphoric and rhetorical usage
generally are basic to both, as are literal statements.[23] Yet far
more crucial, we think, for collapsing any boundary distinction
between ideology and science is the recognition that meaning can
never be disinterested. Meaning is not reducible to self-interest.
Yet neither is any meaning possible—scientific, poetic, or other—
that is unrelated to the fact that all of us are born into a set of
social circumstances and have our own personal histories. Combined with our intent in any given action, and our interests in
figuring out how to realize our intent, our knowledge of the world
must inevitably give us a particular perspective. There is no
presuppositionless view of reality, no Archimedean point; we
must all stand somewhere to do our looking.

But the fact that we must look at a house from one side does
not mean necessarily that we have a false view of the house. It
simply means that we have a partial view. Nor does it mean that
the house is not there. More to the point, it does not distort the
view to look at the structure of American society from the
perspective of how it actually affects the middle and working
sectors; it reveals, rather, dimensions of the structure that will not
be seen if we look at it from an upper class position.

Viewing ideology in this way is not tantamount to relativism.
That all knowledge, even social and natural scientific knowledge,
is socially grounded and from an interested perspective does not
make all perspectives equally right or equally wrong. Rather, as
Anthony Giddens suggests, such a view of ideology is quite
compatible with "accepting that social science can deliver objectively valid knowledge. But it involves rejecting . . . [that] the
relation between such 'valid knowledge' and 'invalid knowledge
claims' is the defining feature of what ideology *is*."[24]

This is a crucial issue for the acceptance of our particular
argument. For if ideology is necessary, and indeed science itself is
ideological, then how is objectivity to be defined? Why would
anyone, and certainly the middle sectors, feel compelled to

acknowledge the validity of our arguments? Why not dismiss them as but one more perspective, or, worse, one more biased perspective? Is it possible to imagine a valid non-positivist view of social science?

The claim that science is socially based, involving interests outside those dictated by scientific methodology and theory, does not say that science is determined by those interests.[25] To suggest that would mean we could easily speak in all cases of bourgeois or proletarian social science. A position of this sort, however, is tantamount to saying that science reflects the mode of economic production.[26]

How, then, can one escape the positivist assumption that doing authentic social science is a presuppositionless, disinterested process, without abandoning all claims to having something valid to say? Is it possible to construct a non-positivist view of objective knowledge? Positivism argues for the unity of natural and social science on the basis of their common search for laws. These laws consist of empirical regularities which permit prediction. In the social sciences, the principal alternative to positivism is the interpretive tradition. It argues for a radical distinction between society and nature and, thus, between social and natural science. Since we attribute meaning to our world and make choices based on our thought, society may have rules, but it will never be a lawful realm like that of nature. The role of social science is to understand this world of human meaning and to explain it.

We are sympathetic to this non-positivist stance. We, too, insist on the importance of meaning and an understanding of human nature that sees people as active interpreters of their world. The necessity of interpretation means that all action is a product of human choices and society is seen as a human product. Human beings are not simply determined by social circumstances; they actively coproduce and even transform them.[27]

In rejecting positivism, however, we cannot simply replace it with the interpretive position. The problem with the interpretive view is its "ceding natural science to positivism."[28] Positivism is no more descriptive of natural than of social science. The crux of the matter is the positivist tendency to equate natural (or social) law with empirical regularities. Roy Bhaskar argues persuasively to the contrary that laws refer to mechanisms that underlie empirical patterns, rather than being equated with them. Natural and social law, then, are "tendencies," not readily proved or falsified by any given empirical example.[29]

Yet Bhaskar does not wish wholly to reject positivism either, and here is the point at which his argument bears on the issue of the validity of science. For if we can speak of laws for both nature *and* society as tendencies, then there are grounds for reconceiving the unity of natural and social science in a non-positivist way.[30]

Simply to adopt the interpretive position is to limit the task of social science to understanding what people believe about their social world. To do so, however, is to equate the understanding of society with society itself. That ignores the reality that the society we have collectively created, in turn shapes and conditions our thought about it. By denying that society is more than its meaning for us, we short-circuit any attempt to be critical of those meanings. The interpretive position cannot recognize the false consciousness that results from a misreading of social forces hidden from our view as actors.[31]

We need to recognize that society is an emergent level of reality, based in the thoughts and actions of individuals, but also capable of acting back on us. It shapes us in ways that are not always immediately evident. Our actions may be intentional, but they have unintended consequences which lie outside of our direct awareness and control. There are structural reasons, for example, why the middle layers of American society are such ardent believers in individualism. But it is only by acknowledging the existence of underlying structural mechanisms that produce individualism, Bhaskar's tendencies or laws, that it is possible to discern whether belief in individualism itself is an accurate or false reading of society.

This means that the social scientists' reading of the middle layer's view of society, is itself socially conditioned. In order to assure an accurate explanation of society, it is necessary to appeal to empirical data not addressed or accounted for adequately by alternative explanations. We must also be self-critical of the social context, assumptions, and value-commitments that shape our own theory.[32] Positivism, unfortunately, inhibits that process by imagining itself to be value-free.[33] The irony is that by claiming to be value-free, positivists assure their own subjectivity; the claim to be free of ideology is itself an ideology and leads to false consciousness. To be objective, then, does not imply that we are value-free but rather that we constantly acknowledge social influences on our explanations of society. This does not guarantee objectivity, but objectivity is not possible without it.

Economic Paradigms and Ideology

Economic paradigms or models are also ideologies, stories that can either reveal or conceal the real economic world. Economists believe that their paradigms highlight the essential features of some particular aspect of the economic system. Such models are used to analyze and understand the economy so that when problems arise they can be dealt with using appropriate policy actions. But policies are defined as being appropriate in terms of the model rather than the real world itself.

It is easy to underestimate the ideological power of paradigms and think of the real world as being too complex to understand in any holistic way. The prevailing ideologies in the social sciences pressure us to grasp the world a piece at a time by constructing ad hoc models. In the social and natural sciences these models are quite formal. All of us, however, hold equally ideological models more informally in everyday life. Both the formal and the intuitive models play an extremely important part in the management of the world. John Maynard Keynes, for example, claimed that "[p]ractical men . . . are usually the slaves of some defunct economist. Madmen in authority, who hear voices in the air, are distilling their frenzy from some academic scribbler of a few years back."[34] Lord Keynes' dictum suggests two things about economic models. First, they serve as the basis for national policy, and second, the policies that flow from them cannot claim to be value-free. Economists think of their operative paradigms as revealing, as opening up the world of economic decisions to rational understanding and explanation. However, once a particular paradigm purports to explain all of reality rather than one perspective, it tends to conceal, not reveal. The

assumptions that undergird any economic model become effectively hidden from view as that model becomes the dominant
ideology for economic analysis and policy.

Chapters 2 and 3 considered the assumptions that underlie
the most dominant Western economic models, particularly assumptions about the role of individuals. "Madmen in authority"
have been distilling their frenzied policies from such models for
some time in the United States. The behavioral assumptions
about the role of the individual economic decision maker and the
structural assumptions about the number, size, and power of
those decision makers bear little relation to institutional realities.

During the nineteenth century the market model reached
center stage among economists in industrial countries. In the
United States both economic analysis and national policy had
accepted the market ideology by the beginning of the twentieth
century. Thus, any action seen as "enhancing" the market was
immediately recognized as "good." The mystical claims of the
market economy have led to a false perception and consciousness, which hide the reality of our world.

Obeisance to the market has blinded us to the fact that
models "work" only when their assumptions match the mechanisms of the real world. Such a claim cannot be made about the
basic assumptions that undergird the effectiveness of the market
as an institution providing efficiency in allocation. An effective
market, according to Adam Smith and his followers, requires
competitive conditions with large numbers of small producers
and sellers of a product. The product itself must be homogeneous, and it must be relatively easy for producers to enter the
industry. It is questionable whether these rather rigid assumptions ever held sway, even in the less monopolistic nineteenth
century. Certainly in our own world, dominated by monopolies,
oligopolies, and transnational corporations, the assumptions do
not hold. Try to fit them, for example, to the modern automobile,
oil, or nuclear submarine industries.

If economic paradigms were nothing more than toys that
theoretical economists play with, we could dismiss the market
paradigm as naive and move on to dealing with the real world.
Unfortunately, policymakers become wedded to particular mod-

els. As that happens, their ability to be pragmatic about appropriate economic policy is dramatically reduced. Their choices are limited by a particular, but not necessarily appropriate, economic model. Monetarists always choose monetary policy because its conservative assumptions agree with their ideological vision of the way the world ought to be, not because any objective evidence shows it to be more effective policy. Supply-siders choose tax-cut policies because they believe that taxes reduce productivity, not because objective evidence reveals a relationship between reduced taxes and increased societal welfare. And liberal economists always suggest income redistribution policies because they believe that the more fortunate ought to take care of the less fortunate in spite of some evidence that indicates that existing programs may institutionalize the conditions of poverty.

It is unfortunate when professionals fall prey to the temptation to believe that their models mirror reality. It is worse when they sell these models as the only appropriate mode of analysis for national economic policy. Too often they fall into the positivist trap of treating their models as presuppositionless. People who earn a good living are likely to believe what the economists say about the market model; because the market works for them, they believe it works for everybody.

Matching the assumptions with the real world conditions is a necessity for making the market achieve the desired goal of serving societal welfare. In the absence of those preconditions, a market is nothing more than a collection of individuals and businesses all seeking their own self-interest. Nothing leads from that self-interest to societal welfare. How often has any advocate of the glories of the market economy explained its supposed benefits in this way? They fail to do so, not because they are trying to mislead the public or maintain us in ignorance, but because they are fervently committed to the market and blinded to its inadequacies.

It is in this sense that economic paradigms become ideologically concealing. Ideologies as worldviews or interpretive perspectives are revelatory insofar as they allow us to understand and be critical of the reality of our world; they are concealing when they lead us to interpret evidence in ways that hide that reality. When economic paradigms urge continued belief in a world that does not exist, they are concealing. When those same models become the basis for national economic policy that affects us all, they become dangerously concealing.

Some examples of "dangerously concealing" paradigms and their consequences will help to clarify this point. Consider again the recent influence of the monetarist perspective in the Federal Reserve System. Their basic behavioral assumptions include a belief that decisions affecting the size of the Gross National Product are directly influenced almost exclusively by the size of the money supply. They also hold that it is essential to have a currency with a stable value in order to build a strong economy. Since 1979, the monetarists have influenced national economic policy more than any other group. They have urged and achieved a very slow rate of growth in the money supply in order to combat inflation. There is little doubt that their restrictive monetary policies have dramatically slowed the pace of inflation from the double-digit rates that prevailed in the seventies. Unfortunately, one of the side effects of their policy choice has been the deepest recession since the 1930s, an agonizingly slow recovery, and unemployment that remains well above acceptable levels.

The monetarists would not regard their position as ideologically concealing, and certainly they would see their economic paradigm as opening up understanding of the real world. The problems mentioned above are seen, if they are discussed at all, as unfortunate side effects that must be borne if the economy is to solve its significant problems. Any alternative explanations or policy proposals are rejected because they do not fit the "right" assumptions, assumptions that are rarely examined by the true believers.

There are at least three other assumptions under which monetarists operate. First, private "individual" decision making is always more efficient and preferable to public sector decision making. Second, it is individuals who make most of the economic decisions. And third, the market always works to achieve social welfare. If you accept all of these assumptions, then stabilizing the monetary conditions creates a good environment within which to make individual decisions. Operating from this base, however, the monetarist paradigm cannot effectively explain a real world in which most of the major decisions are made by corporate and governmental bureaucracies. Clinging to the model in the face of conditions to the contrary plays a doubly concealing role; it hides both the nature of the real world and the alternative policy choices that it necessitates.

The liberal economists of the 1960s and 1970s provide another example of policy makers being wedded to economic models which then conceal reality. As we have noted, these liberal legislators and administrators put a complex web of taxes and transfer payments in place. This web was designed to redistribute income from the middle and upper classes to the poor. The intent was to protect the poor against the vagaries of an economy over which they had no control.

Several assumptions lie behind the liberal economists' model for improving societal welfare.

1. Welfare is most effectively measured in material terms.
2. Material welfare is basically equivalent to ability to buy consumer goods.
3. Income redistribution is the most effective way to enhance that ability to buy.
4. The market can solve problems of inequity in social welfare provided that income inequities are eliminated or reduced.

These assumptions ignore, and thus hide, any possibility that the real problem that creates the initial inequities might be something other than an income distribution issue. The legislation and programs of the sixties and seventies never raised the possibility that our basic economic structure might be incapable of creating equity. To those who believe that the basic problem is lack of income, redistribution schemes seem appropriate. However, if the basic problem is that the poor have no ability to control or change their economic circumstances, then redistribution simply glosses over the problem by making its consequences less offensive.

As a result, liberal redistributive economic models are also ideologically concealing. They direct attention away from the real problem by making us believe we are "doing something" about poverty. As much as we might like the moral tone of such models, the fact that they ignore elite control and mass powerlessness means that the real problem persists. The data presented in chapters 2 and 3 about economic accumulation indicate that powerlessness is increasing. The distribution of power is becoming even more distorted. Under these conditions, how can the poor, the most powerless of us all, ever hope to create conditions that protect them against intense poverty? The power of the elite to alter, quickly and radically, the conditions and location of production, means that the poor, much of the working fraction, and many of the middle fraction can never have any real economic security. Even those who believe that social welfare is best defined in material terms will surely agree that the existing system ensures that material well-being will never be very stable for a large part of the population.

Where does this analysis of welfare programs lead? Many applaud the goals of such programs. Alleviating the suffering of the poor can hardly be seen as undesirable. However, if the analytic models used to create such programs are based on faulty behavioral and structural assumptions, it may be that the present approach to achieving the desired goal is inadequate. If the commitment to those analytic paradigms is firm, the result is a concealing ideology that not only fails to solve the problem of poverty, but also prevents the discovery of alternative models that might provide a more effective set of policy alternatives.

There is a tendency to define the monetarist model as moderately rightist and the redistribution model as moderately leftist. Yet, there is a sense in which both are conservative, supporting an ideology designed to maintain the status quo. Both models accept the market as the basic arbiter of economic decision making. Their advocates believe that the market, with only limited interference, can achieve the maximum societal welfare.

Again, recall the basic assumptions of the market paradigm, which claims that the economy of the United States is based on individual decision making and defines the individual as either the household or the business firm. It also assumes that there is private ownership, particularly of the means of production. Production activity is organized for profit; that is, the individual decision makers use their ownership of the means of production to seek maximum profit. If the competitive conditions are fulfilled and there are many small buyers and sellers of homogeneous products, with industries that are easy to enter and leave, then the pursuit of profit will require the individual firm to produce efficiently and sell at low prices. Otherwise, the customers will seek other producers. As a result, producers must find ways to use resources as efficiently as possible in order to maintain low prices. If consumers can buy products at low prices with the assurance that resources are being used efficiently, then the material well-being of society is being served effectively by a market economy.

The dominant beliefs lead to the elevation of the market to a position of reverence. That further protects the market from any challenge. However, an examination of the assumptions shows they do not match the real world conditions. In many industries there are only a few very large producers. They work hard to get consumers to believe that their products are differentiated, not homogeneous—that is one reason there is advertising. Furthermore, most large-scale industries require huge capital investments in order to operate efficiently, thus effectively preventing new firms from entering the industry.

As a society, we have been socially conditioned to interpret our world from a perspective which gives material economic success a place of pre-eminence. But that means, once again, that we view the United States from the vantage point of the existing elite. Because the system has served this elite well, there is a tendency for all of us to claim, "the system works." If we look at things from the viewpoint of the poor and laboring class generally, we see a very different picture. Which perspective is "right"? There is obviously no value-free answer to that question. But since the first perspective does not adequately explain extensive and continued poverty, while the second explains both poverty and wealth, it would seem that viewing our world from the perspective of the laboring class is more revealing than viewing it from the perspective of the elite. The elite want us to think about what our market system does for us. The alternative perspective wants to know what it does *to* us.

Institutional arrangements ensure that a mismatch must

emerge between the assumptions of the free market model and the actual conditions of society. The pursuit of profit is one of the goals of the market system. The entrepreneurs who receive the profit soon discover that the amount of profit available to them is directly related to the degree of control they have over the means of production. More control flows from increased ownership, and ownership flows from accumulation. There is a very strong incentive for the individual business firm to use its profit to buy more capital and/or land, enhancing control over the means of production. Unless we assume that all entrepreneurs are equally gifted and have equal access to resources, this process of accumulation implies that some businesses will become large and powerful relative to others. But then the competitive conditions are violated, and the market begins to serve the interests of the economically powerful rather than societal welfare. Once we realize that, we might begin to ask what it does to the rest of us.

The working fraction and the poor do look at things from a different structural perspective. But even though they are the most disadvantaged by the failure of the market to serve societal welfare, they, too, can fall prey to the promise of economic opportunity that is open to anyone in the market system. That promise effectively hides from them the reality that very few ever succeed in dramatically altering their economic conditions. It may also lead them to blame themselves, rather than the system, for their individual failures to move up. Finally, the middle sector has been bought off. We do not want to recognize the failures of the market system because we do not want to sacrifice the material comfort that an oligopolistic system has brought us.

Thus the market ideology is triumphant. It has concealed and continues to conceal the reality of gross inequities in the distributions of income, wealth, and power. Differences in well-being are seen as benign results of differences in ability. In reality, they are the malignant consequences of differences in wealth and power. The market exacerbates these differences through its emphasis upon and its rewards for accumulation. Despite the promises of the market, the poor can never "catch up"; the structure of the market simply will not permit it.

Theology and Ideology

One reason why the social sciences want to distinguish their work from ideology is to preserve the validity of their conclusions. A similar impulse has been at work in traditional Christian scholarship. Both biblical scholars and theologians have had their own bouts with value-free objectivity.

The need for certitude has taken hold in relation to biblical interpretation. The prevailing assumption is that one can be free of bias and identify the true grounds upon which the message of faith can be affirmed. Often in very different ways biblical scholars present themselves as able to interpret the meaning of the biblical tradition without the distortion of ideology. One movement focuses upon verbal inspiration and the literal accuracy of the Scriptures. The words of the Bible are the Word of God. The Word is immediately accessible and self-evident in its meaning. When one asserts "the Bible says," one is claiming "God says." The linguistic convention of capitalizing words such as *Scripture, Bible, Word of God* is an indication of this. Somehow it is affirmed that the "Word of God" is entirely free of an environment affecting its meaning and that hearers of the Word can appropriate it without reference to their sociohistorical circumstances. Elisabeth Fiorenza describes this approach: "Just as we have instant coffee without grinding the beans and filtering it, so we can have instant inspiration and guidance from the Bible without bothering with the obstacles of a historical understanding."[35] The Word of God is value-free and transfers from one time and place to another without attention to either.

Another movement is a reaction to the first and resembles the sciences in the desire to achieve historical certitude. Here, however, the objectivity is not in the Word but in events as they really happened. The assumption is that faith requires historical facticity, the true determination of an occurrence. What the Christian and the theologian need are "the facts." The truth rides on a reconstruction of historical events in a way that makes faith absolutely credible. If one can determine that the Exodus really happened, one has legitimated the faith that the Hebrew tradition affirmed about the actions of God in their lives. Similarly, nineteenth-century attempts to produce a "life of Jesus" were driven by the assumption that faith would be more secure if a historically accurate picture could be constructed.

These two forms of the quest for certitude in biblical interpretation have in common a conception of religious discourse that is not abused by ideology. In one way or another the Bible is seen as standing on its own. One can relate to it without a consideration of where a person is standing. There is no need of mediation; one's perspective ought not play any role in shaping what is there. Understanding is not something that occurs through having a point of view but by virtue either of the "Word" with its own capacity for clarity or by the historical facts that legitimate the faith.

Theologians generally share with biblical scholars the aspiration to be ideologically free. While biblical scholars want to avoid having ideology contaminate their reading of the text, theologians are concerned that it may affect the formulation of the faith. Both proceed from the notion that the ways in which the *world* formulates reality are at odds with the ways in which the *Word* formulates reality. The parables of Jesus are almost always constructed on a model that sets the logic of "everydayness" against the logic of the Kingdom. One of the more obvious and perplexing examples is the parable of the laborers who worked different hours but received the same reward at the end of the day. The conventional wisdom of the world is that one gets paid for the labor exacted. The system is set to enact that; it is tuned to the interests of the vineyard owners. But the teachings of Jesus always give priority to human need. Since the need is equal, the recompense is equal. Theologians argue that this passage only appears to be foolish when it is examined through the ideologically distorted lens of what the world views as "right."

Theologians, however, tend to be concerned as well with how ideology is an impediment to the changes they envision for the world. They usually think of ideology as integrally related to the defense of the present and the assurance of its maintenance. They would place principal emphasis on the "evaluative conception" of ideology. In this definition ideology supports the claim that the dominant order is the same as "what ought to be."

The effect of these arguments is to divide up the cultural universe according to its presumed relation to human interests. "Non-ideological" segments of culture, such as religion and science, which provide our basic conceptions of reality, are thought to be ahistorical. They are not directly related to the interests and concerns of individuals and groups with particular sociocultural positions and real historical experiences. The ideological aspects of culture, on the other hand, are always relative to such concerns and experiences. They represent only the particular perspective of a social position or group in interpreting more paramount commonly shared symbols. Ideology advocates or apologizes for the sacred canopy but always remains distinct from it.

A traditional theological response of this sort to ideology can be found in the work of Pierre Bigo. While he claims faith and ideology are similar in their quest for universality and their appeal to being comprehensive, there is a significant difference between them. ". . . [A]n ideology is conditioned by the interests and values of a specific group in a definite historical conflict; faith . . . is not linked to any particular time or culture, even if it has to be incarnated in them."[36] For Bigo, the realm of faith is free of the need to defend the present. Faith is said to work from the vision of an alternative future, such as the Kingdom of God, while ideology works from present constructions of reality.

A good many theologians still have enough Karl Barth in their systems to fear instinctively any earthly alliances and presume that faith can somehow be spared contamination by ideology. Theology should avoid linkages with secular thought or movements. This chapter has argued that ideology is necessary and inevitable; that leads to the position that theology is an ideology. How could it be otherwise? If ideology is a socially generated perspective, it would be difficult to assert that theology as a way of viewing and understanding had an immaculate conception. Theologians cannot lay claim to historical virginity. Biblical events are given to us ideologically, and we appropriate them ideologically.

Theologians tend not to use the term ideology in this sense as inevitable and potentially revealing. For them it only conceals and contaminates the faith. They fear a claim like that of Jerry

Falwell, which gives a divine mandate to the origins of free enterprise or equates bringing America back to God with the election of Ronald Reagan.

Among the many criticisms of liberation theology from the academic and ecclesiastical establishments is the allegation that it is just an ideology. At the same time liberation theologians themselves often feel stung by the charge that they have merged the faith with Marxism. That would be equally indefensible. A distinction needs to be made between giving ultimacy to earthly construction and an earthly construction of faith. To acknowledge that one's viewing is social and historical, that a person stands somewhere in the process of understanding, is not the same as elevating a finite order to ultimacy. It simply means that any understanding of the faith always emerges in a particular setting and reflects it; there are neither messages nor truths in midair. While one might be surprised to hear a group of young persons in a shanty town of Uruguay say "For us, Jesus Christ is Che Guevara," that is a necessary risk. As José Miguez Bonino writes, "in the course of history, the face of Jesus Christ has frequently taken on the features of the man . . . who best represented what at that moment men linked most closely with the Christian religion or with the fullness of humanity."[37] That is an entirely different statement from one that says Jesus was or is a Marxist. The distinguishing mark is between a historical construction of the faith and equating the faith with a particular social philosophy.

Some have argued that theology can only preserve a critical function if it assumes the existence of some "eternal truth" or "essential message" independent of a historical setting. Its claim to question the social order is only legitimate if it transcends that order. For them theology is about something timeless which the theologian makes timely. We argue it is essential to recognize that the ultimate symbols and acts of faith arise out of a particular historical time. Only then can it be seen how those symbols act in another time. They are, however, subject to misuse. The suggestion that religion should become less generous in its "symbol lending" is only partially helpful. In a secular society the church can too easily accommodate itself to wider cultural forces. But the larger issue is the control of the symbol by the biblical context. The authentic utilization of symbols requires a structural similarity between the events of their origin and those in which use is made of them.

Both Martin Luther King, Jr., and recent presidents of the United States have used Exodus-related events to interpret their cause. The difference in the outcomes is that the one produces a critique while the other functions as a rubber stamp. King's use of the Exodus does legitimate the mission of the Black community, but it also critiques the structures of a society that make the mission necessary. A president is apt to exploit the imagery surrounding the formation of Israel by using it to justify an unambiguous American role for the preservation of freedom in the world. The most common form of the argument centers on America's relation to international communism. We are the "new Israel" and the Russians are the Egyptians. But it is at this point that the examination of the biblical context puts a brake on the usage of the text. The story does not fit, since the Soviet Union and the United States are not in an oppressor and oppressed relationship as was the case between Israel and Egypt. The structural similarity between then and now does not hold. By contrast, when King used the Exodus imagery, the relation of Black to white and Israelite to Egyptian matched. The match enabled him to advance a critique of society.

One self-evident consequence of our argument is that theology as ideology does both reveal and conceal. It can help appropriate the reality of existence and the world, or it can render them opaque. It was the Christian faith that enabled Dietrich Bonhoeffer to see and act against the magnitude of the Nazi evil, while Hitler and others were using Christian symbols to conceal what they were doing. Theology can enable one to see clearly, or it can cause blindness.

5
Ideologies from the Middle

We have attempted to critique how ideology has functioned in our own disciplines and to set out a contrasting definition of it. We need now to explore how ideology relates to social transformation, specifically in terms of the social conditions of the middle sectors in American society. In constructing a new ideology it is important to examine already existing middle class ideologies. Some basically accept the present reality, reforming it only by looking to the past, while others offer a more fundamental shift in vision for the future. The fundamentalist evangelism epitomized by the Moral Majority of Jerry Falwell and the principles of Keynesian economics so basic to the liberal policies and "Great Society" programs of the post-Depression era represent ideologies that are reformist. Both have made powerful claims on the consciousness of significant segments of the middle sectors and beyond, particularly by reinforcing individualism. We hope to avoid treating them as straw persons; we recognize the legitimacy of the need and the intensity of their appeal for the middle classes, while rejecting their conclusions.

There are as well ideologies that focus on an alternative future, the environmentalist, anti-war, anti-nuclear, consumer, feminist, and New Left political movements. Although these movements have a firm foot in the middle class, they potentially move us beyond acting as though we were a class, to a closer alignment with the working class fraction and the poor. Unlike the Moral Majority and liberalism, these alternative positions are explicitly critical of the underlying economic and social structures that create poverty, ecological devastation, shoddy merchandise, discrimination against women, and the nightmare of nuclear war. These movements and ideologies also remind us that religious symbols are not the sole means by which the middle layers grope toward transcending our individualism and collaborating with others to realize an alternative destiny.

Reformist Views from the Past

Two reformist middle sector ideologies, the Moral Majority (or the Liberty Federation) and Keynesian liberalism, have vastly different conceptions of middle class interests. Neither, however, is capable of addressing the real concerns of the middle layers, or the wider issues of social equality and justice necessary for the future.

Both the Moral Majority and liberalism misread the present circumstances of American society, and the middle layers in particular. Both perpetuate the false dichotomy between the individual and society, which leads to distorted conceptions of human nature and the character of social change. The Moral Majority embraces the free-market principle on which Keynesian liberalism is also based. This is because they share similar assumptions about human nature and the relationship of the individual and society. In this model, all societies simply replicate and reflect a universal human nature. Human nature is something constructed prior to society. We did not come about in a social context, but were already here existing individually in a natural state. The market model, for example, advances a "social contract" theory of society. Human beings do not inherently need to live in a society, but agree to do so only because the contract with others better enables us to secure our goals. The individual takes priority over society; society is the by-product of individuals and functions to fulfill their needs. John F. Kennedy attacked this view of society in his famous inaugural challenge: "ask not what your country can do for you—ask what you can do for your country."

If human beings are not inherently social, then human nature tends to be seen as fixed and universal. Echoes of this appear in popular literature and song. "A smile means the same thing everywhere," or "love is the universal language." Navajo or Eskimo may appear to be different, but underneath that thin cultural veneer, they are just like you and me. Not only is human nature thought to be universally the same, it is said to be quite specific in its content. For if we are asocial, then we must have sufficient *innate* characteristics to survive without society. Foremost among these supposedly universal, inherent human traits is that we are rational calculators of self-interest. Scratch any person and you will find an economic homunculus predisposed to buy cheap and sell dear. The problem of reconciling the insatiability of human desires with limited means for obtaining them, an assumption of capitalist market systems, is taken also to be inherent in human nature generally.

This view of human nature drives both Keynesian liberalism and the Moral Majority to endorse individualism and to reinforce those expressions of it already in place from other sources. Both positions, and certainly the Moral Majority in particular, speak directly and perceptively to the deep feeling of a lack of social identity. Yet affirming our importance solely as individuals reinforces the circle of isolation and self-centeredness that initiated the search for identity. It has doomed those in the middle to that singular, solitary pursuit of acquisitions, of property, as one of the few tangible markers in our society of the successful person. There is an irony in the Moral Majority's advocacy of the market and the conception of human nature that it implies. How can one reconcile the market model based on the maximizing of self-interest with the traditional Judeo-Christian call for a new human nature founded in selflessness? Falwell, indeed, appears to be lauding the very selfishness of human nature condemned by Christianity as the source of our fall.

In either the religious guise of evangelicalism, or the economic and political cloak of liberalism, such assumptions are insupportable. One can argue on paleontological grounds alone for the *social* nature of human beings. All human primate species now existing, and all of our hominid forebears, including *Australopithecus afarensis* over 3.8 million years ago, have survived in *groups*. There is overriding evidence against any existence in the dim past of some isolated, fully human individuals who came together voluntarily to form society. Indeed, it is the very capacity to be social, and, what is more, to rely *culturally* on others, that has allowed us to evolve as a species. As Clifford Geertz has argued, "there is no such thing as a human nature independent of culture. Men without culture . . . would be unworkable monstrosities with very few useful instincts, fewer recognizable sentiments, and no intellect . . . . [1] Both anthropology and sociology argue that we are who we are as a species, not simply because we created culture, but because we were created in part through culture. Whether based on Adam Smith, Rousseau, Hobbes, Freud, or religious doctrine, theories about human beings once having existed as individuals in a state of nature are without support. William Golding's nightmare in *Lord of the Flies* of the beast that lurks within us is quite thoroughly mistaken. Such a view implies that human individuals have a uniform nature relatively uninfluenced by society. The children in Golding's novel easily revert to their essentially violent nature once the restraints of society are removed. Golding attributes to them fully formed capabilities apart from society. Yet human beings are not capable *as a species* of existing apart from each other. Social cooperation is not a matter of voluntarism, of doing it either for altruistic or utilitarian reasons; it is a necessity.

Our social nature has yet other profound implications for a critique of any theory that posits individualism as integral to human nature. If we are social, and if societies vary, then we, too, as humans must vary. We may share a very basic biological framework, but the overriding characteristic of human beings must be sheer diversity. We depend on learning, and what we learn may be radically different in different societies. To be human, then, is universal only in the sense that we all share the capacity to learn different things. It is far more accurate in such a situation to speak less of Human Nature than of human natures.[2] One cannot assume that human beings cross-culturally will be uniformly possessed of the same goals, interests, or motives. The desire to acquire goods and the profit motive are not universal. From our own particular cultural perspective, we may find it difficult to imagine a group of people indifferent to the prospect of owning the moon. Yet few non-Western societies would even consider it.

The physical anthropological evidence squarely contradicts the liberal and neoclassical economists' views of human nature that undergird both capitalist social systems and the creationist theology of Falwell. There are additional grounds on which to argue against a focus on rational calculation of self-interest. The complete rationality of human beings called for by classical economic models is an empirical impossibility. The most that can be said is that we are "reasonable."[3] We do try to utilize the means that will successfully realize our ends, but we can never foresee all the conditions or have access to all the resources necessary for perfect rationality. The complexity and competing nature of our wants and interests alone preclude establishing them in a hierarchy necessary to such perfection.

Furthermore, the cross-cultural evidence is overwhelmingly against the moral acceptance of such a model of human conduct in *all* human social systems except capitalism. Indeed, the capitalist is an anathema in all traditional ethical systems because he or she sets self-interest and material acquisition over/against the well-being of society. While Western religious traditions, particularly Protestantism, have at times used the notion of stewardship to uphold a rapacious utilitarian attitude toward nature and the production of a surplus, other societies condemn such traits.

Although founded in the same assumptions about individuals and society, Falwell's theology and liberalism erect different historical accounts by which to guide human action. Falwell places a selective emphasis on the priestly and pastoral, at times masquerading as the prophetic. That has led him in the awkward direction of creating and promoting a *sociopolitical* movement to defend what is at heart a privatized and *individualized* conception of religion. Rather than follow the usual sectarian pattern of making religion a matter for individuals and creating an alternative social world in its image for the select few, a Jerry Falwell or a Pat Robertson wants to instill the same vision in the wider society for the rest of us by legislative fiat.

In Falwell's model change is to be achieved not by aiding those who do not conform to the theoretical assumptions of the model, but by eliminating them from consideration. For the Moral Majority, it seems, the American dream should not be for most Americans. It should be reserved for those who fit the uniform fundamentalist assumptions of what all Americans should be, before they even begin to dream. "Fair play" is an ideal only for those who *ought* to be in the game. This again resembles the sectarian impulse. The real problem comes in figuring out what will become of the rest of us who do not fit the assumptions.

Evangelicalism and liberal economics resemble a form of Social Darwinism with its philosophy of the survival of the fittest. While liberalism differs in being more inclusive in determining who is fit to stay in the game, nevertheless it does see competition as the only game in town. Liberalism also is similar to evangelicalism in the relationship it perceives between the state and society. If Falwell grants the state only the right to legislate morally suitable players for the game, then liberalism, such as Keynesian economics, allows for state intervention only to modify market forces, which in turn will create morally suitable players. While more generous in its vision of who might reap the benefits of the "Great Society," liberalism is equally uncritical about many of the presumed blessings. Both tend to assume that not only is the market the driving force of our society, but it should be. This similarity between liberalism and evangelicalism is also seen in their common assumption that reform should begin with the state through legislation. Both assume that changes in the legal system, not economic structures, will bring about the desired changes in the wider society. They maintain this because their views of human nature lead them to see society as a collection of individuals. Like the voluntarism of the middle classes, these models claim that human beings are, or can be, exclusively captains of their own destiny. This leaves little room for the semiautonomous reality of society, as the intended and unintended consequence of *collective* action. We would agree that people have created structures. Falwell and the Keynesians seem to forget, however, that the structures also create individuals, and in their own image. Social structures deny access to resources and resist attempts at change. To the extent that some of us in the society are powerless before our collective creations, we are not just influenced by them, we are determined.

We have argued that there are two fundamental flaws underlying the ideology of "fair play" in Falwell's theology and Keynesian liberalism. Both assume the precultural, asocial nature of human beings. Because of this, they have postulated a false and restrictive view of what motivates us as humans: all humans act *naturally* out of self-interest, rationally calculating personal profit. This leads to another false assumption: the priority of the individual over the structures of society. They affirm the efficacy of individual action, in a view of free will defined by economic self-interest. They place power only in the midst of discourse. Power is strategic, not institutional, for them. They tend to see it principally in its enabling dimensions, ignoring how power can also be structurally obdurate. They generally argue, therefore, that individuals are powerful—if we want something we can come up with ways to get it—rather than relatively powerless in the face of institutions.

When we accomplish something in our individual work with others on a job, we have used power to achieve goals. Yet power is an aspect of institutions, the routinized patterns of collective action, which do enable us to exist, but also limit individual action. We are, collectively, the creators of institutions, but they stand over against us, virtually impervious to our individual attempts to change them. It follows that the old middle class view of voluntaristic change is without foundation. Change by its very definition must be collective, social, involving the use of power by some in contention with the entrenched power of others. Whether intentional or not, change does not occur through individual transformations in a series of isolated, unrelated sequences. It must occur through modifying or uprooting the structures that shape action. Falwell's call for a change of heart is like the liberal emphasis on a change in personal values; both fail ultimately because they wish to convert individuals without realizing the semiautonomous nature of our institutions. A clear example of the liberal emphasis on values and individual change was the counterculture of the hippie movement. It is no accident that the hippies with their echo of the Beatles' "All You Need Is Love" were an archtypical middle class movement.

Breaking with and Transcending Individualism

Since neither the Moral Majority nor Keynesian liberals have an effective solution for the dilemma of American society, what is an alternative vision? What kind of ideology will depict accurately the structural position of the middle layers and lead to an understanding of their real class interests in the social reconstruction of American society? We argue that an ideology concerned with "fair shares"—that is, with equal access to basic resources, and with social justice for all in the laboring class—is crucial for a genuine renewal of society.[4] It is far more sound in its depiction of social reality, and of the social conditions for most Americans, than is the predominant image of "fair play" in any of its conservative neoclassical, evangelical, or liberal Keynesian forms. A typical formulation of "fair play" "stresses that each person should be equally free from all but the most minimal necessary interference with his [or her] right to 'pursue happiness.' . . . All are equally free to *pursue*, but have no guarantee of *attaining*, happiness."[5]

We in the middle sector will continue to be victims of the prevailing ideology as long as we are blind to its existence and to the role it plays in shaping our lives. To become aware of the system under which we all live, to critique it, and to act on that critique, therefore, calls for new ideological perspectives. New ideologies begin with an escape from the dominance of the existing ideology, which reflects the interests of the capital-owning class. To get to a position of "fair shares," for example, it is necessary to critique the notion of individualism. It is consistently interpreted in our society in ways that ensure the maintenance of the capitalistic economic system and the power of the capitalist. This can be seen in the persistent belief that individuals on the bottom need only work hard in order to "pull themselves up by their own bootstraps." Success and the personal acquisition of an economic surplus become virtually synonymous. To be successful you need to have more goods and services than you need. The dominant economic models are predicated on the assumption of a perfectly competitive market in which the play of individual self-interest, and the effectiveness with which individuals compete and use their own resources, determine their rewards and position in life. That neatly absolves both the system itself *and* more fortunate individuals from any responsibility for the creation and maintenance of the conditions that spread poverty. Failure is not the system's fault, in this view, for the system works for those who want success enough. Poverty is a failure of will or of moral rectitude. The poor stay poor because they just don't have the savvy, guts, or discipline to get ahead.

The middle fraction, with Adam Smith, Hobbes, and Rousseau, tends to view the individual as separate from, and more important than, society. This view of the individual does not fit actual circumstances, which are far more ambiguous. Clearly there are real areas of individualism and individual freedom. Indeed, these are essentially a result of the earlier rise and expansion of the middle layers in the nineteenth century. With the growth of industries and bureaucracies, some could experience real upward mobility through education and other more individualistic means. Compare that, however, with today, when the increased centralization of wealth and power in society essentially precludes upward mobility much beyond one's own class; indeed, many in the middle are moving closer to those at the margins.

As all of us become increasingly aware of the powerlessness inherent in the middle layer position, it is possible that we can see the important economic interests shared with other powerless people in society: the poor, women, ethnic and racial minorities. It is in the interests of all to restructure the system, diffuse power, and build a more humanly fulfilling society.

To do this implies a different ideological story about the individual. One can no longer entertain a sense of individual competition or a neoclassical economic view of self-interest. Nor can people see themselves religiously in an individualistic light. Rather, it is important to recall different beliefs about the cooperative nature of human beings and mutual interdependence.

There are many sources for this view. They include an understanding gained from sociology and anthropology about our fundamentally social nature as animals and our extremely malleable reliance on learning. The view also draws on human history in noting that over ninety percent of all human societies have emphasized an egalitarian way of life. Our own class-based, individually competitive society is the exception, not the rule. Class-based societies essentially have been the result of the accumulation of an economic surplus, usually based on the development of intensive agriculture. Since the domestication of plants has occurred within only the last 12,000 years or so, and even then is not found in all existing societies today, nearly all of human existence has been spent in subsistence-based societies.

Such societies by necessity tend to be more egalitarian and communally focused than our own. In societies such as the !Kung San, the hunters and foragers of southern Africa, sharing takes place in a wide variety of institutionalized forms and is essential both to their survival and to being defined as a good person. A strong case can be made that such sharing is entirely distinct from the altruism applauded in our own society. Indeed, altruism, and forms of it like charity, can only take place in class-based societies that emphasize private property. Only in such societies can those who control their own property decide voluntarily to be generous to the poor. Westerners may appreciate the sharing found among the !Kung yet deprecate it as caused by poverty. In this view, they may be cooperative, but our affluence is far more preferable. To be sure, we do have a host of technological and other innovations. Yet we should not be too quick to assume out of hand that we have a superior quality of life to the !Kung and other hunting and foraging groups.

It has been argued that ours is not the original affluent society.[6] The very way in which affluence is defined must be sensitive to different cultural contexts. The tendency is to assume ethnocentrically that our human forebears such as *Homo sapiens neanderthalensis*, or all the contemporary hunting and foraging societies, have lived at best a hand-to-mouth existence, racked by a perpetual search for food. Near starvation and hard work are their lot in life. Indeed, this assumption is essentially a Hobbesian view of such unfortunates; their lives must be nasty, brutish, and, perhaps mercifully, short.

Marshall Sahlins debunks this image first by questioning just how hand-to-mouth and near starvation hunters and foragers really are, and second, by raising profound doubts about our own way of defining affluence relative to theirs. Sahlins draws extensively on Richard B. Lee's work among the !Kung. Though the annual rainfall is only six to ten inches, Lee noted that there was a "surprising abundance of vegetation" in the Kalahari region of the !Kung. "Food resources were 'both varied and abundant,' particularly the energy-rich mangetti nut—'so abundant that millions of the nuts rotted on the ground each year for want of picking.' "[7] While 60% of the population engage in subsistence activities, they do so for one-third of the time Americans spend. Each adult !Kung works only about fifteen hours a week, or two hours and nine minutes per day.[8] "The daily per-capita subsistence yield for the Dobe [!Kung] was 2,140 calories," well above their estimated requirement of 1,975 calories.[9]

The significance of these statistics increases when it is realized that the circumstances of the contemporary !Kung, restricted as they are to the least desirable land, are far worse than those of our hunting and foraging ancestors. The same is true for other areas of their life as well. Medically, for example, many of the diseases from which !Kung and other indigenous groups now suffer have been introduced by the West and are particularly virulent because of the lack of migration on reserves. Groups that are able to maintain their traditional diet and living patterns continue to be much less afflicted by illness generally and certainly "diseases of development," such as diabetes, obesity, hypertension, circulatory problems, mental disorders, nutritional deficiencies, and dental problems.[10]

In light of this portrait of life in non-Western hunting and foraging societies, one ought to reconsider the ease with which Americans speak of themselves as the most progressive society in history. Much of our chauvinism may come from not knowing where we actually stand. Having been taught just how fortunate we are, we tend to use ourselves as the yardstick to assess others.

Yet even among industrialized nations, Americans do not measure up in a variety of basic areas central to a good quality of life. Michael Parenti sums this up starkly:

> The United States has been portrayed as a land of prosperity and well-being, but closer scrutiny brings little cause for celebration. In life expectancy, 20-year-old American males rank 36th among the world's nations, and 20-year-old American females rank 21st. The infant mortality rate in the U.S. is worse than in thirteen other nations. In eleven countries women have a better chance to live through childbirth than in the United States. One out of every four Americans lives in substandard housing. One out of every five American adults is functionally illiterate. Almost 80 million Americans live on incomes estimated as below a comfortable adequacy by the Department of Labor, and the U.S. Census Bureau reports that almost 32 million Americans live below the poverty level. Of the latter, less than half get either food stamps or free food. Racial minorities suffer disproportionately in every area of life, including housing, health, education, or employment. Thus, a Black child has nearly one chance in two of being born into poverty and is twice as likely as a White baby to die during the first year of life.[11]

In light of such statistics, the definition of affluence takes on added significance. The Western tendency is to define affluence as being able to produce much. While human wants are potentially infinite and the means scarce, through technology and industrial output the gap can be narrowed. A different definition of affluence is possible, however: that of desiring little. This definition is much more characteristic of hunting and foraging societies. It assumes "that human material wants are finite and few, and technical means unchanging but on the whole adequate. Adopting [this] strategy, a people can enjoy an unparalleled material plenty—with a low standard of living."[12]

It is the liberal economic assumptions, based on the earlier market model of classical economics, that have led to the kind of class division and poverty that Parenti describes above. Societies like the !Kung "have few possessions, *but they are not poor.*"[13] For if affluence is defined as an abundant diet, good health, closely knit social relationships, a sense of individual empowerment, and a secure sense of identity, then the !Kung are wealthy indeed. We are not trying to romanticize the !Kung or other hunting and foraging groups. They face their share of human problems. They have learned, however, how to satisfy very basic needs for all their members in a far more satisfactory way than does our own system. After all, the hunting and foraging way of life *is* very successful, environmentally sound, and has been in existence for millions of years. Does it not smack of adolescent arrogance that we in the West, with our capitalist industrial way of life barely 400 years old, should assume our own superiority? One would think that ecological imbalance and nuclear precariousness, let alone the issue of inequality, would be convincing arguments to the contrary. As Sahlins concludes, it is we who have invented poverty.[14]

One of the first steps in building a new ideology as a base for fundamental structural change is the recognition that capitalist economic structures are neither natural nor divine. Only a relatively small number of societies in the world's history have ever held that such structures should be dominant. To be sure, some of the societies that have created those structures have become rich and powerful. That condition, however, does not result from any moral superiority or long-term ecological stability of capitalism. As we suggested in our discussion of the Reformation, capitalism leads to wealth and power because it makes accumulation of material wealth a predominant and status-conferring goal which then translates easily into political power. Yet, in doing so, capitalism certainly does not serve the well-being of all.

A program for change must address the existing dominance of the economy and redress the imbalance in the distribution of power. Systematic flaws cannot be instantly transformed; new social, political, and economic systems centered on justice rather than self-interest emerge slowly. The non-responsiveness of bureaucracy and the strength of vested interests provide powerful sources for the maintenance of "what is" in the face of "what ought to be."

Consider the original Sullivan Principles designed to lead to a change in the condition of Blacks in South Africa through changing the terms of their employment by American-based transnational corporations. The Rev. Leon Sullivan can stand individually for a quite, even fundamentally, different set of values than the General Motors Board of Directors on which he sits. Yet there is also a basic difference in the consequences of Sullivan's and GM's actions as two entities. Even when the individual affects the organization, as clearly we can, and Sullivan has, there are yet larger institutional orbits to consider. Each corporation itself is embedded in a wider structural order, which also resists changes in individual corporations. The Sullivan Principles, as he has acknowledged, have failed to dismantle apartheid. But that is not an example of individual villainy, the malevolence of corporate managers subverting the principles. It is the result of the logic of capitalistic structures of investment and political structures of racism. The true banality of evil, then, is not the individual unquestioningly following out the order of another individual. It is all of us following out the dictates of structures we created, attributing more importance to the system itself than to the individuals living under it. We are like Alan Greenspan remarking that our society can "tolerate" high levels of unemployment.

How does this bear on the involvement of the American middle layers in a movement for social justice and liberation? At a theoretical level, it invalidates all ideologies of individualism. It implies the inevitability of social structures standing over against individuals, requiring social movements of change. It points to the social origin of injustice and deprivation. One can no longer blame the victims of oppression as "just being lazy." Raising oneself up by one's bootstraps is an impossibility in a system with structures that are out of the control of those who are poor or powerless.

The prominence of individualism in American society is evident in the priority given to personal freedom. The enduring crime is infringement upon a person's rights; nothing should abridge one's options. The human prospect is seen as a function of human initiative and innovation; the person is accountable for the plight or the possibilities of existence. The assumption is that what needs to be done and can be fixed is all in the arena of the single self. What is curious about this fixation on the individual is that it does not correlate with any thoughtful analysis of how society works. The very person who thinks in an individualistic way functions collectively through participation in structures. The most crucial decisions for personal lives are in the political sphere. As José Miguez Bonino put it in *Toward a Christian Political Ethics*, " . . . individual lives are nuclei determined by the crisscrossing of complex lines of economic, scientific-technological, communication, and cultural structures."[15] The sense of human autonomy is itself possible because of causal links made binding and durable by the system of order. The individual is incorporated in a web of social, political, and economic networks. The irony is that the very corporate executive who knows our collective complexity nevertheless holds only the individual accountable. Yet we are not autonomous individuals but are part of structures over which we have little control. It is interesting to note further that whenever partisans of their own privilege speak of countries whose societies and economic systems deviate from our own, they attend exclusively to the loss of personal freedom. They seldom appreciate the elevation of the common good in a country and the emergence of a higher quality of life.

There is an important connection between the affirmation of individualism and the individual's sense of powerlessness. The failure to rise above egoism contributes to the condition of helplessness. Liberation theologians break with both their existentialist ancestors and their cultural framework when they focus upon a "liberated humanity." That resets the person in the context of the social prospect. The concept of "liberated humanity" gives priority to a collective reality within which personhood is enacted. Identity is relocated more in public involvement, not private rebellion. Liberation theologians did not invent from whole cloth their emphasis on the social framework of the individual. The antecedent is the biblical tradition. There the individual and the corporate are never sharply separated. *Shalom*, for example, in the Old Testament does not simply refer to a condition of individual well-being but is to be enacted in the whole community. The welfare of the one and the many cannot be separated. "Israel consistently proclaimed that no individual fulfillment was possible apart from seeking the welfare of the whole community."[16] Wholeness and harmony have a social dimension that precedes personal fulfillment. That the social prospect is the framework for personal destinies is no accident given the pre-capitalist, kin-ordered origins of Israelite society.

Return, thus, to the story of Abraham. For both the Old and New Testament communities, his story is *not* one of some individualistic search for power, wealth, or self-identity. He represents the corporate hopes and responsibilities of the community. For the early Hebrews, "the great ancestors of Israel, Abraham, Isaac and Jacob, are a remarkable blend of the typical Israelite with the nation, and thus fittingly its representatives. . . . "[17] It is only by acting in the collective interests of us all that we can hope to gain a measure of individual voice and security.

Some might want to argue that the first person singular is in abundance throughout the biblical record, particularly in the Psalms. That might seem to count for a measure of individualism. As we have just argued, however, one needs to understand that for the Old Testament an "I" in isolation is unthinkable. What undergirds the sense of the individual is what H. Wheeler Robinson calls the Hebrew conception of corporate personality.[18] One of the forms of that argument is the unity of the individual with both his or her ancestors and successors in the clan. "The people *are* their ancestors" in a fundamental, not merely representational, sense.[19] At another level, the king can wage war with another leader of a rival country, and the outcome is defeat or victory for all. All are in the one. Even though the Old Testament in particular seems to focus upon prominent individuals or leaders, their reality is not that of an isolated self. Each springs from a society and embodies it. This tradition of a "corporate personality," which is elaborated on in the New Testament as the "body of Christ," has human solidarity, not individual rights, as the transcending category. The question for the biblical faith is not "what do I deserve?" but "for whom am I responsible?" Put another way, the first question is predicated on the second. As with the golden rule, we would like others to do unto us in a fair way; that depends, however, on how we respond corporately to one another.

Toward a Reciprocal Future

Theoretical interest and pragmatic choice conspire to focus on the potential of religious symbols that support the involvement of the middle sectors in laboring class coalitions for change. There are, however, other sources for new social stories. In part, this is due to the same process of capital accumulation that has given society such a fractured existence generally. With the split of the private and social, and the angst-ridden search for personal identity, the middle layers began to question the old all-encompassing religious order of things. The consequent rise of secularity and multiplying sources of meaning have been well documented. What is the consequence of this for ideologies of social change? Given the secularism and "cultural marketplace" characteristic of our existence, religious stories by themselves don't stand a prayer of uniting major sectors of the laboring class. Even for the middle layers alone, it is necessary to remain well aware of alternate sources of symbolic stories and social organization. These sources enable the middle sector to think in terms of alliances with other fractions of the laboring class. Examples of those sources include the New Left, the anti-war and anti-nuclear campaigns, environmentalism, and the consumer rights and feminist movements. We intend to explore their underlying concern with wider class issues, while also arguing that many of them could more explicitly move beyond their narrow preoccupation with middle layer interests alone.

There is a starkly negative side to the self-image that all of us in the middle sector hold. We think of ourselves as conformists and organization people. Because of our vast experience in the bureaucracy we use the color gray or even being colorless to typify our lives. We see this reflected in sociological texts on "the lonely crowd" and in a virtual industry of fictional literature and the arts. We are the "man in the gray flannel suit"; Willy Loman and Eleanor Rigby are our enduring symbols of the ordered emptiness of life. T.S. Eliot, perhaps, sums up the tone best in "The Love Song of J. Alfred Prufrock," who "measured out [his] life with coffee spoons."[20]

The middle layers, however, have also been a real source of criticism, reform, and even rebellion. We are more than just drones. Much of what is referred to as the "New Left" has its origins and primary support from among the middle layers and particularly from professional and managerial groups.[21] Even a significant minority of the Old Left and especially its leadership in American socialist politics before World War II came from the "professional-managerial" class (PMC).[22] This can be accounted for, in part, by the partial independence of the middle layers. Particularly during periods of expansion, they had control over significant resources. More important, however, was their dominant presence in education as teachers and supervisors and their monopoly over specialized knowledge. They thought of themselves as experts on how the system worked, as well as how to dismantle and change it.

This has led to ambivalence in the attempts of the middle sectors to cooperate with other fractions of the laboring class in political coalitions. On the one hand, the traditional faith placed in reason and education led those in the middle layer interested in social change to assume that they were the rightful leaders in any laboring class movement. On the other hand, there has been a tendency to reject any notion of the existence of a middle class. Their way of life seemed bourgeois, and they felt that the best alternative was to become the proletariat and poor. Middle class romanticism and guilt saw "head work" as parasitic and threw it over in favor of the authenticity of "hand work." This led toward the position that the middle layers ought to be subordinate in relation to the poor and especially the working class fraction. Anti-intellectualism became an important aspect of such coalitions; to participate with other laboring class fractions it was felt necessary to reject one's middle class origins. Much of the rise of New Left politics in the civil rights movement, and especially in the Vietnam War protests of the 1965–75 period, illustrate this ambivalence.

The New Left arose when the conflict between the middle sector values and social reality caused so many American youths to protest the Vietnam War. The elite universities were its initial locale because they were the places caught in the paradox between teaching the old values and doing the Pentagon's research. The student rebellion quickly spread, however, to other universities with students from working class and minority families. The New Left now stood against the universities. It increasingly supported Black working-class-based movements that rejected the traditional PMC attitudes toward the working class.[23]

During the anti-war and student movements, the middle layer was groping toward a genuine coalition with other laboring class fractions. There was not, however, a clear set of ideological images by which to envision a truly equal, cooperative movement. First thinking of themselves as an intellectual elite, and then abandoning that image for an anti-intellectualism, the middle fraction struggled to come to terms with their own class position and find adequate grounds for protest. Trapped in individualistic imagery, they tended to view the world as either personal or social, mental or manual, intellectual or anti-intellectual, without clearly realizing the interpenetration of these characteristics.

The struggle was in the right direction. Out of the civil rights movement and then the anti-war period came not only New Left politics, but also a much more broadly based middle layer concern with nuclear disarmament, ecology, and the consumer rights movements. All of these have been essentially grassroots efforts, consisting of loosely knit and overlapping groups. The same people might be on all the membership lists. The possibility that a loose network could exist is indicated to many of us by the fact that if we join one organization our mailboxes are soon filled with literature from most of them. In terms of day-to-day activities and lobbying efforts, however, there remain significant differences between groups. The ideologies that animate them also may differ. A significant proportion gain their membership through the churches and synagogues and are rooted in a Judeo-Christian understanding. Others are informed by a strictly humanistic vision. In both the secular and religious communities, there is a split between those who are concerned on humanitarian grounds and those who see the struggle along class lines.

These movements tend to deal with issues that transcend the narrow interest of one class fraction, even though their supporters may be drawn from one segment. The Vietnam War protest, nuclear disarmament and freeze campaigns, consumer activism, and environmental movements are all closely identified with middle fraction politics. The ecology and anti-nuclear movements, with their highly visible participation of professional scientists and physicians, are usually viewed in the media as middle class. Other consumer-focused groups such as "Science in the Public Interest," "Common Cause," and "Public Citizen" are also predominantly middle class.

Such concerns are typically regarded as single-issue movements, which reflect particular interest groups in society. Rather than representing a class-based criticism of society, they are seen popularly as groups vying for power in a pluralistic democracy. Nevertheless, while they may be organized by a particular fraction, the issues addressed by each movement are common to the laboring class generally.[24] Such politics by the middle layers are not simply self-serving. Anti-war, anti-nuclear, consumer rights, or environmental protection organizations all basically *serve* interests of the laboring class and *oppose* the economic elites.

If the goal is a genuine coalition representing the basic common interest of all three laboring class fractions, then it is essential to learn what we have in common. We must discern the wider issues around which we can unite. The middle layers must avoid the tendencies toward intellectual elitism and anti-intellectualism in order to cooperate as equal partners with other fractions. Two of the most systematic attempts at this type of coalition have been the civil rights and feminist movements. This is particularly interesting because in both cases they have bridged fractional differences by appealing to a common identity and ideological stories based in racial unity or the solidarity of gender. Fractional unity may occur in finding a story that transcends differences, without ignoring them. Martin Luther King, Jr., did this in two ways. First, the civil rights movement sought to unite people, regardless of class, by appeal to the religious and secular stories that "all people are created equal." And, in the latter days of King's life, tempered by the Vietnam War, the Southern Christian Leadership Conference and others began to mount "poor people's campaigns." Here the unifying symbolism was explicitly one of being part of the underclass, Black or white.

A similar attempt to unify disparate groups has occurred in the women's liberation movement through appeal to a gender identity that cuts across class boundaries. Much can be learned from the nature of their efforts, even though unity has not been fully accomplished. The new feminism has firm roots in the middle layers. *The Feminine Mystique*, by Betty Friedan, or *Ms.* magazine, for example, represents important attempts to deal with the isolation and lack of identity of many middle sector women. Highly educated but often confined to familial roles, such women had real interest in working outside the home as a sign of their independence. This is bound up with economics, to be sure, but it also was expressed in terms of the classic middle sector desire to "be one's own person."

The mass media, and to a certain extent the white, middle sector of the women's movement itself, focused less attention on the early origins of feminism in the nineteenth-century working women's movement for economic rights. The fight for unions by the largely working class and immigrant women in the garment industry is a case in point. So, too, the early importance of women of color in the feminist cause often went unnoticed.[25] Finally, valuable lessons can be learned from the way in which the women's movement has addressed the real feminist concerns among working class women today, both in the United States and the Third World. These concerns do not always parallel those of middle layer women. Working class women here and peasant and working class women abroad are far more concerned with basic class issues of the feminization of poverty and exploitive working conditions than with questions of self-worth or an independent identity.[26] They reveal the similar position of working women everywhere as they become involved in the international division of labor created by transnational corporations. For, when corporations based in the United States move abroad, it is often women who are hired on their assembly lines.[27]

The feminist movement generally has responded to this challenge of recognizing the fractional division of interests, even among women. Certainly the academic and activist feminist literature is replete with explicit analyses of the cross-cutting interests of women. Recognition of this is rarely found in other movements significantly involving the middle sector. Nevertheless, feminists continue to struggle with ways to bridge the interests of class fractions. This is particularly clear in attempts to unionize women workers, whether represented in new organizations such as Nine to Five for clerical workers or the increasing efforts by traditional trade unions. Martin Oppenheimer suggests there is a familiar problem affecting the stability of such alliances. Beyond unity built around short-term issues such as opportunities for equal employment or equal pay for equal work, the women's movement is unlikely to attract a wide following among blue-collar women workers. There simply is too much mutual suspicion: " 'Liberation' issues are trivial to many lower-income women, while the unions themselves are considered discriminatory by many women's groups."[28] Many men in trade unions distrust feminism, arguing that it threatens to disrupt family.

These conditions call for a new view. The long-term issues of liberation are basic to the short-term issues of economic access, equality, and poor working conditions. We have already tried to show how the concern of the middle layers with a search for identity must itself be rooted in an understanding of economic conditions. While the working class fraction and poor are affected by individualism, it is quite understandable that a search for identity is not going to be their first priority. When you are hungry, unemployed, or barely making ends meet, basic economic goals and empowerment are not "short term." Indeed, it is only by forming a coalition around such issues that we will all then be in the position of addressing issues of meaning as well.

What is so valuable about the feminist movement is the degree to which it has considered such broadly based interests and wrestled with concrete political and economic strategies to realize them. Other movements such as the consumer, ecology, and anti-nuclear campaigns have been less successful in pushing beyond a fractional basis to an understanding of how their issues affect all of us. Finally, the individualism of American society traps many of these groups in single-issue movements. That dissipates energy and reinforces the old ideology of special interest groups.

Part of our interest is pushing toward ideological stories that will recognize the points at which such apparently disparate concerns connect as overarching interests of a laboring class. Both the church and elements of the New Left are beginning to talk about such linkages; witness the July-August, 1984, special issue, "Religion and the Left," in *Monthly Review*. The formation of numerous grassroots "peace and justice" networks is another promising sign. Finally, Jesse Jackson's 1984 and 1988 Rainbow Coalition points toward increasing attempts in a variety of distinct sectors to get beyond the redundancy and parochialism of traditional fractional politics.

Working toward political coalitions of the entire laboring class will bring about a much more accurate understanding of just where everyone stands, and the degree to which we all share common problems. The ideologies and symbols by which these similarities are realized will not be the same. The Judeo-Christian stories of the Exodus or Last Supper may galvanize some. For others, it may be a more secular concern for community or the fate of the earth. The stories may differ, but the experience and problems to which they point have been made remarkably similar by a common socioeconomic system. If our experience as a class is really quite similar, then beginning to work on new stories becomes less risky than it initially seems. Forsaking misguided individualism for a new laboring class view really does give safety in numbers. "Hanging together or hanging apart" remains as apt today as it did for the heroes of the American Revolution.

6

The Middle Sector and Liberation Theology

Theology is most vital and creative when a community begins to recognize that its conception of the world and the actual conditions of historical existence are at odds. Martin Luther prepared the way for Reformation theology with his "criticism of the Roman system of mediations and degrees in the name of the decisive biblical categories of judgment and grace. . . ." [1] In his own experience there was a contradiction between the human need for grace and the concentration upon law in the posture of the church. Centuries later Karl Barth triggered a transformation of theology with the publication of his commentary on Romans. At play in his own life was a contradiction between the emphasis upon human goodness as conceived in liberal theology and the experience of evil as the Nazi movement emerged in Germany between the wars. James Cone facilitated the emergence of an explicit Black theology when he discerned the alliance of white theology with its own interests of domination. Black theology created a new agenda for the community of faith by drawing the real condition of oppression and the invisibility of Black culture into prominence. One might say that theology undergoes transformation when the members of a community feel compromised; creativity and innovation emerge "as persons encounter contradictions in life about which they cannot be silent."[2]

Paul Tillich has argued that the church needs a theology that moves between "message and situation." The function of theology is to interpret the eternal truth of faith for each temporal situation of humankind. The message of faith has to be conveyed in a given situation. Situation means all the ways in which individuals and groups express their understanding of existence in a given time and place. When that is neglected, theology no longer speaks meaningfully. However, when the situation dominates, it can relativize the message and make it inauthentic. Theology at its best "moves back and forth between two poles," between what is revealed and the environment in which it is received.[3] Both poles are necessary, but one of them is loaded with eternal truth. While all would not agree with this "method of correlation," the notion of the two poles has been widely affirmed. Even Karl Barth implicitly acknowledges it by warning Christians not to fall asleep on either the newspaper or the Bible, on the events of the day or the stories of faith.

The Shift from the Academy to History

Liberation theology breaks with that formulation in ways that are decisive and threatening. It is unwilling to give absolute primacy to either Scripture or tradition as a starting point. Both mainstream Protestant and Catholic theology are at odds with liberation theology. The underlying move of the older theologies is from a right understanding of Scripture or tradition to application and implementation in the world. There are, of course, quite divergent formulations of the interface. Even when the "situation" can serve a shaping function, however, it does not radically disturb the "eternal truth." That is a fixed point which needs only to be reformulated by the demands of the situation. Access to it is in large measure a problem of using language that works; the presumption is that eternal truth is "there" for translation.

The problem with beginning in the authority of Scripture or tradition is that the reading of the one and the formulation of the other tend to be loaded with the interests of the dominant class. The "eternal message" is not politically neutral. The understanding of it may have gathered up into it a strong bias. It makes a difference who has been doing the reading, the translating, and the conceptualizing. There are oppressive consequences of treating the text of Scripture as an "Archimedean point." For example, the perspective of the translator has determined the translation and contributed to the invisibility of women in the biblical record. If we examine the text with new eyes, the position of women as equals emerges.

A clear and compelling example of degrading women at the level of translation emerges in relation to Phoebe. "Whenever Paul uses the title *Diakonos* to refer to himself or another male leader, the exegetes translate it 'minister,' 'missionary,' or 'servant.' In the case of Phoebe they usually translate it 'deaconess.' "[4] An obvious bias is reflected when the same word is translated one way for a male and another for a female. The offense is compounded in that "deaconess," over time, becomes invested with less and less importance, and in fact becomes a gender-specific role. Some of us can bring to that our own memories of the time when the deaconesses prepared the elements for Communion while the deacons administered them. To envision Paul as a minister and Phoebe as a deaconess shows a bias of substantial proportion in the translator, but it also evokes a misunderstanding in the reader that compounds the denigration of women. Inaccurate interpretations of Scripture and tradition have contributed to oppression.

What this makes clear is that while the crisis of theology has a perennial quality, the nature of the crisis has undergone a significant contemporary shift. Theologians historically have wrestled with the issue of articulating the faith in the presence of those who are set against it. The problem has been one of establishing a wedge into that mind-set that precludes entertaining the validity of faith claims. Schleiermacher, for example, wanted to penetrate the "cultured despisers" of religion by identifying a universal consciousness they could not dispute and derive from it the religious realities.[5] The agenda in one way or another is to gain a hearing for the faith.

Liberation theologians tend to be indifferent to such "secular monsters" which threaten the religious community; they do not focus on finding a way to deliver the "eternal truth" to a hostile audience. The essential issue for liberation theology is not cognitive but historical. It focuses upon the bondage of people, their powerlessness to enact their own lives in particular times and places. It is there that the questions of faith emerge as the people look for a connection between their struggle and the reality of God. The question is not whether God is believable but whether God is with those who struggle for liberation.

Liberation theology is something done when the sun goes down. It is unusual to pre-empt Scripture and tradition as starting points for theological reflection and articulation. However, liberation theologies are bold and decisive in arguing for theology as the second act. The theologian begins in solidarity with those who are victims of the prevailing order.[6] Theology, then, is reflection upon a commitment. Liberation theology advocates a new method rather than a new content.[7] The task is not to address nonbelief or the credibility of faith, but to be involved with the marginated, the nonpersons, and discover the meaning of faith in the light of their condition. The first act is to be faithful to the human situation of oppression as it is available to our experience and subject to our social, political, and economic analysis. What is important is that liberation theology chooses to notice margination and invites an explication of it through the social sciences. The radical components from the vantage point of conventional or academic theology are the new partnerships with the oppressed rather than the "eternal truth" and with the tools of social analysis rather than philosophy. Understanding the reality of one's situation in history becomes for liberation theology a necessary condition for grasping the symbols of faith.

It might appear that liberation theology is inviting Christians to enter the struggle as if they had never heard of Scripture or tradition. None of us can or should cast off our history. We are who we are in part because we have been connected with the Judeo-Christian story. Our action on behalf of the oppressed is driven by and confirms what we have heard. We enter the struggle in cooperation with the powerless because the story identifies that as the place where God is in human history. Then our understanding of the reality of God, Jesus, and all the themes of faith emerges from the streets rather than the library. The fundamental issue is not only where you are but whom you have in view when the faith is set in theological categories.

Some might argue that it is no more legitimate to read the Bible from the "underside of history" than from the vantage point of privilege. There is a built-in perspective either way. In each instance one set or another of interests dominates the reading. However, that does not mean one view is as good as another. Scripture gives us no reason to believe that the Lord will be met "in the great ones of this world . . . (instead) we shall meet him in the poor of Latin America and of other continents."[8] The embodiment of God in the biblical story is not in the chambers of the Pharaohs but in the deprivation of the poor. Jesus is an oppressed Jew. He rode into Jeruselem, the citadel of worldly power, on a donkey with a palm branch, not an MX missile, in hand. Those who do theology after the sun goes down on their action in the streets see him as liberator of the oppressed and not a legitimator of the powerful. For theology to be a second act after the first act—being involved in the human struggle—does not substitute social realities for the themes of faith. It articulates the faith from the only vantage point that permits an authentic interpretation.

One consequence that might be drawn from this is that a middle sector American, especially one who is a white male, cannot write theology. Is being an oppressed class a necessary condition for theological reflection? James Cone comes close to that position when he defines revelation as a Black event.[9] The disclosure of God occurs where oppression is being overcome by liberation and in America that is where Black power challenges white dominance. But the argument can be turned to say that whites can become Black—that is, become part of the struggle for freedom—by their solidarity.[10] Whites can still do theology after the sun goes down if while it is rising they engage in the cause of the oppressed.

We propose to move beyond that position in ways Cone might be reluctant to embrace. A white middle layer American, especially a male, simply does not live under the conditions of the Black community. We are not oppressed. But there is a similarity. A major factor that drives oppression is powerlessness, and this emerges in the experience of the middle sector as well. When we consider where we experience some degree of freedom, we always find it exists within a broader framework over which we have no control. We are like the little child who is free to run away from home but not free to leave the block. The environment is a conspicuous example. We can recycle paper and other waste materials, but industrial America fouls the environment in ways we seem helpless to restrain. In large measure it is the nature and dynamic of the economic order that controls the framework within which we can make only rather inconsequential decisions. What makes us powerless, in its more extreme form, causes others to be oppressed. As long as we in the middle are involved in the struggle against the realities that make us powerless, and as a result seek solidarity with the oppressed, we can be faithful to the method of liberation theology.

Liberation Theology and Middle Sector Powerlessness

It is in the nature of liberation theology as it develops in Latin American communities to conceive that content of the Christian faith in the context of the social reality. Against a history that has its genesis in the legacy of Spanish and Portuguese colonialism, a liberation theologian interprets the faith from within communities committed to liberation in Latin America for the oppressed and exploited.[11] The transposition of that methodology to the first world in terms of racism and sexism has been accomplished without a loss of cadence. But a liberation theology in the context of the American middle sector reality does not fit as comfortably. The necessity of doing theology from within communities of the middle layer is more obviously needed than enacted. Villains such as poverty, racism, or sexism are more muted or seem "more complex," and anger as a "liberating grace" is conspicuously absent.[12] We are confused about from whom or what we should be liberated. The term *liberation* does not recall any self-evident experiences. The perception of many persons is that they are pursuing dreams that are attainable in some measure—if they try hard enough. They do not feel surrounded by any significant limiting situations. What they want is theirs, if they want it enough. They adopt as their own story that of the little red engine: " . . . I think I can, I think I can . . . I know I can, I know I can."

What seems true about that story, and any appropriation of it, is false at a deeper level. Most of us understand ourselves to be "individuated centers of being."[13] In the measure that we are self-actualizers we can achieve to the extent of our capability and initiative. But that vision masks a deeper reality. Individuals and collections of individuals in the middle sector are remarkably impotent. Some may be able to dart and dodge in pursuit of personal goals, but on a wider scale we have little sense of being able to shape or control the history in the midst of which our lives are lived. No one is sure how to stop a nuclear holocaust, how to break the cycle of environmental destruction, or how to suspend conflict in areas like the Middle East. Those issues are part of a structure that as individuals we are unable to penetrate. Personal aspirations aside, we do not know how to bring about "a just and livable society" within which those aspirations could come into being.[14] We are not confident of our ability to alter events. We feel powerless. Our ancestors had a crude sense at least that they were designing history; we have to live with the sense that a computer error might end history. The irony is that even those who "get to the top" are unable to "get on top" of events. John Kennedy said he wanted to be President because that is where the power is—and then a year later confessed surprise at how little he could effect from the Oval Office.

One might wonder why the evidence of our middle layer impotence is not more prominent. It has not made the cover of *Time* magazine; "Sixty Minutes" has not probed it; it is not table talk in either tract homes or suburban spreads. Why is what we see as so obvious and pervasive seemingly so obscure to the great majority? A dominant reason is the "religion of civility."[15] We survive by etiquette. It leads us to submerge certain dimensions of our experience. We have not only tailored our three major religions but also all our visions of class reality to conceal the deeper truths about our existence. A priority to giving no offense dominates our rhetoric and our behavior. Tact and taste control us rather than the norm of truth.

Several features of our middle sector experience escape the screen of civility, and they as much as anything provide a clue to the depths of our alienation from the power to shape our common life. The first feature is our susceptibility to false villains. The ease with which we are convinced that "the Russians are coming" and that every conflict is part of a global conspiracy is evidence of that vulnerability. We are also susceptible to the argument that we are being "had from below." All our social programs can be conceived as being for cheats who are lazy and eat away at our hard-earned tax dollars. One has only to watch Jerry Falwell a time or two to sense the scapegoating. Everything that is wrong with our lives can be traced to the liberals, secular humanists, and communists who want to murder babies, promote pornography, prevent prayer, and push sexual encounters. We consistently are susceptible to these false villains.

The second feature of our experience is even more revealing. It is the false victim. The pervasiveness of brutality to women and abuse of children are examples of turning against our own out of frustration.[16] In 1966, many watched with disbelief the burning of Watts and the self-inflicted wounds on Blacks. Some of those same watchers are now the wife or child beaters whose impotence is inverted into violence. We are frustrated by an amorphous system that defines our reality; we respond with aggression against ourselves. The middle sector burns down its own Watts.

The religion of civility protects us from explicitly identifying the sources of impotence, but it cannot restrain these frustrated expressions of it. The false villains and the false victims are manifestations of loss of control. We can be told whom to blame and instinctively we victimize.

When one probes the American middle sector story it may in fact resemble Albert Camus' *The Plague*.[17] Dr. Reuex knows he cannot cure the plague, but he marshalls his energies toward restraining its spread. In time he learns that he is the bearer of the very plague he has exhausted himself in resisting. We are not in control; the shape and direction of our lives and our societies are not of our designing. Resignation follows close on the heels of a sense that history is out of our control. While we think of ourselves as potential victors, in reality we are at a deeper level powerless. Out of a commitment to individualism we are unable to assemble a society that is fair and just.

Concurrent with the sense of powerlessness is an inevitable experience of vulnerability. Loss of control and insecurity reinforce each other. For the middle layer person the dimensions of that sense of uncertainty are many. Inflation and tax policy make "playing the game" less productive economically. Or, one may be able to buy many more goods than ever anticipated yet have the real satisfaction fall far below expectations. A person may have perceived a college degree as a down payment on assured mobility; in time that degree becomes so commonplace it does not differentiate. And when unemployment is up, only a small percentage of June graduates know where or if they will exercise their vocation. Religion is supposed to be the ultimate ground of security. And yet ambiguity appears to reign here as well. The faith of Paul, in that great "nevertheless" made possible by God, now seems dissipated. Rather than have the world called into question by the Word, the Word is called into question by the world.

Whenever persons experience their present state as adrift or amiss, they inevitably begin to search out the past, to identify roots through which they may sustain themselves. But our uses of the past can either foreclose possibilities for the future or facilitate them. We can turn to the past and appropriate it, either "to remain in its limits," or "to point to new futures."[18] We can distinguish between a "closed" and an "open" past.[19] The first is seductive and the other points to the future. All one can do with a closed past is be drawn within and appropriate it for repetition. An open past fetches new futures.

Jerry Falwell and this book are both directed at social change and focus upon the middle sector. Falwell addresses insecurity by an appeal to his reading of tradition, both religious and national (which often are identical for him). There is no uncertainty in his references to the Bible. The economic order is substantiated for Falwell, for example, by the assurance, apparently in Proverbs, that God instituted and blessed free enterprise. Thus, we have to live within the limits of that divine economic order (with Ronald Reagan as messiah). Falwell wants to restore the past as he sees it and believes that will help overcome what ails the middle sector.

Our argument draws upon a more comprehensive biblical past, and its impact upon the present is not the same. Rather than engender confidence, it creates discontent. Martin Luther King, Jr., provides a compelling example. As we have suggested earlier, he focused on Moses and the Exodus story; when he overlaid that on the Black condition it stabbed inexorably into all that is unfulfilled for Black people.[20] The reality of bondage and the prospect of liberation were laid bare. The pitch of Jerry Falwell is directed toward middle class needs to be at home in the world. Our book is directed toward middle fraction aspirations for a new future. Both call for heroism; one individual, the other social. Rambo and Martin Luther King, Jr., are different models of the heroic.

The Exodus and Justice

To do liberation theology in the context of the American middle sector reality, one must "own" the Exodus story. Because it "is the key event that models the faith of Israel," it must be allowed to decipher our experience.[21] What we learn from the story is that oppression and liberation are a historical reality and that divine revelation unfolds in that context. It is obvious how Dr. King and the Black movement could appropriate that story as their own. Both Israel in Egypt and the Black community in America are involved in "the struggle of an oppressed people in quest of their rights and spurred on by the hope that the victory will be real because their god is at their side for the struggle."[22] The point of entry for middle layer America is not so clear. Those in the middle are neither Israel nor Egypt, but have elements of both.

The significance of the Exodus for the middle sector is that it applies to what is going on even though it is equivocal on who we are. The fact that we are neither the powerful nor the powerless is not in itself important. Rather, our significance and uniqueness are that we are so many in America. In the Third World the people in the middle constitute a much smaller group, and that creates a clear dichotomy between the rich and the poor. In our world the middle is the majority. The conversion of the middle layer to the cause of a "just and livable society" is a necessary condition for the liberation of others. There is no way in which Blacks and women will become free until the middle segment embraces the agenda of freedom. "None are free until all are free" gathers force when it is the majority who have become mired in a lack of power. Our theological position calls us to be on stage, but our structural position blocks our presence.

This is the point at which the earlier sense of the middle fraction is relevant; we are the people who feel that history is out of our control. Events are not of our designing. We cannot throw our weight with liberation and against oppression because we are not in control of ourselves. This is not to deny complicity with oppression or even vulnerability. It is to argue that discernment of powerlessness must precede involvement in the struggle. The form of our involvement for now is contention with our own experience. Probing the origins of our malaise is a precondition for entry into what God is doing in the context of history.

What the Exodus suggests to the middle sector in America is that we have become the peripheral people. We cannot struggle toward the promised land because we do not have a collective sense of agency. We are a mass in the midst of the liberation struggle and cannot grab the reins of events with enough confidence to give direction. We are neither Israel nor Egypt but bystanders unable to become part of the action. The middle layer is a majority at the periphery. While not deprived like the masses in the Third World we are as submerged as they in a history out of our control.

In an earlier chapter we claimed that social change results from collective actions of real individuals in light of perceived injustices. What, then, are the natures of the perceived injustices that motivate middle layer involvement in social change? That is, what are the historical realities in the world that have called and are calling the middle sector to action? One motivation results from a kind of piggybacking on the problems of the rest of the laboring class. Thus, along with the middle fraction commitment to social justice in the civil rights movement there was also a sense of voyeurism—a sense that their problems were not our problems. Perhaps that is why so many of the societal responses to the issues of civil rights were solutions imposed from above by legislative fiat rather than created from below by the drive for human freedom and justice. Perhaps that is also why so many of the programs have created tokenism in place of real change.

Another motivation has its roots in the firm middle class belief in the story of individualism. For example, the consumer movement plays itself out in terms of not getting a "fair shake" in dealings with big business and big government. "How can *I* make them respond to *my* needs?" is a dominant, although not exclusive, theme. Preventing the system from doing injustice *to me* is a much more powerful motivating force than preventing the system from doing injustice *to us*.

A third level at which the middle fragment perceives injustice does carry with it the notion that "we're all in this together." In the nuclear freeze and environmental movements the middle layer values of compromise and civility are sometimes stretched to the breaking point. We grow angry with the injustice of dominant groups making decisions about the use of their power without consulting or considering the people who will be temporarily hurt, permanently damaged, or killed by that use of power.

It is not difficult to think of examples of perceived injustice that fit into one or more of the three categories. What is much more difficult is to search for and discover the causal links that bind all these injustices together. Our stories, our value systems, our beliefs, all act to push us toward the conclusion that injustice arises, at worst, from a correctable flaw, an oversight, in the construction of the system. Most of the time we believe that injustice is most likely to occur as a result of individual, and hence legally punishable, malevolence. The Nuremberg trials represent a classic example of the dominance of this individualistic view of injustice. "Find and punish (or change the heart of) the person responsible."

Social justice is social; it has to do with the society as a whole. Justice cannot and must not be defined abstractly and ahistorically. The middle sector in America firmly believes that the criteria for justice can be divined in the rule of law. That is, if the law establishes no barriers to all enjoying the same rights, then the system supported by that law is morally right and fair. This is an ahistorical criterion for judgment which ensures not the creation of justice, but the maintenance of the *status quo* with whatever injustice is inherent within it. It is ahistorical because it ignores the reality of the existence of political, economic, and social institutions that make it difficult for some groups and individuals to exercise the rights to which they are legally entitled. When laws are unjust, they reflect the injustice of the institutional arrangements of society. Despite the fact the laws may guarantee equality, an unjust system will not grant that equality, no matter how the laws are adjusted.

Justice can be conceived of as something that is prior to and must come before the law.[23] That is, the economic, political, and social systems must be informed with moral rightness before it is possible to devise a legal code that supports and enhances justice. If, for example, the just distribution of political power is an important issue, it is not acceptable to begin with some given set of laws which provides a framework for politics and then determine the "most just" conditions within those laws. Rather, we must start with political justice in a particular setting and then create a legal and institutional framework to sustain it.

Observing existing conditions does not necessarily make us historical. Both political conservatives and liberals in the United States have been caught in that trap. They observe the human condition, but they don't understand the reality of that condition. Both sides, in fact, try to define justice in terms of equality rather than equity. The right believes that justice exists with the creation of a legal "equality of opportunity," discussed earlier. The liberals believe that justice can be achieved by the creation of "equality of outcomes." This position is also ahistorical, because it attempts to create equal outcomes within a society whose political, economic, and social structures are set for inequality. A fundamental tenet of individualism is the importance of the incentives created by the inequality of the reward mechanisms. To posit "equality of outcomes" for this society as it is currently constructed is to be hopelessly out of touch with historical reality.

Virtually all would agree it is unjust that the poor are so much more likely to be found guilty when accused of crimes and to receive much stiffer penalties, particularly prison sentences, than are the non-poor. As a case in point, it was the widespread existence of economic and racial inequity in the application of the death penalty that led to the 1972 Supreme Court decision invalidating all the existing death penalty laws in the individual states. In this instance there is a belief that moral rightness and equity, hence justice, are served best only when conviction and sentencing are based on the circumstances of the crime, not the racial or other socioeconomic circumstances of either the perpetrator or the victim. The thrust of our formative stories tells us that we are all equal before the criminal law, but historical reality draws a very different picture. However, given the existing structures of the legal system (e.g., the cost of lawyers, judicial overloads, plea bargaining, and politically motivated prosecutors), there is not much hope for an end to this kind of injustice. The answer must begin a pre-legal move. There must be a radical restructuring of the system of criminal law and of the power to use that law before we can expect that system regularly and routinely to serve justice and attack injustice.

Another example of injustice in the United States is the existence of malnutrition among children. This can be traced to the poorly balanced diets and the lack of calories forced on some families by poverty. Recent statistics show that in 1985, 14% of the total population and 20.1% of the children in the United States were living in poverty.[24] Yet the society produces material abundance in terms of both food and other items. What, then, is the reason for the malnutrition and its associated problems of poor physical and mental health and decreased learning capacity? The Declaration of Independence tells us that we have the right to life, liberty, and the pursuit of happiness. Surely, poor children do not have equal access to those rights. Why do we choose to control, utilize, and distribute our material abundance in ways that emphasize the selfish over-indulgence of some and permit the tragic denial of others? The pattern of ownership and control over the means of production and the use of those means for the pursuit of private profit make such denial endemic to the system. Poor people cannot mount an effective demand for proper nutrition. Their needs, therefore, cannot be regularly and efficiently served by a private enterprise, profit-motivated system.

The hunger question starkly focuses the serious "*tri-lemma*," discussed in chapter 2, that the middle sector faces with regard to issues of justice. First, the economic malaise of the seventies and early eighties makes some parts of the middle segment increasingly vulnerable to the unemployment and poverty that create hunger and malnutrition. In that sense they are at least potential victims of systemic injustice. At a second level, the middle layer finds that its work activity, particularly its activity of low-level management in large corporations, gives it a complicity in that pursuit of profit which is such an important part of the denial of the social needs of the poor. Thus, the middle fraction is in some degree responsible for the injustice of the system; we are part oppressor. Third, and perhaps most significantly, the middle sector finds itself to be powerless to change either its vulnerability to or its complicity with injustice. Even when we perceive the injustice, we are so steeped in the ideology of individualism that we quite literally cannot conceive of the systemic responses that are necessary to right the wrongs. As members of the system, we cannot secure our rights or control our destiny in the ways that the story of individualism promises. As individuals we can do nothing to change the system.

This "tri-lemma" reveals the need for liberation. We have to be freed from the abusive use of our limited authority. Powerlessness in the face of the system implies a lack of opportunity and ability to choose something else. In this sense, liberation means an empowering that frees us to choose alternatives. But most importantly, liberation for the middle segment creates the opportunity to do justice. It is not so much the freedom from oppression but the freedom for justice that must inform any middle sector heroism.

Jesus and Jerusalem: Cleansing the Temple

In liberation theology the opportunity to do justice is a priority that is evident in its selection of texts and their interpretation. The charge has been made often, and with a measure of validity, that liberation theology has a disproportionate reliance upon the Old Testament for its biblical legitimation. The Exodus, in particular, is the focus of that allegation. The argument gathers force with the centrality of bondage and oppression in the story. Again, that places some distance between the narrative and the American middle class reality. But the significance of the Israelites' life in Egypt goes beyond their slavery. Egypt provided benefits, and that had its own attractiveness. Part of what is lost by giving oppression and bondage the prominence they deserve centers on the reality of "the fleshpots" in the land of Egypt "when we did eat bread to the full" . . . (Exod. 16:3, KJV). There is no reason to believe that the Israelites were totally isolated from the luxury that permeated the aristocracy. This is not to imply in any measure that it was a "promised land," for its corruption was comprehensive. But evils can be appealing. "Egypt was a center of wealth and good living; it makes sense to suggest that many Israelites admired the very people who oppressed them, copied Egyptian ways, curried Egyptian favor."[25] There was surely some of the good life to be had, even if the framework was slavery. The risk of rebellion was partially centered in the sacrifice of affluence. Like the American middle sector, most Israelites had something to lose in their revolution. In that sense the Exodus is our symbol, as well as a symbol for the oppressed, and includes a dimension of our experience.

Symbols of challenge to the status quo, however, can also be found in the New Testament. Whenever theologians want to bring into focus the reality of Jesus, it is always in relation to something perceived to be central for understanding him. We read about "Jesus and the kingdom of God," "Jesus and the future," "Jesus and the poor." None of those themes is strange or without defense. What is curious is that one so seldom sees the theme of "Jesus and the temple" developed. This is particularly surprising when one realizes that "[f]rom every point of view the temple was the most important Israelite institution in the time of Jesus."[26] We need to establish its centrality for understanding Jesus. One way to approach that is to highlight the importance of Jesus' going to Jerusalem. The significance of Jerusalem is reflected in the insignificance of Galilee. Nothing of religious or intellectual prominence was in evidence there, and in no sense could it be associated with the exercise of power in any form. Indeed, "[t]o be a Galilean Jew was already to be one of the ignorant, insignificant, and despised of the world."[27] Galilee was the epitome of rejection. For God to choose that as the point of entry into the world for Jesus is the height of folly in human terms. It was not a great place to be from insofar as one's origins identify one's importance.

Jerusalem was everything Galilee was not. Jerusalem was the ultimate symbol of established power. It "was the center of the powers that excluded and oppressed the masses, . . . the center of religious domination . . . the center of economic, political, and military domination."[28] All the forms of domination were fully present in the city, and they were joined to add force to one another. Jesus had to go to Jerusalem in order to confront the sources of injustice. It was, after all, a city under the jurisdiction of a foreign military power.

When Jesus entered Jerusalem he went first to the temple. In large measure it is the issue of the temple that makes clear the nature of his message and the political consequences that follow from it. Indeed, it goes a long way toward explaining why he had to die. In a prelude to the end, even as a sign of it, Jesus said to one of his disciples: "Do you see these great buildings? There will not be left here one stone upon another, that will not be thrown down" (Mark 13:2). This prediction of the destruction of the most venerable religious institution of the time becomes part of the charges as Jesus is brought before Caiaphas. False witnesses told the council that Jesus had said, "I am able to destroy the temple of God, and to build it in three days" (Matt. 26:61). Even on the cross, in excruciating physical agony, he is taunted, "You who would destroy the temple and build it in three days, save yourself, and come down from the cross" (Mark 15:29–30). Once again, in the trial of Stephen, this follower of Jesus is held accountable for his proclamation that "Jesus of Nazareth will destroy this place" (Acts 6:14). The one unforgivable dimension of Jesus was what he said about the temple; that sealed his fate and justified it.

From within our American framework, it is difficult for many of us to grasp the enormity of the offense. In our minds we substitute church for temple. We pay attention only to a single dimension, that both are places for worship. Therein lies the flaw in our response. What makes that equation false is the distinction between the temple and the synagogue in biblical times. Both were religious institutions, complementary ones, with distinguishable functions. The temple was the place of sacrifice; the synagogue was the place where the law was proclaimed and exposited. The temple served an economic function, while the synagogue served a teaching function. The temple was centralized; the synagogue was dispersed. For a Passover festival the population of Jerusalem might increase fivefold as pilgrims made their way to the temple for sacrifice. Worshipers at Passover (A.D. 66) needed approximately 255,600 lambs.[29] Thus, the temple was the center of economic activity, while the synagogue was more a place of assembly for hearing the meaning of the law.

All of this discussion is germane to understanding Jesus' cleansing of the temple. While the story is uncomplicated, its significance is not self-evident. The setting of the event is the celebration of the Passover. The people of faith are pouring into the temple to celebrate the Exodus events, the great act of liberation for the slaves. Jesus is on the way to the temple as well. For reasons not entirely obvious, he takes cords in hand and proceeds to drive out the merchants and tax collectors. Sheep, oxen, and pigeons, the objects sold for sacrifice, are expelled; coins are strewn on the temple floor, and the tables on which transactions occur are overturned. It is not pre-eminently an act of violence as is so often argued, but an act of righteous anger. We miss the importance of Jesus' action if we identify the activity of the temple with bingo and church bazaars. That would be to equate peripheral activities with integral economic and political functions. The cleansing of the temple has to be seen in relation to Jesus' words about its destruction.

The cleansing is a symbolic act, obscure until we decipher the role of the temple in the society. Jesus is not addressing the spiritual insensitivity of the priests or a lapse of taste. The temple drew together every dimension of the life of the country and as such was the center of power. "The temple was thus, at one and the same time, a bank and a marketplace, the seat of political authority and the source of regulation of religious symbols, a place of prayer, and an enclosure in which every type of human transaction took place."[30] The intertwining of all dimensions of personal and institutional, religious and secular existence was comprehensive and intense. Separate spheres and institutions did not exist.

What brought this all together was the fact that the temple was the heartbeat of the economic system and therefore a political force of inordinate proportions. For Jesus, its religious function was eclipsed by the prominence of commerce. What is far from apparent when read in our own setting is the role of the temple as a bank.[31] There was substantial capital accumulation in its treasury. Money was generated and made safe there. It was also made available to fund necessary projects in the country and to serve the self-interested goals of political figures. Wall Street would be amazed at the capital formation, and Congress would covet the access to such extensive resources. It should not surprise us that confiscating temple deposits was a recognized prerogative of the king.[32] Political power rides in part on fiscal control exercised by the king and the temple; it perpetuates domination and enforces powerlessness.

In the act of cleansing the temple Jesus suspends briefly the banking operation of Jerusalem, brings commerce to a halt, and threatens to jeopardize the economy—all without authority. It was not long before operations returned to normal, but a statement had been made. The attack goes to every level of the society but focuses unambiguously upon the economic order. It unmasks the sacred sanction the temple provided for institutionalized greed. Those who dispute the competence of Catholic bishops to comment on the economy in our day would have been more than

offended by Jesus' act in his day. It is in the nature of symbolic acts
that they are not sustained assaults, but are paradigmatic thrusts.
Reading the cleansing of the temple story against the reality of its
time is evidence enough that Jesus mistrusted the power of
institutions and identified the economic order as the pulse of
domination. The cleansing was a political act of the first order,
one given depth and meaning for having occurred during the
celebration of Exodus events.

What would it mean for those of us in the American middle
to see our reality through the temple episode? One way to
approach that is to identify what it precludes. Issues of justice are
not addressed by charity, directing some surplus luxury at the
needy. Issues of justice are not addressed by a change of heart,
opening ourselves emotionally to those who are in pain. Issues of
justice are not addressed by incentives to do good, promising
rewards for acts of compassion. With the temple episode in
Jerusalem, Jesus directs our passion for justice into the sphere
from which injustice is generated. We are called to discern the
false ideologies in the institutions that we support by silence; we
are called to a new consciousness at odds with that which drives
the dominant culture; we are called to be a community that
counters the status quo and envisions an order of human solidarity rather than individual self-advancement.

Religious Symbols and the Spirit of Our Age

The temple cleansing enables us to see our complicity in
oppression through the economic order and energizes us to create
a new one in which the needs of all supersede the privilege of a
few. A new order, however, requires us to contend with a secular
spirit of the age. Some would argue that religious symbols and
god-talk are no longer meaningful. Liberation theologians in both
the first and Third worlds have been indifferent to secularity as a
dimension of *their* reality. Faith is not seen as undermined by a
secular, cultural mood but by the conditions of historical existence. Langdon Gilkey describes cultural mood as "that fundamental attitude toward reality, toward truth, and toward value
which characterizes an epoch, and within whose terms every

creative aspect of life, including a period's religion and its theology, expresses itself."[33] Liberation theology in general has not related to the ways in which the spirit of an age can severely interrupt the language of faith. In the late 1960s Gilkey argued persuasively for the existence of a cultural mood marked by contingency, relativism, transience, and autonomy.[34] Those themes set the terms for what can be grasped convincingly and meaningfully. As a pre-conceptual framework they preclude assertions about "ultimate order, coherence, or meaning" and define history as a human project.[35] Secularity means the heavens are empty and earth is of our making.

One of the more revealing differences between theologians in North America and those in Latin America emerges around the question of God. Several decades ago mainstream America gave some considerable attention to "the death of God." The movement may have had a strong media component; few would deny, however, that it flashed a signal that the reality and content of transcendence were in dispute. Some in the academy were willing to risk the conjecture that the theological venture was impossible without reference to this challenge. By contrast the question of God for Latin Americans centered on the "death of idols"; they concerned themselves with exposing false gods. Idolatry, the worship of something finite, eclipsed atheism or agnosticism as a dominant problem. It is not entirely surprising that the issue clustered around "the creation of gods and of idols that sanction oppression and anti-life forces," as Pablo Richard and his co-authors put it in *The Idols of Death and the God of Life*.[36] The true God rather than no God was the consuming dilemma for victims of oppressive systems. Survival presses to the fore different issues than affluence drives a person to consider.

It is very clear that the symbols of faith work in Latin America. The task of liberation theologians is to alter for whom the symbols work. The mandate in part is to withdraw transcendence from false pretenders, to articulate how the "God of life" shatters the "idols of death." In North America we cannot assume biblical symbols are in full force. We do not experience God as dead, but neither can we assume that the invocation of the divine name will have transforming power.

The symbols of faith can be instrumental in social transformation, but they are impaired by the spirit of the age. In a typical middle sector community one might expect to find this dilemma expressed in several ways. Those within the churches sustain a relationship with the Judeo-Christian symbols that is at most contained within the sphere of their private lives. Yet even that inner attachment to the symbol may be tenuous. Celebrating the Lord's Supper may not differ dramatically from the more frequent coffee hour after the service. While missing an Easter service may be unthinkable, thinking about its deeper meanings is unlikely. What strikes one about those outside the church, on the other hand, is that they are so seldom hostile to its claims. Religion is rarely even seen as a worthy enemy, something from which one needs to protect oneself.

Some years ago one of the authors asked social activist Saul Alinsky why he always seemed to be aligned with churches and synagogues. He responded that these are the people whose Scriptures contain the symbols of revolution and that all one needed to do was awaken them to the meaning of their cherished images. We agree, while noting that other traditions also have such symbols. The problem is, how can the middle sector connect with the discourse of faith so that it functions to overcome the sense of powerlessness and enable the emergence of a new society?

Liberation theologians drive us to come to terms with our own reality. They teach us to suspect the representation of that reality that dominates in our society. The argument threaded through this book has been that things are not as they are thought to be. There is a profound contradiction between conception and experience. We have been working toward unmasking our existence as individuals and communities. One can hardly expect the symbols of faith to precipitate change when we are not in touch with what needs changing. The story of Abraham will not make sense to those for whom present realities are utopian. For the middle class what blocks the force of the biblical story is a false consciousness. At the same time it is important to expose the environment of the texts in order to be awakened to their relevance. The earlier discussion of Jesus and the temple is an example of that. The story can work on us once we understand its setting and come to an awareness of our own. The importance of laying bare both our context and that of the biblical faith needs further consideration.

It has been argued that revolutions occur when persons sense themselves as moving from being "cramped" to being "wronged."[37] While that has been true, it does not seem immediately applicable to the task of converting the middle class to the project of creating "a just and livable society." The problem for the middle layer is that we do not feel cramped; we feel numbed. And that is not the stuff of militancy. We need to recognize and address the fact that we *are* at an impasse. At least one cause of this malaise is that prophetic biblical symbols are not activating the religious community; they have been soothed by the priestly and pastoral.

The religion of civility has intervened in our reading of the biblical record and attuned us to only half of our daily confrontation with both life and death. In Deuteronomy God says, "I have set before you life and death, . . . choose life" (Deut. 30:19). If we make that choice, however, without attention to death, the life that is chosen has neither depth nor significance. Biblically, death is a prominent metaphor for the human condition. Death has sovereignty over our existence in all its forms. Of course, the word calls for specification, and one might be tempted to limit its jurisdiction to the end of physical life. By contrast, William Stringfellow writes that ". . . when the name of death is used, I intend that it bear *every* definition and nuance, *every* association and suggestion, *every* implication and intuition that *anyone* has *ever* attributed to death, and I intend that the name of death, here, bear all meanings simultaneously and cumulatively."[38] To be alive biblically is to resist death, to stand against "the principalities and powers" through which death achieves sovereignty over life. The deeper theological meaning of the powerlessness of the middle layer is that we are marginated; we are a people who cannot join the liberating action of God in human history. We are in a "Babylonian captivity" to social structures that prevent the creation of "a just and livable society." Our history as a class is one in which we have failed to resist death.

To create an appropriate metaphor for our life as a class, a new ideology must draw on a doctrine and a ritual that are instrumental in the transfiguration of death. What do the resurrection of Christ and the celebration of the Lord's Supper mean in the light of our American reality?

Under the impact of the individualism which dominates society, the resurrection is interpreted as an answer to the need for a "blessed longevity." The individual acquires eternal life independently of life in the orders of the world. The meaning of the resurrection, however, is not captured in the survival of the individual. In the New Testament death is more than a biological symbol; it requires a political conception of the resurrection. The resurrection cancels the power of death over us as a people or a class. Pilate claimed he had life and death control over Jesus, and biologically he did. But the deeper truth, to which the resurrection points, is that Pilate had no control at all. He could condemn Jesus but he stood powerless before the Kingdom of God.

The resurrection faith gives Christians a new vision of reality. It substitutes life for death as a generative theme in historical existence. The resurrection, then, is like Jesus saying in effect to Pilate, "You think it is this way, but it is that way." The resurrection is an unmasking of what and who constitutes reality. It is a testimony, Gutierrez claims, that Christ is "alive in the poor and oppressed . . . alive in the very midst of the death that seems dominator . . . [and that creates the possibility] of living subversively the gladness of Easter right at the heart of a people's movement crushed and repressed."[39] A political conception of the resurrection means that the immobility forced on us by structures of the social order does not have to be that way. Expectation of a new order replaces resignation to the existing disorder. The resurrection has "set in motion an eschatologically determined process of history. . . ."[40] History is now driven by its future rather than constrained by the conspiring of past and present. Revolutionary praxis dooms all determinisms, the cynicism of the inevitable. It requires hope for the open possibilities of history.

If, as Lehmann says, "the future draws the present toward

itself from the past," then the real illusion is the sovereignty of death, our domination by the structures that be.[41] The political and sociological consequence of the resurrection is that "a liberating humanity" can gain control over the realities that control it. "I set before you life and death—choose life" means that we can rein in what has been reigning over our lives. What is really dead is death.

The way in which we have privatized the resurrection has a parallel in our conception of the Lord's Supper. As "the medicine of immortality," it has been fused with our individual needs. We may take communion together, but it is as individuals that we conceive its benefits. If it is not death, it is the quest for personal peace that fashions our expectations and shapes the experience of the table. Rather than the act of communion being an event of social conditioning, the ritual itself has been socially conditioned. For all its surface centrality in even the highest churches liturgically, communion has been altered to suit the needs of dominant groups in the church.[42] And they have become either blatant or subtle custodians of the status quo. The Eucharist in a middle sector church serves to keep us politically immobilized, indifferent, and complacent.

But the Lord's Supper was and can be a revolutionary ritual, one in which we act out our faith that the future of God shapes the past and present. "It is not a simple memorial. It is not confined to the past, a sort of sorrowful and nostalgic recollection of the Lord. It is openness to the future, full of trust and gladness."[43] Those who come to the table as biblically conceived come to resist death. The Eucharist is an act of political subversion when freed from its captivity to the private.

What is most commonly forgotten, or conveniently suppressed, is the Old Testament background of the act. "Jesus instituted the Eucharist on the night of the Jewish Pasch. It was a national feast, a celebration of their independence, their liberation from slavery in Egypt."[44] Even as the deliverance of the Jews was a political event, so the origins and thrust of the Eucharist are political. It is unambiguously an act that declares that the liberation of humankind is the mission of God in the world, then and now. On the one hand, the taking of bread and wine involves the creation of mutuality. It is anti-individualistic. It is one form of declaring that we are the body of Christ, we are one. This communitarian factor was once upon a time risky and led to the persecution of the church. "The principalities and powers" fear human solidarity. Being one in Christ is dangerous; any human bonding can "get out of hand."

What makes the Eucharist liberative is its alliance with the future and its power over oppression and our numbness. It is the premier celebration of the death of death. At the table we declare that the Pentagon is dead, Wall Street is dead, imperialism is dead, structural indifference to human suffering is dead. And what is alive is the one who said, "The Spirit of the Lord is upon me, because he has anointed me to preach good news to the poor. He has sent me to proclaim release to the captives and recovering of sight to the blind, to set at liberty those who are oppressed" (Luke 4:18). What happens in the taking of the body and blood of Christ, who is our future, is the "unmasking of injustice" and an empowerment for resistance.[45]

When the Eucharist is faithful to its origin in the liberation of the Israelites from the Egyptians, its practice becomes the creation and celebration of a liberating community. Communicants can no longer accept the constructions of reality maintained by the structures of society; we are delivered from their power by "he who comes." Taking bread and wine becomes an act of defiance.

Revolution is ritualized in the Lord's Supper, even as it is a consequence of the resurrection. Those who take the risen Christ into their lives at the table "can no longer put up with reality as it is, but begin to suffer under it, to contradict it. Peace with God means conflict with the world, for the goad of the promised future stabs inexorably into the flesh of every unfulfilled present."[46] We cannot domesticate the Christ identified with the liberative act of God in the Exodus; by that Christ we can be driven to "militant compassion." With faith in the resurrection celebrated in the Lord's Supper, we as a people take aim at the formation of a social order "truly free of servitude" and where persons can become "active shapers of their own destiny" in community.[47]

7
Heroism as a Social Act

The images of life and death have been used as symbols that identify the struggle of the middle sector in America. Ours is "a time in which the power of death is pervasive and militant and in which people exist without hope or else in pursuit of transient, fraudulent, or delusive hopes."[1] The signs of death can be seen starkly in the physical and emotional violence which has become more a way of life than a last resort. We in the American middle layers numbly embrace the forms of violence in our lives, without passionate aversion. Powerlessness, lack of identity, and economic precariousness conspire to make us indifferent to the possibility of death prevailing over life. There may be instances of highly individualized gallantry, but social heroism had its last hurrah with the Reformation and the attendant rise of capitalism. The new middle sectors have lost control and become trapped in the circumstances set in motion by the earlier heroism of the old middle classes.

It has been argued that the middle sector in America can re-align itself with the forces of life. The orders once created by, and now hostile to, the middle fraction can be dismantled and replaced by ones that serve the interests of justice and meaningfulness. Human solidarity can re-emerge as conditions are set to promote community and to resist the forms of individualism which isolate people and instill competition. Christian theology and the church could have a promising role to play in nurturing a new heroism of the middle layers.

This chapter suggests some preliminary moves toward such a heroism. We have envisioned the possibility of a liberation theology from the middle. But in what sense can that provide a base for a civil religion? It is, after all, impossible to maintain a permanently prophetic religion, one solely focused on the issuing of jeremiads. Therefore, a new liberation theology will have to consider its role not only in promoting change, but in living with the consequences of it. For example, what would be the relationship of a prophetic theology with the dominant social institutions *after* major changes have occurred?

We want to set out some of the issues that we think might be involved in the journey toward a different society. What are some particular images that might galvanize the church and the middle sector in thinking about the future? How can we dismantle the economic and bureaucratic edifices that have caused so much of the damage in the first place? What might be some points at which we in the middle could begin concretely to rebuild? Are there specific moves we can make, individually and collectively, to regain some control over our day-to-day lives and the structural framework of our existence? Can we relinquish the old false sense of being middle class in order to create the mutuality and reciprocity that come with the more accurate view of ourselves as laborers?

Liberation Theology, Civil Religion, and the Emerging Church

The argument in this chapter is shaped around the prospect that social justice will become the mandate for society and that new institutional arrangements will emerge to secure it. We need to think about a time in which what we have been envisioning begins to take hold and become a reality. One of the ways to begin centers on civil religion as it has been and as it could become. The issue is whether the religious symbols of this new liberation will become a type of civil religion.

A major contention of Robert Bellah's "civil religion" is that there is no such thing as a purely secular state. Even the more strident critics of his concept acknowledge that no nation is without a civil religion. Civil religions may differ in content and in quality, but they are a "functional universal."[2] In simplest terms civil religion means that we understand ourselves as a people through religious symbols. They draw us together around our heritage, cementing us as a people; they articulate the meaning and purposefulness of our "whence" and our "whither." Every nation has this common faith which explains and animates. The symbols of a civil religion are usually those available in the culture from the dominant religion. The Judeo-Christian tradition in America has provided the symbols for national self-understanding.

In the early days Americans understood themselves as the "new Israel," and we continue to profess to be "a chosen people." Our origins and mission take on ultimate significance which we state with biblical imagery that legitimates the national reality.

Doing liberation theology in North America can be seen as hinging on "a creative use of America's civil religion."[3] In John Coleman's view, existent reality is a boundless resource for the aspirations of the theological posture we have been advocating. What civil religion has to offer is a usable past. It sets out the task of retrieving the national heritage as a force in the struggle for a new future. Civil religion holds up ideals and dreams and through them fashions a new day. It is not a mindless patriotism, shallow and self-serving, but a deeper national loyalty to the best; it is a source of both vision and energy.

Coleman contends that in Latin America liberation theology is struggling to create a civil religion by making community synonymous with the church and continent. The force of this blending creates the prospect for a more just society. In North America, on the other hand, there already is a civil religion which should be a bold resource for liberation theology. The national heritage and self-image have "large doses of messianic expectation" which promote an alternative future.[4]

For the purposes of this study, it is not clear that American civil religion is an asset of indisputable value. It is more likely to preserve a past we do not accept than create a future we can affirm. The prevailing effect of American civil religion has been to sanction and legitimate the status quo. It instills the false confidence that America is favored among the forces of history. In seeing the nation as the "new Israel," we are assured an unambiguous role as the guardian of freedom. Such a closed view of history, however, turns us into an agent of death rather than of life. It seldom challenges the order that institutionalizes poverty and injustice. The "god" of American civil religion is very slow to anger; indeed "his" patience is inexhaustible. The purposes of liberation theology are not likely to be advanced by alignment with such a civil religion.

American civil religion, and liberation theology in the context of the middle class, do have in common the Judeo-Christian symbols. Yet one of the reasons we reject the existing civil religion is precisely the use it makes of those symbols. There is a notable distortion in the way civil religion attaches the American reality to biblical imagery. It is only possible to continue to associate America with the "new Israel" by radically compromising the settings that produced the symbols. At best, the fit is inappropriate. The economic order and its consumerism create a reality strikingly similar to "the fleshpots of Egypt."

One of the things American civil religion does to biblical symbols is empty them of their original content. An early and important discussion of civil religion charged that transcendence in civil religion was "symbolically empty" and preempted "particularity of content."[5] It is precisely this particularity that is essential to the conscientious use of biblical symbols.

If the symbols offend no one, how can they effectively advocate justice? As argued earlier, the context of a symbol, story, or metaphor is crucial in defining the content. We have to be clear about both the biblical setting and our own before we make bold to put them together. Idolizing the nation is a consequence of being indifferent to historical realities. However, it becomes more difficult to misappropriate the symbols when we see ourselves under "the God of justice," who persists in creating "time and space . . . for freedom"[6] through the long journey of humankind. The symbols we thought would keep America above criticism may in fact subject us to it; the civil rights movement was a conspicuous example of biblical symbols being transposed from sanctification to judgment.

Civil religion is inevitable. But we reject the contention that it is a ready asset for liberation theology. Liberation theology, however, could become a new civil religion in American society. One of the ways in which that new version would be different is in its disposition toward suspicion. Liberation theology has been marked by a prophetic distrust of the prevailing order and the ways in which it institutionalizes privilege and creates oppression. Social transformation alone will not ensure that the interests of some will coexist easily with the vulnerabilities of others. New systems and orders reflect the persons who created them and are never free of their perspectives. The new civil religion will not lower its guard on self-interest and its intensification in institutions. "Our" people and "our" values at the centers of power do not guarantee the implementation of liberation. The habit of suspicion cannot abate simply because "the city" has "new foundations" and new leadership.

A civil religion shaped by liberation theology will both undermine the structures fostering individualism and affirm and celebrate community. "The body of Christ" professed in the Eucharist has a public and therefore a political content. Part of what that means is that *we* are a people before *I* am a person; indeed, personhood emerges in the framework of human solidarity. The body is one and not a collection of parts. The understanding of a shared reality means that our own "good" and that of others are inseparable. The book of Acts speaks of a day in the early church when "the heart of the multitude of believers was one and their soul was one, and not a single one said anything of what he had was his, but all things were in common. . ." (Acts 4:32). This is usually envisioned as a condition in which private resources are pooled. As individuals we "kick in" what is ours. If, as we have argued in relation to private property, the universe is on loan, then everything belongs to all, and distribution should follow need rather than greed. What being "born again" really means is not personal salvation but social solidarity. It is not a private process of getting the soul right with some ultimate entity but assuming one's place in a community and accepting the responsibility for neighborly need. The meeting of that need does not mean charity or good works but human interdependence and mutuality.

It might appear as if we are thinking of a time in which the nation has become a church. That should not be the consequence of liberation theology as a civil religion. Neither do we propose to make the church obsolete. Rather, its nature and mission will undergo significant transformation. One of the clear developments that will occur in North America we already see in Latin America, where liberation theology poses a threat to the traditional ecclesial order. There the power base is emerging from below through the basic communities, and the Vatican establishment is responding as though threatened. When Father Leonardo Boff of Brazil began to suggest how the Gospel, which had been transforming the world, would transform the church he was silenced for a year.

In North America we are also envisioning a "people's church" with considerable authority residing in the laity. Decentralization of American churches has its risk factor; it could parallel what has happened when certain functions were defederalized and left to those closest to the scene. Localization can be a setback. The difference is that members of grassroots organizations such as basic communities are the ones who have participated in setting out social justice. They are likely to demand what the local elite often mouth platitudinously.

Part of what we are saying is that the hierarchical nature of the church will be dismantled and the community of faith will reflect its own interests and mission. What will be distinctive about "the church from below" is that human solidarity and sensitivity will be given full play. The faith will not be articulated in reference to persons and their private talks with God but to the community and its sense of justice for all. The dominant reality will be a liberated humanity, not saved souls.

The church, then, is a community of discernment. Its function through the ages has been to announce the forces of life and denounce the forces of death. And the proclamation of the resurrection Gospel is the faith that through "the justice of God" life defeats death. This means that liberation theology has focused on the prophetic, yet there is a pastoral ministry to be assumed as well by the people for one another. We suggest that the model of the Good Samaritan, rightly understood, might control the style of the caring. What strikes one about the Samaritan is that he was so "efficient and unsentimental."[7] For a man beaten, robbed and left to die, he simply did the things that needed to be done. When he left the victim at the inn to recuperate he agreed to pay if more was needed. Nothing is said in the story about the man's motives. Certainly the question of a charitable deduction never arose. The Samaritan responded because he was needed. The parable is distorted if we think it is a lesson in private heroism. Biblical writers always think from within a community and the flow of life between person and person. The pastoral ministry of the church likewise should be not only lay-centered but marked by this kind of reciprocal response to need as it arises.

Liberation theology not only establishes the primacy of the prophetic and requires a change in the pastoral ministry, it also affects the priestly ministry in its celebration of the faith and our life in the world. What will be different is what it celebrates. The church has a habit of becoming an apologist for the status quo. The malignant alliance between the power structures in Latin America and the Roman Catholic clergy is only more subtly manifest in the alignment of Jerry Falwell with Ronald Reagan and Billy Graham's relationships with Richard Nixon and Lyndon Johnson. The church shaped by a liberation theology will not celebrate the life of the nation or revel in any association with the elite; it will celebrate the victory of life over death and stand guard over the exercise of power. The role of the church is not to bless the prevailing order but to proclaim a "Crucified God" who suffers under the conditions of historical existence and acts always and only for the triumph of justice.[8]

Idolatry, Transcendence, and Sustaining a Horizon

It is precisely what drives the new order that is at issue in a dimension of the Exodus story we have not considered. The Exodus has functioned both as a discernment of the condition of powerlessness, and as a way to attach a people to their destiny as a "liberating humanity" under a "liberating God." However, between the slavery of Egypt and the glory of the promised land lies the time of our lives in which we are drawn back to what was before as well as attracted to what lies ahead. The present is the moment in which a people are forever electing the past or enacting the future. The cultural tradition of the Israelites included the realization that the burden of choice was theirs. While they understood themselves to be set in motion by a God who heard their cry of suffering, they also knew they had again and again to choose to be chosen.

The ownership of liberation is apparent in the story of the golden calf; it becomes the choice of Yahweh as a domesticated idol or as a constant horizon. It may never have occurred to Moses that his delay on Mount Sinai would provide his people with the opportunity to forfeit their destiny. His brother Aaron responded to the people's anxiety and uncertainty in ways Moses would not. While liberation from slavery was a source of joy, living with freedom and its responsibilities became a burden. Being free of Moses and the mission to which he held them was almost irresistible. The people approached Aaron with the words, "Up, make us gods, who shall go ahead of us; as for this Moses, the man who brought us up out of the land of Egypt, we do not know what has become of him" (Exod. 32:1). The unspoken message in their words suggests their wish for a swift and immediate substitution. They wanted to replace Moses with "gods, who shall go ahead of us." They no longer wanted to be led by one who held them to the future but by an idol who would reassure them. Aaron responded, "Take off the rings of gold which are in the ears of your wives, your sons, and your daughters, and bring them to me" (Exod. 32:2). When they offered their jewelry "he received the gold at their hand, and fashioned it with a graving tool, and made a molten calf; and they said, 'these are your gods, O Israel . . .' " (Exod. 32:4). And they worshiped them.

In understanding the event, it is important to recognize that "[t]he golden calf did not represent 'another god,' nor did it purport to be a representation of Yahweh. The Israelites were simply constructing the seat, the throne, the symbol of the presence of Yahweh in their midst."[9] In a real sense the Israelites wanted to be free of the God of Moses in order to have Yahweh under their control. They wanted to transform God from "God-leader-out-of-slavery" to "God-consoler-in-oppression."[10] The golden calf gave them a god on their own terms, not one who would set terms for them. Idols comfort; transcendence claims! The Israelites might not have understood what theologians take for granted: that the ways in which we think about God determine the ways in which we think about ourselves. But it was evident to them that if they could get a god "in their midst," diminish the transcendence in God, they would be liberated from a liberating mission. A domesticated god one can live with; a transcendent god one must live toward. Idols consort with complacency; the God of the horizon sets us toward a promised land.

The American middle sector is composed of those for whom "the liberating God" is not a symbol that gathers in meaning or mobilizes purpose. And there are others whose fixation on God is not connected at all with the image of *liberation*. We would not advance an argument that attempts to establish the truth of language about God. Rather, we are interested in what is made true by the actions of the middle sector in history. The significant referent for those in the middle sector ought to be primarily "liberating" rather than "God," as Sharon Welch puts it in *Communities of Resistance and Solidarity*.[11] We do not want the truth to rest on the divine nature or existence of God but on what enables human liberation. Historically, "[t]he truth of God-language and of all theological claims is measured not by their correspondence to something eternal but by the fulfillment of its claims in history, by the actual creation of communities of peace, justice, and equality."[12] The golden calf was a creation of a people who no longer wanted to understand themselves as obligated to enact the conditions of liberation. We take the word "God" and the transcendence it represents as the means by which we hold ourselves to a horizon which can never be reduced to something "in our midst."

All who are members of the middle "class" may recognize ourselves as readily in the golden calf episode as in any dimension of the Exodus narrative. Our tolerance for the transcendence of God is as fragile as that of the Israelites. We may be even more vulnerable in that we have no memory of slavery and have been surrounded by the convictions that we are already in the promised land. However, the choice between life and death is ours daily; doing liberation is a mission we can both own and reject. While the image of slavery does not fit our plight, we do have entrapments. These entrapments are evident in three experiences. The conjunction of highly individualistic values and the reality of American society leave us experiencing a *lack of identity* and an increasingly *precarious economic existence*, within a system that makes us *powerless* to bring about change in our daily lives. Like the Israelites, the American middle class has turned the status quo into its own golden calf. Even though it is exasperating when these experiences limit horizons, they are embraced because they make no demands.

The three problems experienced by the middle sector do interconnect. Identity is at risk because our lives and our work serve goals that are not personally and humanly fulfilling. Our individualism and the nature of our socioeconomic system lead us to think we should create our identity in terms of our work experience. Yet, if our identity derives from profoundly unfulfilling experiences, then it is little wonder either that we feel a lack of identity, or that we are engaged in a frantic search for identity.

When we examine why our identity is so unfulfilling, we come up against the problem of powerlessness. Most of us in the middle layer of American society have responsible jobs and earn reasonable incomes. We are limited, however, in the ability to control the conditions under which we do those jobs. Oftentimes we cannot even make important decisions about the job itself, about the questions that will be addressed or the kinds of decisions that will be made. This creates frustration and anger but gives no constructive outlet for those feelings. We know intuitively that our existence should be different, that we should be more in control, but we think we are unable to change the conditions of existence. Despite the fact that we are comfortable materially and seem to have at least some derived power, this deeper malaise makes everything we do appear unimportant and meaningless.

Powerlessness places material comfort at risk as well. If we work in the private sector, we never know when our employer may declare bankruptcy as the steel company, LTV Corporation, did in 1986, or when the whole operation may move to another state or country, as have so many firms in the computer industry. We can do nothing to influence such decisions and, once made, those decisions may have extensive and unpredictable effects on our lives. The fact that our search for meaning is influenced by our economic existence makes the outcome from precarious economic circumstances all the more devastating. The loss of a job can deal our fragile egos and identities a crushing blow.

If we work in the public sector, dramatic changes in circumstances are also possible. The Reagan administration has decimated the social service agencies of the federal government. Many people have suffered job loss or demotion and have witnessed the virtual destruction of programs in which they have invested much of their working life. That has meant a dramatic change in their economic circumstances, but it also appears to trivialize their accomplishments. They, too, have found themselves powerless to resist the impulses and decisions of the political elite. The destruction of their work has created a sense of meaninglessness every bit as deep as that experienced in the private sector.

Given the interconnected experiences of loss of identity, precarious economic circumstances, and powerlessness, what can the middle layers do about it? Is there any different way to organize the structural relations in the society so that we can begin to empower the whole laboring class, create a meaningful identity out of a renewed class consciousness, and turn economic precariousness into economic security? Can we make these experiences work for us, turning them into an upward spiral improving the human condition rather than the present whirlpool that is sucking all of us into dehumanization?

The golden calf episode in the life of Israel represents a moment in which they forfeited their mission and settled for a modest advance over their past. They chose a domesticated Yahweh as an idol who comforted them within their limits. The Israelites tired of a God whose transcendence instituted impatience and rage against an order in which justice was sacrificed on the altar of security. The God of Moses held them to the future, and to the suffering always brought on by the birthing of the impossible. For the American middle class the golden calf represents a choice. We can choose our own submersion in history, accepting the lack of identity, the economic precariousness, and the powerlessness. Or we can melt down the golden calf and do liberation. We can seize a social heroism in which a vision of ourselves as part of a larger class overcomes our lack of identity, and empowerment for freedom shatters our economic precariousness.

The argument of this book has moved from the premise that a new social heroism is needed in America and that the middle fraction in solidarity with other segments of our society is integral to that mission. We are those people who have stood within the system and accepted its terms and the limited future it defines. But as part of the laboring class we can stand against the present order of American society and radically transform the circumstances of our existence.

We share with Robert Bellah and his colleagues in *Habits of the Heart* a sense of urgency and frustration. We do not agree that the prospect of "a morally coherent life" is simply contingent on "the kind of people we are—on our character."[13] While the social order may be an expression of "the habits of the heart," we do not believe that simply tampering with beliefs and practices is the solution. The true scale of the problem is not addressed by a modification of individualism and commitment. The prospect of a new future rides on the determination to understand ourselves as part of a class and create new orders and institutions in American society. The social heroism we seek calls upon all of us to restore mutuality and reciprocity as the themes of human existence and to construct social orders that express and sustain them.

The debate between individualism and collectivity is as old as it is futile. The formation of the issue generally implies that we have either to sacrifice our uniqueness or our bonds with one another. That is an alien dichotomy to the biblical tradition as well as others. Americans like to think of existence as drab in socialist countries; the presumption is that the price of giving some primacy to the common good is the demise of individuality. Any review, however, of corporate attire and social mores in American business leaves one wondering where the real representation of drabness exists. The images of mutuality and reciprocity join personal and social identity in ways that presume both individualism and human solidarity.

The biblical tradition differs from contemporary society in that it never attends simply to the question "Who am I?" Biblical writers are concerned with the question "Who are we?" Social identity is primary; individual identity is derivative. Tracing the story of the Exodus as it threads its way through the life of Israel reveals a people who are forever remembering what God did to make them who they are. Personal identity was fashioned in the context of mutuality of social identity. The contrast between the biblical mentality and our own emerges at an interesting point. While we are interested in the boundaries of personality, they are intent upon the boundaries of community. The issue is not where do my individual rights end but who is included in our community, who is our neighbor? The issue of limits hinges on the social rather than the personal realm.

As long as individualism is a dominant mode of existence, efforts to address lack of identity and a pervasive powerlessness expressed in economic precariousness are exercises in futility. We are like addictive mall shoppers who hope that one of their purchases will finally establish who they really are. The social heroism proposed here does address the three haunting human experiences in the American reality. Beginning in mutuality, it confronts our lack of identity with the notion we are part of a class, our powerlessness with the empowerment that comes as we choose together to set the conditions of our future, and our economic precariousness with the security of a people joined together in a more equitable community.

Signposts on the Journey

In thinking about the future we wish to avoid the pitfalls of providing one more utopian blueprint. Continuing the biblical analogy, we do not want to tender our own vision of the promised land. To do so would only be a return to all of those misguided middle class visionaries of the past, from at least the Enlightenment on, who so willingly assumed the mantle of intellectual leadership in movements for social change. It is this kind of presumptuousness, based on arrogant assumptions of the superiority of "head" workers, that we want to avoid.

Ours is the more modest, yet still formidable, goal of suggesting possible signposts on the journey. We lack the utopian certainty of a Fourier, for example, confidently providing descriptions for his "phalanxes" of the future, down to the disposal of the garbage. Our signposts represent tentative options, rather than detailed prescriptions. If we in the middle agree that our position is increasingly meaningless, precarious, and powerless, then these guides may be plausible alternatives for how we might act given our similarities with other laboring class fractions.

By providing a sketch of alternatives we do not presume to write for the working layers or the poor. Any coalition of the laboring class would have to involve a conversation among the participants. That is essential to the meaning of coalition, as an alliance based on the recognition of both common and disparate interests. This same modesty, however, in the matter of signposts, must also apply to the middle layers. Conversations with peers in the middle generally should also take the form of a dialogue. There is no point anywhere in this process of thinking about social change where either the "word" or the "Word" can come down from on high. Justice begins from below. It is in that spirit we offer our own contributions to the ongoing conversation and action.

As we confront our situation, it is important to remember that there are institutional arrangements that increasingly lead to the concentration of economic and political power in fewer hands. The powerlessness of all in the laboring class fractions needs to be explored in relation to those arrangements. In a similar way, the continued economic insecurity of the poor and working fractions and the growing insecurity of the middle layers need to be examined against the corporate, financial, and property structures which serve to increase and concentrate the economic security of the few.

All of that takes place in a framework where the dominant values are those of the elite. The middle fraction in particular worships individualism because we see individual members of the elite who have wealth, income, power, and lifestyles we envy. We accept material wealth as the measure of success and as the outward manifestation of the difference between those elites and ourselves. In some subtle and not so subtle ways we have a derivative identity, not grounded in our own existence, but in a vicarious attachment to the lifestyles of the rich and famous. When we do search for meaning in our own existence, we cannot find it; we expect meaning to come in the form of the same wealth, income, and power which the elite has and we covet.

Changing all of that requires both individual and structural moves. Bellah is correct in contending that the search for individual meaning in society requires a change in the "habits of the heart." We can find or create new meaning for ourselves which accords with the reality of our existence. The search for that new meaning, however, must take place in present historical conditions with all their structural entrapments, not in some idealized past. Despite Bellah's claims, the American past probably never did contain a golden era of community that can be recovered by returning to some historical values.

In this book, we claim that the search for new meaning must be accompanied by corresponding changes in those institutional arrangements that concentrate power and economic security. These new meanings, for us, must also be ideological stories by which unjust institutions can be restructured. If not, such a search for new meaning would seem to be another of those personal tasks that reinforce individualism. That is the other flaw in Bellah's approach, a failure to understand that some of the reasons for middle Americans' derivative identity rest in the tight box of institutional arrangements that keep us from imagining anything different.

Changing things, then, requires two intertwining courses. One looks to the small, individual things that can be done to realign human values and help to create a more meaningful identity. The other asks us to build the political, economic, and social coalitions that are necessary to create counter-institutions. These can challenge and supplant those existing structures that create powerlessness, feed insecurity, and force the adoption of derivative identities. We cannot pursue either course by itself. The first would only lead to an asocial consciousness without changing the powerlessness and precariousness of the many. The second would seduce us into believing we were creating change when all we would really do is replace one set of dominant and dehumanizing institutions with another.

Must the middle sector become schizophrenic? Or are there some choices that will move us along both courses at the same time without splitting up our energies so that drives for change trail off into nothingness? There are some steps that can at the same time move us forward and keep us whole. First, what are those institutional arrangements that are the most limiting and dehumanizing? Then, are there some individual moves that will allow us to create an authentic rather than a derived identity? Next, are there counter-institutions that can grow out of that individual behavior and create an effective alternative to those limiting and dehumanizing institutions that are now dominant? Finally, can we develop or recapture symbol systems that will give rise to new ideological stories that will allow us to engage in social heroism?

Institutional Obstacles

We have discussed at length a variety of existing institutional arrangements that limit the possibilities for human fulfillment.

The task here is to identify the most serious structural problems, which should be the first targets for change. Among economic institutions, private property and large corporations offer particularly pernicious obstacles to the search for a more socially responsive society.

There are four elements in this analysis that we consider to be important: (a) the almost unlimited rights to private property, (b) the concentration of economic decision-making power in the hands of very large industrial corporations, in part at least reflecting the extension of property rights to those corporations, (c) the tight control over financial assets and credit exercised by a very small group of extremely large financial corporations, and (d) the powerful role of both public and private bureaucracies in providing information and making decisions that dramatically affect all of our lives.

Private property is symbolically important in American society. We have explored reasons for that in some depth in chapter 3. If private property is to continue to exist and become a socially useful institution, then the rights to use corporate property must be sharply curtailed. All the legal arrangements with regard to property rights must begin to move toward diffusion rather than concentration of ownership. Much of the concern about the negative quality of private property relates to its use or misuse by corporations. It is necessary to reorganize our legal arrangements in order to make corporate private property rights subordinate to, rather than equal to, individual property rights.

Much of the concentration of economic power that contributes to powerlessness and insecurity comes about because of corporate ownership of the means of production. Under any new set of private property arrangements, ownership of the means of production cannot reside with the corporations in the same way it does now. Such ownership will have to be more diffuse, either through a broad-based program of worker ownership, public ownership, or some mix of both. Current patterns of concentrated ownership and management create oligopoly industries such as national defense, autos, appliances, or steel. Firms in these industries often look only for acceptable rather than max-imum profit. The principal goals of corporate leadership tend to be survival and the maintenance of the power of the managerial elite. But those goals do not necessarily serve the interests of workers or the general needs of society. If corporate decisions about the use of capital plant and the implementation of new technology are subject to approval by broadly based worker co-alitions or by the public sector, then much of the abuse that cur-rently flows from concentration of ownership can be eliminated.

Finally, one of the abuses that sanctification of private property creates is the elevation of property rights over human rights. Again, legal structures must be recreated so that no right to property can be so sacrosanct that society must countenance poverty, homelessness, and malnutrition rather than infringe upon the right to use property as we wish.

The power of industrial corporations to make economic decisions flows from the concentration of corporate ownership. Since the ownership of the means of production confers such power, it has created an adversarial relationship between a corporate elite and the working fraction of the laboring class. This shows up in the rise of the labor union movement in the early 1900s, in labor-management relationships, and in the current efforts to blame non-competitiveness in American industry on "high" labor costs. The middle fraction of the laboring class has consistently operated the bureaucratic structures for those in charge. We in the middle have aligned our values with those of the elite, and this has blinded us to our similarities with the rest of the laboring class. One result has been a reflection of the elite–working class adversarial relationship in our own relationship with the working fraction. We are too ready to blame the unions and labor for all the ills of American industry. Once again, it is a structural relationship—our own bureaucratic positions and the material comfort which flows from them—that puts the blinders on us. It keeps us from recognizing that the elite manipulate most of our symbols and thus control our destiny.

We are powerless because power has been concentrated in the structural relationships under which we live. Very large industrial corporations, operating on the basis of their own internal logic, make decisions about the kinds of products to be produced and the organization and location of the production process, without consulting the members of the laboring class. Whether we are part of the poor, working, or middle fractions of the laboring class, our opinion and our needs are not important for the corporation. What is important is the maintenance of a reasonable rate of return, the locus of decision-making power among the elite, and the right to make whatever moves they consider desirable. All of these goals are achieved most of the time because the legal status of business corporations protects them from interference.

In 1986 the second largest American steel company, LTV Corporation, claimed protection from its creditors under Chapter 11 of the federal bankruptcy statutes. Corporate mismanagement and a depressed market for steel left the company unable to meet its debt obligations. As a result, many employees lost their jobs, some supplying corporations were forced out of business, and retirement and medical fringe benefits were seriously at risk for employees who had given most of their working lives to the corporation. At the same time, in a kind of "Alice in Wonderland" illogic, the LTV 1985 annual report shows that the corporation's chief executive officer received a $162,000 "performance bonus" in addition to his $530,000 annual salary. Just exactly what chief executive "performance" is there to be rewarded in a corporation that lost $781 million in one year?

There is ample evidence to indicate that LTV as well as the entire American steel industry is facing an enormous crisis brought on by two factors: the slow growth in the world market and the rapid decline in productive efficiency in comparison with Japanese, Korean, and Western European producers. The first problem is a predictable cyclical phenomenon in capitalist economies. The second, however, results from the confluence of strong markets in the 1950s and 1960s and oligopoly power in the American steel industry. As the dominant steel producers in the twenty-five years following World War II, the relatively small number of American companies could share the world market and go on making comfortable profits even though their physical plant and their technology were rapidly becoming obsolete. Since they had to answer only to themselves, their decisions about the use of resources and the reinvestment of profits reflected only a private use mentality. As a result, they were able to ignore the interests of workers as well as general social needs.

When the stagflation of the 1970s struck, the world market began to shrink, and more efficient steel firms in the rest of the world began to take the lion's share of the market. The United States simply could not compete, but not because labor costs were too high or the Japanese engaged in unfair competition. In fact, the real source of the problem is an outmoded technology and a dilapidated physical plant, both of which have slowly deteriorated into obsolescence due to years of neglected investment. Instead of plowing profits back into investment projects that would make the industry healthy and efficient, big steel management chose to engage in mergers and acquisitions, distribute more profit to stockholders, and pay excessive management salaries. This accompanied a strategy to create labor peace with high wages and large fringe benefits. Even after the 1981 Reagan tax cut generated large new cash flows and after-tax profits by increasing depreciation write-offs in an effort to stimulate business investment, the steel industry did not respond by modernizing. Rather, it engaged in a wave of mega-mergers both inside and outside the industry, none of which seem to have made either the individual firms or the industry better able to compete with foreign steel.

Reharnessing the productive power of America to make it serve human need must involve an end to the kinds of corporate structures and legal arrangements that allow situations like that of the big steel companies to emerge. If the growth of oligopoly power in the steel industry had been sharply curtailed, individual firms would have been forced by domestic competition to modernize their plants and become more efficient. We would not have had to wait for an international market crisis to reveal their inferiority and inability to compete with foreign steel.

It is equally important to be wary of unbridled competition, since that tends inevitably to lead to the very accumulation that creates oligopoly and monopoly power. In the late 1970s, the Congress and the economists were congratulating themselves on the fantastic benefits resulting from deregulation of the airline industry. Despite their reluctance to face deregulation, the airlines found themselves in an era of higher profits and lower prices. That rosy picture has been tarnished by large-scale losses because some carriers cannot fill up their flights even with very low prices. There is now a wave of mergers hitting the industry, which some analysts believe will leave us with as few as seven major carriers, all considerably larger and more powerful than they were before deregulation. Consumers may be happy with current low airfares, but that pleasant condition will not prevail for long once the new giants in the industry begin to flex their oligopolistic muscles.

It is not simply size or competitiveness that damages the social welfare as business corporations pursue their own well-being. The damage is due more fundamentally to the nature of the private property rights and the extension of those rights to corporations, together with the lack of any social control over investment decisions. It is these phenomena that allow corporations to grow larger in the first place, and then to use the power of size and accumulated wealth to protect themselves from competition. No matter what is done to reorganize the management and internal distribution of power in corporations, as long as their property rights remain unchallenged, the businesses will continue to serve their own interests, often in contradiction to the common good. Reorganization of corporations to allow more egalitarian decision making and a different distribution of profit will at best only temporarily alleviate the problem. While corporations maintain complete control over the investment in and use of capital, the same abuses of corporate power will continue to exist.

Industrial corporations, of course, are not the only source of economic power in the society. Much of that decision making is dictated by financial institutions, and their power is stronger today than ever before. That is why problems like Third World debt and weak savings and loan institutions in the United States pose such a threat to the existing economic arrangements. Easy and constant availability of credit is the lifeblood of modern industrial societies, whether they are capitalist or socialist. Anything that threatens that availability poses a far greater threat to our economy than recession. Since the power to control credit is concentrated in the hands of a small number of banks and insurance companies, a few failures or bad decisions can severely damage the monetary fabric of the society.

Just as in the case of industrial corporations, financial institutions have accumulated vast wealth because of extensive private property rights. Their use of that wealth in the pursuit of more wealth is often at odds with the best interests of the society. Yet neither the laboring class in general nor the middle fraction in particular can do much to counteract this power. When they make too many loans to Mexico and are then threatened by Mexico's inability to pay, the rest of us are damaged by the unavailability or high cost of personal credit. We are also hurt indirectly as the corporations for which we work find credit harder to get and more expensive. That can cost us income and jobs.

Here, too, deregulation in order to create more competition does not necessarily help. The Deregulation and Monetary Control Act of 1979, ballyhooed as the harbinger of a new era of competitiveness in American financial markets, has instead led to a wave of mergers. Financial institutions have fought to acquire more oligopoly power and thus protect themselves against competition.

Reduction in the size of financial corporations, and more social control over their investment and lending decisions, are necessary if we are to turn the power of financial ownership to the service of social need. The current trend toward the merger of financial, industrial, and retail corporations must certainly be stopped if we wish to avoid a society held hostage to the interests and bad decisions of financiers.

The preponderance of bureaucratic power is the final element that must be addressed to restructure the arrangements that dominate and condition our lives. Earlier chapters have argued that bureaucracy is necessary in a society like ours in order to simplify the economic, political, and social decision-making process. At the same time, bureaucratic structures tend to take on a life of their own and reshape society in their own image. They may also continue to exist long past the time when they have served out their usefulness to society.[14]

There is a tendency to think of bureaucratic problems in terms of the government sector, and there are certainly a number of areas where public bureaucracy damages the social welfare. Consider all those institutions that establish rules that defy common sense. How many of us have gone to get a driver's license or a building permit only to be shunted from office to office in a maze of red tape? The damage may be compounded when two or more agencies establish bureaucratic rules for some activity and the rules conflict. State development agencies make all sorts of concessions in order to attract new industries and new jobs. At the same time, state environmental protection agencies are trying to protect their populations against increased pollution. The differences in the application of these development and environmental strategies among states often leave the people unable to control the situation. That is, we are trapped between our needs for jobs and our needs to be protected from environmental damage, and the bureaucracy provides us no help in coping with our situation.

The final area of concern with public bureaucracy may be the most subtle and, therefore, the most dangerous. This occurs when an agency seems to have responsibility for establishing rules to protect the public but actually fails in that protection because certain problems fall through bureaucratic "cracks." The Federal Drug Administration is an example. We assume that FDA testing assures the safety of various medical products. We are constantly discovering, however, already approved products that cause cancer, birth defects, or other medical problems.

We often forget that the private sector has bureaucratic structures that give rise to equally dehumanizing and socially pernicious behavior. We all know someone who has bought a new car that was a lemon. Instead of an appropriate response from the auto manufacturer, the victim often gets a run-around among the sales department, the customer relations department, the legal department, and so on. No one wants to take responsibility for the consumers' problems, and the bureaucratic nature of the decision-making process allows each department to avoid accountability. Similarly, when we find an incorrect charge on a credit card bill, a long, involved process is necessary to get it corrected. Sometimes, the computer becomes a bureaucratic obstacle, one that will not listen to its human masters. When that happens, the problem may hang on for months.

Of course, each of these private-sector examples is only annoying. They may make us feel individually powerless, but do not by themselves make all of the laboring class fractions unable to control what is happening. More dangerous bureaucratic quagmires arise when large corporations have so many semi-autonomous subsidiaries that the decisions of one are counteracted by the decisions of the others. There has been a serious concern about hazardous waste disposal in the United States in the past ten years. That dangerous chemicals are dumped is not simply the result of a conspiracy among corporate leaders. With the approval of top management, a corporation's environmental department sets down stringent rules about safe disposal. At the same time, corporate headquarters demands cost-cutting to increase profit. A production division is caught between costly demands to dump wastes safely and the pressure to raise profits. The result may be unsafe dumping and serious damage to the environment and societal welfare. It is important to recognize this as not an individual evil, but rather an institutional evil, a kind of corporate "sin" caused by a conflict between bureaucratic goals.

Correcting the problems of bureaucracy has been the subject of innumerable books and monographs as well as a series of Presidential commissions. It seems to us that most of these are wrong-headed in the sense that they attempt to reduce the existing bureaucracy by eliminating government agencies or business departments and subsidiaries. A more useful approach is to create conditions that more automatically control the spread and thus the power of bureaucratic decision making. For example, in the public sector, a simple expedient would be that no department or agency could be created without provision for an automatic review and evaluation after a certain number of years. The legislature and executive would have to make a positive decision to keep each agency at its point of review, not simply a "no decision" which allows it to continue to exist. Failure to serve the social welfare effectively would be sufficient grounds not to renew an agency.

The same logic might also prevail in the business sector among both industrial and financial corporations. In addition, the suggestions made earlier about limiting corporate size and property rights, and creating more social control over the use of the means of production, would also serve to limit the negative impacts of bureaucratic decision making in the private sector. It is important to reiterate that we do not and indeed could not advocate the elimination of bureaucracy in either the public or private sector. It serves too many useful functions in rationally organizing the economic, political, and social decision-making process for anyone ever to contemplate a total elimination of it. Instead, we in the middle sector must strive to control the ability of bureaucracy to constrict our lives as individuals and to render us powerless as a class.

Individual Moves Toward an Authentic Identity

Since we in the American middle layers have such an attachment to individualism, it is assumed that the process of change must begin with the individual. Social structures, however, do take on a life of their own. Nevertheless, if society and the individual are inherently connected, social change must imply changing individuals. If individual moves do not result in structural change they will ultimately change nothing. Where, then, can a person in the middle fraction find an opportunity to initiate meaningful change?

When we explore the role individuals can play in moving toward significant structural change, we must examine the kinds of decisions they make. In the economic sphere, persons decide which goods to buy and about borrowing, depositing, and investing personal financial resources. To a limited extent they decide where and for whom they want to work. Politically, individuals decide whether they want to vote and for whom. In addition, there are often state and local issues including tax levies and constitutional and legal changes on the ballot. They also have choices about joining and being active in political parties and special interest political action groups. Even the choice to run for various political offices is partially open to the individual. In terms of social relationships, individuals are free to participate in at least some of a wide variety of interpersonal interactions. Of more concern for our purposes, there are a myriad of social and civic organizations available for membership.

When we, as individuals, make decisions about buying goods and services, it may be possible to buy them from businesses that do not have large-scale corporate structures. We *can* buy our food from local grocers or from food co-ops. In our financial decisions, we *can* do careful research in order to borrow, deposit, or invest with those financial institutions that have the least amount of interaction with the financial conglomerates that control the international money markets. We *can* do our best to make certain that our deposits and financial investments are not being used to further the international arms race or to support the regime in South Africa. Although decisions about place and kind of work are more constrained by availability and by the need to support ourselves and our dependents, we *can* nevertheless try to find jobs where work activity neither overtly nor implicitly supports worker exploitation.

These moves are not without personal cost. Buying "local" rather than from national chains may be more expensive. The same is true for relationships with financial organizations. The cost of credit and the return for investment is, at least in part, dependent upon the quantity of financial resources available. Large financial institutions have far more resources available; they can lend more cheaply and find the best opportunities for investment, thus often paying the highest rates of return. Even when there are "local" suppliers of goods or financial services—for example, the co-op or the credit union—they are often connected with large corporations and the international money markets as sources of supply and credit. The work and time involved in doing the research that allows these decisions to be made makes searching out the small, non-conglomerate producers and financial institutions even more expensive. Nevertheless, such moves represent a significant personal choice which can ultimately help to change the overall societal structures. It would be foolish to claim that such decisions by an individual would be sufficient. However, when many individuals start to make such choices, their effect will be felt.

Many Americans in the middle fraction have some contact with politics. We vote, are active in supporting or fighting local issues, and make contributions to political candidates and causes. These political actions are not usually conceived of as playing a role in reshaping the society. Nonetheless, they can. In acting politically, whether in the form of personal votes, or in support for candidates and causes, we are sometimes able to make choices that express more communal and less individualistic values. We can write letters, join or create political action groups, and engage in civil disobedience, all aimed at the reordering of society's priorities. Again, actions by one individual are not significant, but if we can convince more and more of the middle fraction in particular and the laboring class in general to join with us, the political structures can be changed.

In chapter 1 the American middle fraction was described as "the joiners in a nation of joiners." While that is true, it rarely has had any fundamental political or structural consequences. Participation tends to be either altruistic or focused on single-issue politics. Civic organizations may sponsor need-based college scholarships or raise money for local food pantries. We may even recycle or focus on environmental problems. In almost all cases, however, joining is viewed as an individual act, and the organization is seen as a group of individuals doing something for the society or community. The notion of doing something *to* the community or society is very foreign to us. Groups like Kiwanis, Rotary, or Lions often provide scholarship money *for* the local community. They are never engaged in trying to change the *nature* of funding for education, an action which might do something *to* the society by fundamentally changing the educational conditions for many.

As a joiner, then, one can find those organizations that seem to be doing the most to challenge the status quo. It may indeed be a sign of the times that organizations that would once have been part of the counterculture, such as "peace with justice" committees, now are filling their membership roles with people from the middle sectors. It is even plausible to join "establishment" organizations such as Kiwanis, Lions, and Rotary and try to direct their actions in ways that are more overtly political and aimed at change. The May 1987 United States Supreme Court decision forbidding sex discrimination by Rotary International came about when the local Rotary club in Duarte, California, admitted women in violation of Rotary bylaws. The club's charter was revoked in 1978 by the state and national organizations. Litigation continued[15] until the recent decision by the Supreme Court struck down the prohibition against female membership.

While these moves begin with things that individuals can do to help bring about structural change, most of them involve at least some implicit cooperation, if not the overt creation or redirection of organizations. Our world contains many pernicious institutional and structural arrangements that serve to intensify the insecurity, powerlessness, and lack of identity that characterize the lives of all of us in the laboring class. These individual actions can be effective only if they lead to the creation of counter-institutions aimed at replacing private ownership and the corporate power ethic with a system that has mutuality, reciprocity, and community at its center.

Counter-Institutions

In American society there are also organizations that began as strangled cries by or for oppressed groups. When such groups focused their efforts on the appropriate dominant institutions, they were able to create counter-institutional power and use it to bring about fundamental structural change. Some good examples are the abolitionist movement in the mid-nineteenth century and the labor union movement during and after the 1880s. And, of course, the civil rights organizations of the 1950s and 1960s brought about essential structural reforms by using their power to create access to public facilities and political office for Blacks in America.

These examples provide us with both models for bringing about institutional change and some caveats about the results. Change requires organization, mass, and perseverance. Movements such as labor unions were able to mold large numbers of individuals into a cohesive body, well organized over long periods of time, and finally to wear down their opponents. In each case, however, warnings are in order; the victories won were incomplete and the victorious became part of the establishment, stopping the pressure for change. The abolitionists did indeed help to bring about an end to slavery, but they never followed through with the kind of institutional changes necessary to create full human status for the former slaves. As a result, freed slaves and their descendants spent at least another one hundred years with declining economic circumstances, virtually no access to power, and an identity partially derived from the dominant white society.

The union movement of the late nineteenth century established the right of laborers to organize for contract negotiations and for mutual protection from exploitation. Their victory was accomplished only with violence on both sides followed by an uneasy peace. In many cases, however, that uneasy peace gave way to a pattern of corporate/labor union cooperation which for a long time ensured profits to management and high wages to labor. Some of the costs were higher prices for consumers and a pattern of racism and sexism in hiring that was clearly to the detriment of Blacks and women.

The point of these reservations is not to castigate the abolitionists or the labor unions. It is instead to point out the seductive attraction involved in accommodation with the existing power structure. Co-optation is a very real danger, and any organization attempting to act as a counter-institution faces that danger as a constant threat. The use and abuse of private property rights by large corporations, the corporate accumulation of wealth and power, and the spread and indifference of public and private bureaucracies are the source of economic precariousness, powerlessness, and lack of identity. Accommodation to those forces is not acceptable if we are to change our society into a humane and mutually cooperative one.

Many different organizations can become the counter-institutions that we believe are a necessary response to the problems of individual malaise in our society. The "peace and justice" groups mentioned previously are organizations that have espoused counter-institutional values in their demands for a nuclear-free world and social justice both domestically and internationally. Such groups seem, for the most part, to have understood the interconnection between the existing sources of power and the continued dominance of violence and injustice in our society and the world. Other organizations can also serve to "conscienticize" the middle layer's own ambivalent position vis-à-vis the dominant elite in our society. Individuals could combine, for example, to form a credit union as a way of protecting themselves against the concentration of financial power in the hands of big banks. The credit union could become more of a counter-institution by making its own investment and lending practices non-discriminatory and promoting worker control and other alternative businesses and business arrangements.

Individuals by themselves and especially as members of groups can bring pressure to bear on institutions of which they are a part. Such pressure can urge the institutions to take a stand for justice and humanization and to follow out that commitment in their economic, political, and social actions. Institutions can and should make statements upholding their fundamental moral, social, and political beliefs. "Institutional neutrality" is an ideological code word called forth by the establishment to pressure institutions into supporting the status quo. You never hear anyone claiming that institutions should be neutral when a college or a civic organization comes out in favor of current government policy or in support of dominant corporate interests. It is only when such organizations attack the positions of the elite that they are held up for scorn. The powers that be have never denigrated a foundation for buying stocks in corporations that do business in South Africa, but they certainly do not like it when institutions suggest divestment. In both cases, the foundation is taking a moral position, so the question is not taking positions, per se, but, what positions do you take?

The conscientization process, the mobilization of individual commitment, and the creation of counter-institutions will all take time. Because they are slow and painstaking processes, they may seem to be only evolutionary and thus doomed to co-optation and failure. But they can in their slow, inexorable way become "non-reformist reforms." These are reforms that seem on the surface to be only adaptations but create a new ideology and a new value system which ultimately cause the more fundamental structural changes necessary to build a new society.

Multiple Stories for a New Heroism

If society is *really* to be changed, then those in the middle layer must replace the dominant ideology of individualism and its associated values that allow the primacy of private property and the economic dominance of corporate power. We will conclude by identifying some new symbols that might give rise to a new ideology. Such a new ideology is necessary if we in the middle are to keep our focus and maintain our efforts to bring about real and radical change in American society under the leadership of a united laboring class.

The attempt to articulate a liberation theology in the context of the middle fraction is quite distinct from Black and feminist theologies, since there are not clear-cut social movements with which we can link. Our task is complicated by our lack of a social identity equivalent to those presupposed in other liberation theologies. When James Cone, for example, wrote his first book, he connected his theology with "Black Power."[16] Solidarity among Black Americans has been achieved to some significant degree by a movement whose initial goal was to create a social identity as an oppressed people destined for freedom. Cone's early work attached the language of faith to what was happening already in the Black community. He could argue that the coming together of Black people to affirm their dignity and rights is the movement of God, the breaking of the kingdom of God into human history.

In the first stages of Mary Daly's work, she tapped the

dynamic of the emerging women's movement and articulated it with theological and philosophical symbols.[17] The nature of the divine reality as a process of becoming, for example, was not only in accord with the coming of women to a separate identity but undergirded it as well. To think of God as "The Verb," rather than a noun, gave a dimension of ultimacy to the journey of women toward the fullness of their own humanity.

There is no comparable social bonding or political movement among the middle layers in American society. The most striking element is fragmentation. While we cannot claim to be oppressed, victimization is evident in the degree to which the creed of individualism and the dynamic of capitalism set us apart from each other. We are enclaves rather than a people. There is no pervasive social heroism upon which liberation can draw. As individuals we may have a personal identity, but it is not grounded in a social identity with any heroic aspirations. We may see ourselves as Americans, Ohioans, or Protestants, but those do not act as transforming identities. They are self-evident categories, not demanding images.

In the attempt to do liberation theology in the context of the American middle layer, there is a stark contrast with the first century and the biblical understanding of community. The individualism so dominant in American experience leads to an apparent preoccupation with uniqueness and self-actualization. We begin with a sense of separateness and seldom touch our strength in interrelational bonds. An authentic biblical existence would find us embedded within a community and ultimately empowered by our connections with that community. When entering a room of people, even a family gathering, we must find a way of emerging from self and some means of connecting with another "individuated center." The real moment of terror is the fleeting apprehension that we may not be able to get in touch or attach ourselves to another in a group. Our presumed goal of "standing on our own two feet" is precisely what makes the crowd so lonely and our footing so unsure. There is only passing comfort in the realization that all of us may have created our uniqueness through the same edition of a Talbot's or L. L. Bean catalogue. For Americans in the middle, community is a problem to be solved, and neither dress nor "in" discourse can do it for us. We work toward what we as persons most need; we are unable to assume community and work within it.

In the culture of the New Testament, human existence is understood as embedded in a social framework and characterized by interrelationships. What constitutes uniqueness is not what sets us apart from others, but what sets us within a given group. The community is that which is unique and distinctive, and the challenge is finding a way to be able to act as an individual at all.[18] The starting point was not estrangement but social solidarity. Neither the first-century culture nor the New Testament witnesses have much interest in individualism in our American senses of the term. To the extent that they thought of themselves as individuals, it was "in a sequence of embeddedness."[19] The presumption was that if you knew the community you knew the person. There are clear examples in the New Testament that one was known and understood by virtue of family, village, or city. Of Jesus the question was asked, "Can anything good come out of Nazareth?" (John 1:46) and "Is not this the carpenter, the son of Mary . . . ?" (Mark 6:3). Biblical writers worked from a clear sense of social indentity within which one's personal identity emerged.

Liberation theology in the middle cannot assume a shared social identity or a movement that bonds persons in the manner of women or Blacks. It does, of course, denounce the ideology of individualism. In all its social, economic, political, and psychological forms that ideology can prevent the fulfillment of pressing human needs. Individualism is ineffective in dealing with the structures and systems which perpetuate those needs. Liberation theology announces the centrality of reciprocity and mutuality which for us does not yet exist. The most significant biblical symbols—covenant, kingdom of God, body of Christ, and so on—all presuppose a social identity and solidarity within which personhood emerges. The imagery of faith assumes embeddedness and interrelationships.

Liberation theology does not begin in a concern for authentic personal existence, but in the prospect of authentic *social* existence. When it draws before us "the God of justice," the primary issue is not the rights of individuals, but the responsibility of persons within community. When it conceives of sin it is not some private infraction of the rules, but a violation of what sustains the community. When it envisions forgiveness, it is not a personal pardon, but a construction of new conditions for human fulfillment.

One of the reasons the biblical faith and its expression in liberation theology fail to "take" in American society is that they move from a condition of human solidarity that our absorption in individualism cannot conceive. This is why our argument does not embrace a change of heart as the sufficient condition for a new America. What we call for is a change of location. The call is not fulfilled in personal transformation alone, but the recognition of the middle layer as members of a larger class. Some biblical scholars might argue about whether or not class is an appropriate category within the biblical record, but it is essential to the response of the middle sector to the biblical claims.

In the context of Latin America, "conscientization" involves a people's recognition that they are submerged in history—that is, determined by it—and have a "vocation for freedom." In middle class America conscientization means coming to terms with the necessity of a class consciousness and the recognition that our interests and mission can only be served to the degree we create and sustain a condition of social embeddedness that does not yet fully exist. The laboring class is called to establish a social identity like that assumed in biblical times and brought into being through the Black and feminist movements.

We have struggled in vain for an image appropriate to the middle sector in the way that "Black Power" has energized that community. In time it may emerge. For now, we have to dedicate ourselves to enacting mutuality and reciprocity. Part of what that means is discerning and acting with those existing constituencies in our society that share a sense of embeddedness and interrelationships.

That which does unite the fractured but vibrant voices from the middle today is precisely their common *class* basis as laborers. What allows union rank-and-filers and college students to plan together for demonstrations on Central America, or "middle sector" churches to support the rights of migrant farm workers, is a recognition that we share real interests and have a core of common experiences. These are rooted in our economic system, with its vast social machinery harnessed to private benefit, which leads to or exacerbates the most intractable problems of our society. Racism, sexism, consumer powerlessness, environmental pollution and depletion, or the threat of nuclear oblivion can all in one form or another trace their peculiar shape or sheer presence to the elevation of individual gain in capitalism over social needs.

Yet with the intricate division of labor under which we live today, our protests against such problems take on an equally specialized quality; they seem unconnected, even antagonistic to each other. We might think to ourselves, what does the need for a job have to do with anti-nuclear campaigns? Our social movements tend to mirror our individualism, leading us to perceive society as a series of single issues, not as an interconnected system.

Americans do not like to think in class terms. Unlike Europeans, we are taught early that classes either do not exist, or they are so open as to be meaningless. We use images of America as the melting pot to capture our feeling of racial and ethnic homogeneity, but similar ideas pervade our views on class as well. It seems far preferable to most Americans to think in terms of consensus or homogeneity rather than reciprocity; witness the recent moves to make English the official language of California. Or we prefer to think of our individual uniqueness within a universal Americanness, rather than of class differences. As the Girl Scouts said several years ago on the flip sides of their cookie boxes, "I'm not like anybody else."—"We have a lot in common."

Part of this, of course, is due to the individualism and voluntarism of a capitalist society. But it is also a result of our American origins, founded by an entrepreneurial class shorn of virtually all vestiges of old feudal loyalties. Much of Europe's sympathy to socialism, and our own lack of it, can be explained by their greater familiarity with the mutual benefit organizations and worker's leagues that are a legacy of feudalism. Cut off from the old European class divisions dominated by the noblesse oblige of the aristocracy, Americans have relished our apparent social uniformity and freedom to achieve individually. What we have neglected to understand is how this has led to a new and equally closed class structure. We may lack the titles of the landed gentry, but those in the social registers of America form every bit as much of an elite.

One of the ironies of our society is that while most of us are busily denying any real class hierarchy in America, the corporate elite are quite secure and self-conscious in their maintenance of a class barrier. The upper class forms a very tightly knit series of families connected by marriage, education, club membership, and a whole array of separate cultural institutions.[20] Most of us rarely see the true power elite, and know even less about them. The Carringtons or Ewings of popular culture are poor imitations, which encourage us to think about the much more obvious nouveau riche.

If internal ties within the upper class are so unambiguous, and the boundary between them and us equally clear, would it not make sense to think about our *own* similarities as laborers? At the very heart of our argument has been the contention that, in spite of all the camouflage of individualism and the division of labor, we *are* one part of a larger class. Until we begin to appreciate this common tie with the working and poor fractions, there is virtually no hope for escaping our perpetual search for identity, economic security, and control. Like Sisyphus, we will be doomed to a destiny of labor that goes nowhere.

In thinking about building potential political coalitions with other segments of the laboring class, it is imperative for us to go beyond single issues to their common underlying cause(s). If our predicaments stem from an identity as laborers, it stands to reason that they can be solved only by addressing the basic class problems, not the surface symptoms. Pollution, economic insecurity, or the power of the military may affect each fraction of the laboring class somewhat differently. But they do affect us all. Only by helping ourselves by helping each other, by being *reciprocal*, do we stand a chance of reclaiming some control.

The immediate stumbling block is the conviction that the system is either natural and cannot be changed, or good and should not be changed. Or, cynicism and fear prevent us from being involved in public issues. It is too easy to dismiss those trying to recapture some control as crackpots or "America haters"; we are either embarrassed or angered by them. Even such transparently benign activities as recycling, joining food or other cooperatives, or holding peace vigils can earn the sneers or laughter of our neighbors. We are apt to doubt ourselves in such a situation; individualism makes us so dependent on the approval of others that we quickly feel exposed and deviant, as if standing up for our convictions were really just "making a scene."

Our middle class sensibilities would have dismissed Jesus out of hand. Anyone so boorish as to drive the money changers out of the temple does not even deserve a hearing. Another irony of our predicament, then, is how much of our inaction has nothing to do with concerted opposition by those in charge. How many of us would be mortified to be seen at any demonstration, vigil, or parade? How many of us would "waste our time" or contend with potentially hostile strangers to collect petitions or appear before the city or some other council? It is our own feelings of foolishness, vulnerability, or cynicism that often get in the way. We give up the ghost with barely a fight.

Until we take those first fledgling and very frightening steps, until we are willing to seem so alone and maybe lose the little we have, we can only suffer in silence or grumble ineffectively. And we will not take those first steps as a class fraction, until we are convinced *personally* that we are affected. Only if we can conclude that like the Israelites in Egypt we are in an untenable position, or that like Abraham we have a great deal to gain by setting off into the desert, will we even consider planning for the journey. If we arrive at that starting point, it will mean that we are taking ourselves seriously. We will have decided that by God, or some other imagery, we suffer legitimate grievances. In turning to each other and discovering we are not alone, we also at last discover a new social identity as a class. And *that* Weber would certainly recognize as the first step, once again, toward social heroism.

Notes

Prologue:

1. Max Weber, *The Protestant Ethic and the Spirit of Capitalism* (New York: Charles Scribner's Sons, 1958), p. 37.
2. Robert N. Bellah, et.al., *Habits of the Heart* (Berkeley: University of California Press, 1985), p. viii.
3. *Ibid.*, p. 81.
4. Evan Thomas, "Growing Pains at 40," *Time*, May 19, 1986, pp. 37–38.
5. James H. Cone, *My Soul Looks Back* (Nashville, Tenn.: Abingdon Press, 1982), p. 123.
6. *Ibid.*, p. 130.

Chapter 1:

1. Robert McAfee Brown, *Is Faith Obsolete?* (Philadelphia: Westminster Press, 1974), p. 139.
2. William M. Leo Grande and Carla Ann Robbins, "Oligarchs and Officers: The Crisis in El Salvador," *Foreign Affairs*, Summer, 1980, pp. 1084–1103.
3. Max Weber, *Economy and Society*, Volume 2 (Berkeley: University of California Press, 1968), p. 932.
4. Anthony Giddens, *Capitalism and Modern Social Theory: An Analysis of the Writings of Marx, Durkheim, and Max Weber* (New York: Cambridge University Press, 1971), pp. 164, 167.
5. Weber, *Economy and Society*, p. 932.
6. *Ibid.*, p. 932.
7. See Raymond Williams, *Marxism and Literature* (Oxford: Oxford University Press, 1977).
8. Barbara Ehrenreich and John Ehrenreich, "The Professional-Managerial Class," in Pat Walker, ed., *Between Labor and Capital* (Boston: South End Press, 1979), pp. 9–10.
9. *Ibid.*, p. 12.
10. *Ibid.*, p. 11.
11. *Ibid.*, p. 28.
12. Erik Olin Wright, *Class, Crisis and the State* (London: Verso, 1983), p. 201, emphasis original.
13. *Ibid.*, p. 201.
14. *Ibid.*, p. 62.
15. *Ibid.*, pp. 63, 74ff.
16. *Ibid.*, pp. 78–79.

17. *Ibid.*, p. 81.
18. See Paul Starr, *The Social Transformation of American Medicine* (New York: Basic Books, 1982).
19. This position has been carefully spelled out in Richard C. Edwards, *Contested Terrain: The Transformation of the Workplace in the Twentieth Century* (New York: Basic Books, 1979).
20. *Ibid.*, p. 23.
21. *Ibid.*, p. 26.
22. *Ibid.*, p. 179.
23. *Ibid.*, p. 116.
24. *Ibid.*, pp. 119, 124, 126.
25. *Ibid.*, pp. 127–128.
26. *Ibid.*, p. 179.
27. *Ibid.*, p. 131.
28. *Ibid.*, p. 131.
29. *Ibid.*, p. 144.
30. *Ibid.*, p. 145.
31. *Ibid.*, pp. 146, 148.
32. *Ibid.*, p. 132.
33. *Ibid.*, pp. 191–192.
34. *Ibid.*, p. 193.
35. See Richard Sennett and Jonathan Cobb, *The Hidden Injuries of Class* (New York: Vintage Books, 1973).
36. See Eli Zaretsky, *Capitalism, the Family, and Personal Life* (New York: Harper Row, 1976).
37. Richard Sennett, *The Fall of Public Man: The Social Psychology of Capitalism* (New York: Vintage Books, 1978), p. 261.
38. *Ibid.*, p. 259.
39. Marian Burros, "Diet Game, Where Chances of Winning Are Slim," *The New York Times*, July 16, 1986, p. 13.
40. Sennett, *The Fall of Public Man*, p. 145.
41. Edwards, *Contested Terrain*, p. 205.

Chapter 2:

1. World Bank, *World Development Report 1986*, (New York: Oxford University Press, 1986), p. 180.
2. *Ibid.*, p. 227.
3. U.S. Department of Commerce, *1984 Statistical Abstract of the United States*, (Washington, D.C.: Government Printing Office, 1984), p. 461.
4. *Ibid.*, p. 530.
5. World Bank, *World Development Report 1986*, p. 184.
6. *Ibid.*, pp. 184–185.
7. Myron Magnet, "The Fortune 500 Special Report," *Fortune*, April 29, 1985, pp. 252–319.

8. Lars Osberg, *Economic Inequality in the United States* (Armonk,N.Y.: M.E. Sharpe, 1984), p. 44.
9. Edward F. Denison, *Accounting for United States Economic Growth, 1929–1969* (Washington, D.C.: Brookings Institution, 1974), pp. 94–95.
10. *Ibid.*, p. 16.
11. U.S. Department of Commerce, *1985 Statistical Abstract of the United States*, (Washington, D.C.: Government Printing Office, 1985), pp. 390, 433.
12. Denison, *Accounting for*, p. 54.
13. U.S. Department of Commerce, *1985 Statistical Abstract*, p. 525.
14. William Ryan, *Equality* (New York: Vintage Books, 1981), p. 14.
15. U.S. Department of Commerce, *Historical Statistics of the United States: Colonial Times to 1970* (Washington, D.C.: Government Printing Office, 1975), p. 137.
16. U.S. Department of Commerce, *Survey of Current Business*, March, 1986, p. S-10.
17. Kan H. Young and Ann M. Lawson, "Where Did All the New Jobs Come From?" in *1985 U.S. Industrial Outlook* (Washington, D.C.: Government Printing Office, 1985), p. 30.
18. M. Bruce McAdam, "The Growing Role of the Service Sector in the U.S. Economy," in U.S. Department of Commerce, *1985 U.S. Industrial Outlook* (Washington, D.C.: Government Printing Office, 1985), p. 42.
19. Young and Lawson, "Where Did All," p. 29.
20. U.S. Department of Commerce, *1985 U.S. Industrial Outlook* (Washington, D.C.: Government Printing Office, 1985), p. 36-6.
21. *Ibid.*, pp. 36-1 to 36-12.
22. Ryan, *Equality*, pp. 3–36.
23. Amanda Bennett and Douglas R. Sease, "Getting Lean," *Wall Street Journal*, May 22, 1986, pp. 1, 24.
24. Lillian Breslow Rubin, *Worlds of Pain* (New York: Basic Books, 1976), pp. 37–45.
25. Edwards, *Contested Terrain*, p. 193.
26. Ryan, *Equality*, p. 14.
27. Walter Brueggemann, *The Prophetic Imagination* (Philadelphia: Fortress Press, 1978), pp. 11ff.
28. *Ibid.*, p. 17.
29. *Ibid.*, p. 17.
30. *Ibid.*, p. 17.
31. *Ibid.*, p. 13.
32. Rubem Alves, *What Is Religion?* (Maryknoll, N.Y.: Orbis Books, 1984), p. 73.
33. Ronald Reagan, as quoted in Dean Peerman, "Presidential Proof-Texting," *The Christian Century*, February 20, 1985, p. 176.

34. Gustavo Gutierrez, *The Power of the Poor in History* (Maryknoll, N.Y.: Orbis Books, 1983), pp. 66ff.

35. *Ibid.*, p. 67.

36. Allan Aubrey Boesak, *The Finger of God* (Maryknoll, N.Y.: Orbis Books, 1982), p. 29.

37. Phillip Berryman, *The Religious Roots of Rebellion: Christians in Central American Revolutions* (Maryknoll, N.Y.: Orbis Books, 1984), p. 22.

38. Robert McAfee Brown, *Theology in a New Key: Responding to Liberation Themes* (Philadelphia: Westminster Press, 1978), p. 158.

39. Berryman, *The Religious Roots*, p. 19.

40. Gutierrez, *The Power of the Poor*, p. 90.

Chapter 3:

1. Magnet, "The Fortune 500," p. 266.

2. Osberg, *Economic Inequality*, p. 44.

3. See Creel Froman, *The Two American Political Systems: Society, Economics, and Politics* (Englewood Cliffs, N.J.: Prentice-Hall, 1984).

4. Osberg, *Economic Inequality*, p. 41.

5. World Bank, *World Development Report, 1986* (New York: Oxford University Press, 1986) p. 227.

6. Gutierrez, *The Power of the Poor*, p. 116.

7. Frantz Fanon, *The Wretched of the Earth* (New York: Grove Press, 1968).

8. Gustavo Gutierrez, *We Drink from Our Own Wells: The Spiritual Journey of a People* (Maryknoll, N.Y.: Orbis Books, 1984), p. 38.

9. Josue de Castro, *Death in the Northeast* (New York: Vintage Books, 1969).

10. Susan Schroeder, *Cuba: A Handbook of Historical Statistics* (Boston: Hall Reference Books, 1982), p. 568.

11. World Bank, *World Development Report, 1981* (New York: Oxford University Press, 1981), p. 179, and *World Development Report, 1986*, p. 237.

12. World Bank, *World Development Report, 1981*, p. 177, and *World Development Report, 1986*, p. 235.

13. World Bank, *World Development Report, 1981*, p. 175, and *World Development Report, 1986*, p. 181.

14. Virgil Elizondo, *Galilean Journey: The Mexican-American Promise* (Maryknoll, N.Y.: Orbis Books, 1983), p. 93.

15. José Miranda, *Communism in the Bible* (Maryknoll, N.Y., 1982), p. 21.

16. *Ibid.*, pp. 21–22.

17. *Ibid.*, p. 35.

18. Martin Hengel, *Property and Riches in the Early Church* (Philadel-

phia: Fortress Press, 1974), p. 2.
19. *Ibid.*, p. 12.
20. *Ibid.*, pp. 27, 29.
21. *Ibid.*, p. 87.
22. *Ibid.*, p. 86.
23. Richard C. Edwards, Michael Reich, and Thomas E. Weisskopf, eds., *The Capitalist System: A Radical Analysis of American Society*, second edition (Englewood Cliffs, N.J.: Prentice-Hall, 1978), p. 131.
24. William M. Dugger, "The Continued Evolution of Corporate Power," *Review of Social Economy*, April, 1985, p. 11.
25. Magnet, "The Fortune 500," p. 292.
26. Dugger, "The Continued Evolution," p. 2.
27. *Ibid.*, p. 4.

Chapter 4:

1. Paulo Freire, *Pedagogy of the Oppressed* (New York: The Seabury Press, 1973), pp. 31–33.
2. See Emile Durkheim, *The Rules of Sociological Method* (New York: The Free Press, 1964).
3. Juan Luis Segundo, *Faith and Ideologies* (Maryknoll, N.Y.: Orbis Books, 1984), p. 16.
4. Michel Clevenot, *Materialist Approaches to the Bible* (Maryknoll, N.Y.: Orbis Books, 1985), p. 16.
5. Freire, *Pedagogy*, pp. 19–20.
6. Karl Mannheim, *Ideology and Utopia: An Introduction to the Sociology of Knowledge* (New York: Harcourt, Brace, and World, 1936), pp. 88–90.
7. *Ibid.*, pp. 88ff.
8. See Alfred Schutz, *Collected Papers, Vol. I, The Problem of Social Reality* (The Hague: Martinus Nijhoff, 1962).
9. Anthony Giddens, *Central Problems in Social Theory: Action, Structure and Contradiction in Social Analysis* (Berkeley: University of California Press, 1979), p. 189.
10. See Paul Feyerabend, *Against Method* (London: Verso, 1978), and Alvin W. Gouldner, *The Coming Crisis of Western Sociology* (New York: Basic Books, 1970).
11. Giddens, *Central Problems*, p. 187.
12. *Ibid.*, pp. 193–195.
13. *Ibid.*, pp. 190ff.
14. Raymond Williams, *Marxism and Literature* (Oxford: Oxford University Press, 1977), p. 114.
15. Roy Bhaskar, *The Possibility of Naturalism: A Philosophical Critique of the Contemporary Human Sciences* (Atlantic Highlands, N.J.: Humanities Press, 1979).

16. Marvin Harris, *Cultural Materialism: The Struggle for a Science of Culture* (New York: Vintage Books, 1980), p. 315.
17. Clifford Geertz, *The Interpretation of Cultures* (New York: Basic Books, 1973), p. 194.
18. *Ibid.*, p. 231.
19. *Ibid.*, pp. 213ff.
20. *Ibid.*, p. 210.
21. Giddens, *Central Problems*, p. 192.
22. *Ibid.*, p. 192.
23. Geertz, *The Interpretation*, pp. 213ff.
24. Giddens, *Central Problems*, p. 186, emphasis original.
25. Anthony Giddens, *New Rules of Sociological Method: A Positive Critique of Interpretive Sociologies* (New York: Basic Books, 1976), p. 143.
26. Bhaskar, *The Possibility of Naturalism*, p. 84.
27. See Alfred Schutz and Thomas Luckmann, *The Structures of the Life-World*, (Evanston, Ill. Northwestern University Press, 1973).
28. Bhaskar, *The Possibility of Naturalism*, p. 3.
29. *Ibid.*, p. 12.
30. Contrast with Giddens, *New Rules*, p. 146.
31. See Bhaskar, *The Possibility of Naturalism*, chapter 2.
32. *Ibid.*, p. 87.
33. See Gouldner, *The Coming Crisis*, p. 333.
34. John Maynard Keynes, *The General Theory of Employment, Interest, and Money* (New York: Harcourt, Brace, and World, 1936), p. 383.
35. Elisabeth Schussler Fiorenza, *Bread Not Stone* (Boston: Beacon Press, 1984), pp. 25–26.
36. Pierre Bigo, S.J., *The Church and Third World Revolution* (Maryknoll, N.Y.: Orbis Books, 1977), p. 133.
37. José Miguez Bonino, *Doing Theology in a Revolutionary Situation* (Philadelphia: Fortress Press, 1975), p. 2.

Chapter 5:

1. Geertz, *The Interpretation*, p. 49.
2. *Ibid.*, p. 53.
3. See Schutz, *Collected Papers*.
4. See Ryan, *Equality*.
5. *Ibid.*, p. 8, emphasis original.
6. See Marshall Sahlins, *Stone Age Economics* (London: Tavistock Publications, 1974).
7. All references from Richard B. Lee, "'!Kung Bushman Subsistence: An Input-Output Analysis," in A. Vaydah, ed., *Environment and Cultural Behavior* (Garden City, N.Y.: Natural History Press, 1969), as quoted in Sahlins, *Stone Age Economics*, p. 21.

8. Sahlins, *Stone Age Economics*, p. 21.
9. *Ibid.*, p. 23.
10. See John H. Bodley, *Victims of Progress*, second edition (Menlo Park, Calif.: The Benjamin/Cummings Publishing Company, 1982), p. 151ff.
11. Michael J. Parenti, *Democracy for the Few*, fourth edition (New York: St. Martin's Press, 1983), pp. 28–29.
12. Sahlins, *Stone Age Economics*, p. 2.
13. *Ibid.*, p. 37, emphasis original.
14. *Ibid.*, p. 37.
15. José Miguez Bonino, *Toward a Christian Political Ethics* (Philadelphia: Fortress Press, 1983), p. 16.
16. Bruce C. Birch and Larry L. Rasmussen, *The Predicament of the Prosperous* (Philadelphia: Westminster Press, 1978), p. 148.
17. H. Wheeler Robinson, "The Hebrew Conception of Corporate Personality," in Paul Volz, Friedrich Stummer, and Johannes Hempel, eds., *Werden und Wesen Des Alten Testaments* (Berlin: Verlag Von Alfred Topelmann, 1936), p. 56.
18. *Ibid.*, p. 49.
19. *Ibid.*, p. 51, emphasis original.
20. T.S. Eliot, "The Love Song of J. Alfred Prufrock," in *The Complete Poems and Plays* (New York: Harcourt, Brace, and Company, 1952), pp. 3–7.
21. Ehrenreich and Ehrenreich, "The Professional Managerial Class," p. 30.
22. *Ibid.*, p. 24.
23. *Ibid.*, p. 37.
24. Edwards, *Contested Terrain*, p. 205.
25. Angela Davis, *Women, Race and Class* (New York: Random House, 1981).
26. Domitila Barrios de Chungara, with Moema Viezzer, *Let Me Speak! Testimony of Domitila, a Woman of the Bolivian Mines*, translated by Victoria Ortiz, (New York: Monthly Review Press, 1979), p. 199.
27. See June Nash and Maria Patricia Fernandez-Kelly, eds., *Women, Men, and the International Division of Labor* (Albany, N.Y.: State University of New York Press, 1983).
28. Martin Oppenheimer, *White Collar Politics* (New York: Monthly Review Press, 1985), pp. 129–130.

Chapter 6:

1. Paul Tillich, *Systematic Theology* (Chicago: University of Chicago Press, 1951), p. 5.
2. James Cone, *For My People: Black Theology and the Black Church* (Maryknoll, N.Y.: Orbis Books, 1984), p. 40.
3. Tillich, *Systematic Theology*, p. 3.

4. Elisabeth Schussler Fiorenza, *In Memory of Her* (New York: Cross-roads, 1983) , p. 170.
5. Friedrich Schleiermacher, *On Religion: Speeches to Its Cultured Despisers*, translated by John Oman, (New York: Frederick Unger, 1955).
6. Gutierrez, *The Power of the Poor*, p. vii.
7. *Ibid.*, pp. vii–viii.
8. *Ibid.*, p. xiv.
9. James Cone, *A Black Theology of Liberation* (Philadelphia: J.B. Lippincott, 1970), pp. 90–92.
10. *Ibid.*, pp. 119–120.
11. Gutierrez, *The Power of the Poor*, p. ix.
12. Rosemary Radford Ruether, *Sexism and God-Talk: Toward a Feminist Theology* (Boston: Beacon Press, 1983), p. 186.
13. *Ibid.*, p. 257.
14. *Ibid.*, p. 254.
15. John Murray Cuddihy, *No Offense: Civil Religion and Protestant Taste* (New York: The Seabury Press, 1978).
16. See William Ryan, *Blaming the Victim* (New York: Vintage Books, 1976).
17. Albert Camus, *The Plague*, translated by Stuart Gilbert (New York: Fortress Press, 1957).
18. Ruether, *Sexism and God-Talk*, p. 33.
19. Brown, *Is Faith Obsolete?*, pp. 28–32.
20. Jürgen Moltmann, *Theology of Hope* (New York: Harper & Row, 1967), p. 21.
21. J. Severino Croatto, *Exodus: A Hermeneutics of Freedom* (Maryknoll, N.Y.: Orbis Books, 1981), p. 12.
22. Elsa Tamez, *Bible of the Oppressed* (Maryknoll, N.Y.: Orbis Books, 1982), p. 3.
23. Paul Lehmann, *The Transfiguration of Politics* (New York: Harper & Row, 1975), pp. 250–259.
24. U.S. Department of Commerce, *1987 Statistical Abstract of the United States* (Washington, D.C.: Government Printing Office, 1987), p. 443.
25. Michael Walzer, *Exodus and Revolution* (New York: Basic Books, 1985), p. 37.
26. Hugo Echegaray, *The Practice of Jesus* (Maryknoll, N.Y.: Orbis Books, 1984), p. 31.
27. Elizondo, *Galilean Journey*, p. 53.
28. *Ibid.*, pp. 68–69.
29. Neill Q. Hamilton, "Temple Cleansing and Temple Bank," *Journal of Biblical Literature*, December, 1964, p. 368.
30. Echegaray, *The Practice of Jesus*, p. 31.
31. Hamilton, "Temple Cleansing," p. 365.

32. *Ibid.*, p. 370.
33. Langdon Gilkey, *Naming the Whirlwind: The Renewal of God-Language* (Indianapolis/New York: The Bobbs-Merrill Company, 1969), p. 34.
34. *Ibid.*, pp. 40–59.
35. *Ibid.*, p. 61.
36. Pablo Richard, et.al., *The Idols of Death and the God of Life: A Theology* (Maryknoll, N.Y.: Orbis Books, 1983), p. 1.
37. Lehmann, *The Transfiguration*, p. 247.
38. William Stringfellow, *An Ethic for Christians and Other Aliens in a Strange Land* (Waco, Texas: Word, Incorporated, 1973), p. 69, emphasis original.
39. Gutierrez, *The Power of the Poor*, p. 76.
40. Moltmann, *The Theology of Hope*, p. 163.
41. Lehmann, *The Transfiguration*, p. xi.
42. Tissa Balasuriya, *The Eucharist and Human Liberation* (Maryknoll, N.Y.: Orbis Books, 1979), p. 2.
43. Gutierrez, *The Power of the Poor*, p. 16.
44. Balasuriya, *The Eucharist*, p. 10.
45. *Ibid.*, p. 28.
46. Moltmann, *The Theology of Hope*, p. 21.
47. Gutierrez, *The Power of the Poor*, p. 29.

Chapter 7:

1. William Stringfellow, *The Politics of Spirituality* (Philadelphia: Westminster Press, 1984), p. 69.
2. John A. Coleman, *An American Strategic Theology* (Ramsey, N.J.: Paulist Press, 1982), p. 112.
3. *Ibid.*, p. 115.
4. *Ibid.*, p. 124.
5. Robert Bellah, "American Civil Religion in the 1970s," in Russell E. Richey and Donald G. Jones, eds., *American Civil Religion* (New York: Harper & Row, 1974), p. 258.
6. Lehmann, *The Transfiguration*, p. 289.
7. Harvey Cox, *The Secular City: Secularization and Urbanization in Theological Perspective* (New York: Macmillan Company, 1965), p. 30.
8. See Jürgen Moltmann, *The Crucified God: The Cross of Christ as the Foundation and Criticism of Christian Theology* (New York: Harper & Row, 1974).
9. Richard, et.al., *The Idols of Death*, p. 6.
10. *Ibid.*, p. 7.
11. Sharon D. Welch, *Communities of Resistance and Solidarity: A Feminist Theology of Liberation* (Maryknoll, N.Y.: Orbis Books, 1985), p. 7.

12. *Ibid.*, p. 7.
13. Bellah, et.al., *Habits of the Heart*, p. vii.
14. See Thorstein B. Veblen, *The Vested Interests and the Common Man* (New York: Augustus M. Kelley, Bookseller, 1964).
15. *The Rotarian*, January, 1987, p. 19.
16. James Cone, *Black Theology and Black Power* (New York: The Seabury Press, 1969).
17. Mary Daly, *Beyond God the Father: Toward a Philosophy of Women's Liberation* (Boston: Beacon Press, 1973).
18. Bruce J. Malina, *The New Testament World: Insights from Cultural Anthropology* (Atlanta: John Knox Press, 1981), p. 55.
19. *Ibid.*, p. 55.
20. G. William Domhoff, *Who Rules America Now? A View for the '80s* (Englewood Cliffs, N.J.: Prentice-Hall, 1983).

Bibliography

Alves, Rubem. *What Is Religion?* Maryknoll, N.Y.: Orbis Books, 1984.

Balasuriya, Tissa. *The Eucharist and Human Liberation.* Maryknoll, N.Y.: Orbis Books, 1979.

Barrios de Chungara, Domitila, with Moema Viezzer. *Let Me Speak! Testimony of Domitila, a Woman of the Bolivian Mines*, translated by Victoria Ortiz. New York: Monthly Review Press, 1979.

Bellah, Robert. "Civil Religion in Theological Perspectives," in Russell E. Richey and Donald G. Jones, eds., *American Civil Religion.* New York: Harper & Row, 1974, pp. 161–184.

Bellah, Robert N., Richard Madsen, William M. Sullivan, Ann Swidler, and Steven M. Tipton. *Habits of the Heart.* Berkeley: University of California Press, 1985.

Bennett, Amanda, and Douglas R. Sease. "Getting Lean." *Wall Street Journal*, May 22, 1986, pp. 1, 24.

Berger, Peter L. *The Sacred Canopy.* Garden City, N.Y.: Anchor Books, Inc., 1969.

Berryman, Phillip. *The Religious Roots of Rebellion: Christians in Central American Revolutions.* Maryknoll, N.Y.: Orbis Books, 1984.

Bhaskar, Roy. *The Possibility of Naturalism: A Philosophical Critique of the Contemporary Human Sciences.* Atlantic Highlands, N.J.: Humanities Press, 1979.

Bigo, Pierre, S.J. *The Church and Third World Revolution.* Maryknoll, N.Y.: Orbis Books, 1977.

Birch, Bruce C., and Larry L. Rasmussen. *The Predicament of the Prosperous.* Philadelphia: Westminster Press, 1978.

Bodley, John H. *Victims of Progress.* Second edition. Menlo Park, Calif.: The Benjamin/Cummings Publishing Company, 1982.

Boesak, Allan Aubrey. *The Finger of God.* Maryknoll, N.Y.: Orbis Books, 1982.

Bonino, José Miguez. *Doing Theology in a Revolutionary Situation.* Philadelphia: Fortress Press, 1975.

_____. *Toward a Christian Political Ethics.* Philadelphia: Fortress Press, 1983.

Brown, Robert McAfee. *Is Faith Obsolete?* Philadelphia: Westminster Press, 1974.

_____. *Theology in a New Key: Responding to Liberation Themes.* Philadelphia: Westminster Press, 1978.

Brueggemann, Walter. *The Prophetic Imagination.* Philadelphia: Fortress Press, 1978.

Burros, Marian. "Diet Game, Where Chances of Winning Are Slim." *The New York Times,* July 16, 1986, p. 13.

Camus, Albert. *The Plague,* translated by Stuart Gilbert. New York: Alfred A. Knopf, 1957.

Clevenot, Michel. *Materialist Approaches to the Bible.* Maryknoll, N.Y.: Orbis Books, 1985.

Coleman, John A. *An American Strategic Theology.* Ramsey, N.J.: Paulist Press, 1982.

Cone, James H. *Black Theology and Black Power.* New York: The Seabury Press, 1969.

_____. *A Black Theology of Liberation.* Philadelphia: J. B. Lippincott, 1970.

_____. *For My People: Black Theology and the Black Church.* Maryknoll, N.Y.: Orbis Books, 1984.

_____. *My Soul Looks Back.* Nashville, Tenn.: Abingdon Press, 1982.

Cox, Harvey. *The Secular City: Secularization and Urbanization in Theological Perspective.* New York: Macmillan Company, 1965.

Croatto, J. Severino. *A Hermeneutics of Freedom.* Maryknoll, N.Y.: Orbis Books, 1981.

Cuddihy, John Murray. *No Offense: Civil Religion and Protestant Taste.* New York: The Seabury Press, 1978.

Daly, Mary. *Beyond God the Father: Toward a Philosophy of Women's Liberation.* Boston: Beacon Press, 1973.

Davis, Angela. *Women, Race and Class.* New York: Random House, 1981.

de Castro, Josue. *Death in the Northeast.* New York: Vintage Books, 1969.

Denison, Edward F. *Accounting for United States Economic Growth, 1929–1969.* Washington, D.C.: Brookings Institution, 1974.

Domhoff, G. William. *Who Rules America Now? A View for the '80s.* Englewood Cliffs, N.J.: Prentice-Hall, 1983.

Dugger, William M. "The Continued Evolution of Corporate Power." *Review of Social Economy,* April 1985.

Durkheim, Emile. *The Rules of Sociological Method.* New York: The Free Press, 1964.

Earle, John R., Dean D. Knudsen, and Donald W. Shriver, Jr. *Spindles and Spires.* Atlanta: John Knox Press, 1976.

Echegaray, Hugo. *The Practice of Jesus.* Maryknoll, N.Y.: Orbis Books, 1984.

Edwards, Richard C. *Contested Terrain: The Transformation of the Workplace in the Twentieth Century.* New York: Basic Books, 1979.

Edwards, Richard C., Michael Reich, and Thomas E. Weisskopf, eds.. *The Capitalist System.* Second edition. Englewood Cliffs, N.J.: Prentice-Hall, 1978.

Ehrenreich, Barbara, and John Ehrenreich. "The Professional-Managerial Class," Pat Walker, ed., *Between Labor and Capital*, Boston: South End Press, 1979, pp. 5–45.

Eliot, T.S. "The Love Song of J. Alfred Prufrock," in *The Complete Poems and Plays*. New York: Harcourt, Brace, and Company, 1952, pp. 3–7.

Elizondo, Virgil. *Galilean Journey: The Mexican-American Promise*, Maryknoll, N.Y.: Basic Books, 1983.

Fanon, Frantz. *The Wretched of the Earth*. New York: Grove Press, 1968.

Feyerabend, Paul. *Against Method*. London: Verso, 1978.

Fiorenza, Elisabeth Schussler. *Bread Not Stone*. Boston: Beacon Press, 1984.

_____. *In Memory of Her*. New York: Crossroads, 1983

Freire, Paulo. *Pedagogy of the Oppressed*. New York: The Seabury Press, 1973.

Froman, Creel. *The Two American Political Systems: Society, Economics, and Politics*. Englewood Cliffs, N.J: Prentice-Hall, 1984.

Geertz, Clifford. *The Interpretation of Cultures*. New York: Basic Books, 1973.

Giddens, Anthony. *Capitalism and Modern Social Theory: An Analysis of the Writings of Marx, Durkheim, and Max Weber*. New York: Cambridge University Press, 1971.

_____. *Central Problems in Social Theory: Action, Structure and Contradiction in Social Analysis*. Berkeley: University of California Press, 1979.

_____. *A Contemporary Critique of Historical Materialism*. Berkeley: University of California Press, 1981.

_____. *New Rules of Sociological Method: A Positive Critique of Interpretive Sociologies*. New York: Basic Books, 1976.

Gilkey, Langdon. *Naming the Whirlwind: The Renewal of God-Language*. Indianapolis/New York: The Bobbs-Merrill Company, 1969.

Gouldner, Alvin W. *The Coming Crisis of Western Sociology*. New York: Basic Books, 1970.

Gutierrez, Gustavo. *The Power of the Poor in History*. Maryknoll, N.Y.: Orbis Books, 1983.

_____. *A Theology of Liberation*. Maryknoll, N.Y.: Orbis Books, 1973.

_____. *We Drink from Our Own Wells: The Spiritual Journey of a People*. Maryknoll, N.Y.: Orbis Books, 1984.

Hamilton, Neill Q. "Temple Cleansing and Temple Bank." *Journal of Biblical Literature*, December 1964, pp. 365–372.

Harris, Marvin. *Cultural Materialism*. New York: Vintage Books, 1980.

Hengel, Martin. *Property and Riches in the Early Church*. Philadelphia: Fortress Press, 1974.

Keynes, John Maynard. *The General Theory of Employment, Interest, and Money.* New York: Harcourt, Brace, and World, 1936.

King, Paul G., and David O. Woodyard. *The Journey Toward Freedom: Economic Structures and Theological Perspectives.* Rutherford, N.J.: Fairleigh Dickinson, 1982.

Lee, Richard B. "'!Kung Bushman Subsistence: An Input-Output Analysis," in A. Vaydah, ed., *Environment and Cultural Behavior.* Garden City, N.Y.: Natural History Press, 1969.

Lehmann, Paul. *The Transfiguration of Politics.* New York: Harper & Row, 1975.

Leo Grande, William M., and Carla Ann Robbins. "Oligarchs and Officers: The Crisis in El Salvador." *Foreign Affairs*, Summer, 1980, pp. 1084–1103.

Magnet, Myron. "The Fortune 500 Special Report." *Fortune*, April 29, 1985, pp. 252–319.

Malina, Bruce J. *The New Testament World: Insights from Cultural Anthropology.* Atlanta: John Knox Press, 1981.

Mannheim, Karl. *Ideology and Utopia.* New York: Harcourt, Brace, and World, 1936.

Marx, Karl. *On Society and Social Change.* Chicago: University of Chicago Press, 1973.

McAdam, M. Bruce. "The Growing Role of the Service Sector in the U.S. Economy," in *1985 U.S. Industrial Outlook*, Washington: U.S. Government Printing Office, pp. 38–43.

Miranda, José. *Communism in the Bible.* Maryknoll, N.Y.: Orbis Books, 1982.

Moltmann, Jürgen. *The Crucified God: The Cross of Christ as the Foundation and Criticism of Christian Theology.* New York: Harper & Row, 1974.

_____. *The Theology of Hope.* New York: Harper & Row, 1967.

Monthly Review Foundation. *Monthly Review*, July–August, 1984.

Nash, June, and Maria Patricia Fernandez-Kelly, eds. *Women, Men, and the International Division of Labor.* Albany, N.Y.: State University of New York Press, 1983.

Oppenheimer, Martin. *White Collar Politics.* New York: Monthly Review Press, 1985.

Osberg, Lars. *Economic Inequality in the United States.* Armonk, N.Y.: M.E. Sharpe, Inc., 1984.

Parenti, Michael J. *Democracy for the Few.* Fourth edition. New York: St. Martin's Press, 1983.

Reagan, Ronald, quoted in Dean Peerman. "Presidential Proof-Texting." *The Christian Century*, February 20, 1985, p. 176.

Richard, Pablo, et al. *The Idols of Death and the God of Life: A Theology.* Maryknoll, N.Y.: Orbis Books, 1983.

Robinson, H. Wheeler. "The Hebrew Conception of Corporate Personality," in *Werden und Wesen Des Alten Testaments*, edited by Paul

Volz, Friedrich Stummer, and Johannes Hempel. Berlin: Verlag Von Alfred Topelmann, 1936, pp. 49–62.

The Rotarian, January, 1987.

Rubin, Lillian Breslow. *Worlds of Pain*. New York: Basic Books, 1976.

Ruether, Rosemary Radford. *Sexism and God-Talk: Toward a Feminist Theology*. Boston: Beacon Press, 1983.

Ryan, William. *Blaming the Victim*. New York: Vintage Books, 1976.

_____. *Equality*. New York: Vintage Books, 1981.

Sahlins, Marshall. *Stone Age Economics*. London: Tavistock Publications, 1974.

Schiller, Bradley R. *The Economics of Poverty and Discrimination*. Third edition. Englewood Cliffs, N.J.: Prentice-Hall, 1980.

Schleiermacher, Friedrich. *On Religion: Speeches to Its Cultured Despisers*, translated by John Oman. New York: Frederick Unger, 1955.

Schroder, Susan. *Cuba: A Handbook of Historical Statistics*. Boston: Hall Reference Books, G.K. Hall and Co., 1982.

Schutz, Alfred. *Collected Papers, Vol. I, The Problem of Social Reality*. The Hague, Netherlands: Martinus Nijhoff, 1962.

_____, and Thomas Luckmann. *The Structures of the Life-World*. Evanston, Ill.: Northwestern University Press, 1973.

Segundo, Juan Luis. *Faith and Ideologies*. Maryknoll, N.Y.: Orbis Books, 1984.

Sennett, Richard. *The Fall of Public Man: On the Social Psychology of Capitalism*. New York: Vintage Books, 1978.

_____, and Jonathan Cobb. *The Hidden Injuries of Class*. New York: Vintage Books, 1973.

Starr, Paul. *The Social Transformation of American Medicine*. New York: Basic Books, 1982.

Stringfellow, William. *An Ethic for Christians and Other Aliens in a Strange Land*. Waco, Texas: Word, Incorporated, 1973.

_____. *The Politics of Spirituality*. Philadelphia: Westminster Press, 1984.

Tamez, Elsa. *Bible of the Oppressed*. Maryknoll, N.Y.: Orbis Books, 1982.

Thomas, Evan. "Growing Pains at 40." *Time*, May 19, 1986, pp. 22–41.

Tillich, Paul. *Systematic Theology*. Chicago: University of Chicago Press, 1951.

U.S. Department of Commerce. *1985 U.S. Industrial Outlook*. Washington, D.C.: Government Printing Office, 1985.

_____, Bureau of Economic Analysis. *Survey of Current Business*. Washington, D.C.: Government Printing Office, March 1986.

_____, Bureau of the Census. *Historical Statistics of the United States: Colonial Times to 1970*. Washington, D.C.: Government Printing Office, 1975.

_____, Bureau of the Census. *1984 Statistical Abstract of the United States*. Washington, D.C.: Government Printing Office, 1984.

_____, Bureau of the Census. *1985 Statistical Abstract of the United States*. Washington, D.C.: Government Printing Office, 1985.

_____, Bureau of the Census. *1987 Statistical Abstract of the United States*. Washington, D.C.: Government Printing Office, 1987.

U.S. Department of Labor. *Handbook of Labor Statistics*. Washington, D.C.: Government Printing Office, 1985.

Veblen, Thorstein B. *The Vested Interests and the Common Man*. New York: Augustus M. Kelley, Bookseller, 1964.

Walzer, Michael. *Exodus and Revolution*. New York: Basic Books, 1985.

Weber, Max. *The Protestant Ethic and the Spirit of Capitalism*. New York: Charles Scribner's Sons, 1958.

_____. *Economy and Society*, Volume 2. Berkeley: University of California Press, 1968.

Welch, Sharon. *Communities of Resistance and Solidarity: A Feminist Theology of Liberation*. Maryknoll, N.Y.: Orbis Books, 1985.

Williams, Raymond. *Marxism and Literature*. Oxford: Oxford University Press, 1977.

Woodyard, David O. *Beyond Cynicism: The Practice of Hope*. Philadelphia: Westminster Press, 1972.

World Bank. *World Development Report 1981*. New York: Oxford University Press, 1981.

World Bank. *World Development Report 1986*. New York: Oxford University Press, 1986.

Wright, Erik Olin. *Class, Crisis and the State*. London: Verso, 1983.

_____. *Class Structure and Income Determination*. New York: Academic Press, 1979.

Young, Kan H., and Ann M. Lawson. "Where Did All the New Jobs Come From?" in *1985 U.S. Industrial Outlook*, Washington, D.C.: Government Printing Office, 1985, pp. 29–37.

Zaretsky, Eli. *Capitalism, the Family, and Personal Life*. New York: Harper Torchbooks, 1976.

Index of Subjects

Abraham, 18–19, 137, 207

Basic Christian communities, 68–69, 176
Bellah, Robert, 4–7, 20, 173, 182, 185–86
Biblical scholarship, 117
Black theology, 8, 149–50, 201
Bourgeoisie and the Protestant Reformation, 15, 46, 58, 60
Bureaucracy, 192–95
    and consequences for middle fraction, 25–26, 32–34
    and control, 32–34, 58–59
    and derived power, 61–62
    rise of, 25–26

Capitalism, 15, 171
    and devaluation of women, 37, 205
    and heroism, 172
    and relation of individual and society, 17, 36–37
    internationalization of, 35
    nature of: neither natural nor divine, 134
Church. *See also* Institutions, religious.
    and justice, 68
    and liberation theology, 172, 175–77
    and power from below, 176
    early, individual and society in, 18
    in Latin America, 64, 67–70
    neutrality of, 68
    of the poor, 67
Civil religion
    and individualism, 175

    and liberation theology, 172–77
    as ideology of change, 20
Civil rights movement. *See also* King, Martin Luther, Jr. 22, 88–89, 141–42, 175
Class consciousness, 24, 55–56, 205
Cleansing the temple, 65, 160–64
Computers/information revolution, 32, 40, 53, 55
Conscientization, 101, 204
Consumerism, 38–39, 174
Corporations
    and control, 44–45, 60–61, 72
    and individualism, 137
    and private property, 71–74, 92
    and wealth, 45, 82–83
    as persons, 92–93
    large size of, 45, 82
    mergers of, 84–85, 86–87
    ownership of, 50, 82–83, 95–96
    transnational, 46, 61–62, 85–86
Counterculture, 103
Counter-institutions
    abolitionists, 198–99
    peace and justice groups, 198–200
    unions, 198–99
Cuba, standard of living in, 77

De-skilling, 32, 35
Death as metaphor, 167–68, 171
Deregulation, 192

Economic growth, 48–49, 95–96
    and capital formation, 85
    and labor force growth, 48–49
    in manufacturing, 47–48, 51–55, 96–97